PUBLICS FOR PUBLIC SCHOOLS

Copyright © 2013 by Paradigm Publishers

Published in the United States by Paradigm Publishers, 5589 Arapahoe Avenue, Boulder, Colorado 80303 USA.

Paradigm Publishers is the trade name of Birkenkamp & Company, LLC, Dean Birkenkamp, President and Publisher.

Library of Congress Cataloging-in-Publication Data

Abowitz, Kathleen Knight, author.
  Publics for public schools : legitimacy, democracy, and leadership / Kathleen Knight Abowitz with Steven R. Thompson.
      pages cm
  Includes bibliographical references and index.
  ISBN 978-1-61205-244-1 (pbk. : alk. paper)
  1. Public schools—United States. 2. Community and school—United States. 3. Democracy and education—United States. 4. Educational leadership—United States. I. Thompson, Steven R., author. II. Title.
  LA217.2.A26 2012
  371.010973—dc23
                                                                2012035395

Printed and bound in the United States of America on acid-free paper that meets the standards of the American National Standard for Permanence of Paper for Printed Library Materials.

Designed and Typeset by Straight Creek Bookmakers.

17 16 15 14 13   5 4 3 2 1

CONTENTS

ACKNOWLEDGMENTS

Former colleagues Nick Longo, Sarah Woiteshek, and Stephanie Raill Jayanand-han helped me begin thinking about public conceptions of leadership in 2007. I am grateful for their invitation to do so, and for their good friendship along the way. The ideas they helped to nurture further matured at the Educational Theory Summer Institute in August 2010, where a wonderful group of scholars debated questions of the public in public education. I am particularly grateful to Chris Higgins for his critiques of my work in that forum.

I have learned much from Aaron Schutz and Michael Evans, both of whom have given invaluable feedback about my writing on education organizing. Conversations with Martín Carcasson, Kathy Leslie, and Sarah Woiteshek sharpened my thinking about deliberative democracy practices. Thanks to the Finn family for encouragement when my writing efforts were literally at sea in the spring of 2010. Jason Barry, my editor at Paradigm Publishers, offered helpful ideas and suggestions.

A warm note of thanks goes to Leonard Waks, a fellow philosopher of education who has been a mentor, friend, and book-writing partner. Len provided critical feedback about chapters and gave lots of encouragement in the writing process.

My home department at Miami University has been a productive scholarly community in which to percolate these ideas and is a haven for educational scholars still interested in the public purposes of public education. The university provided me a research leave during 2009–2010, and departmental colleagues helped me focus on my writing during this period. Kate Rousmaniere read early chapters of this work and has always been a role model for producing readable, carefully wrought social foundations scholarship. Richard Quantz has provided friendship, wisdom, and scholarly guidance throughout my tenure at Miami.

Steve Thompson, lead author of Chapter 7, contributed key ideas to the development of this book and helped me link notions of public achievement to the field of leadership studies. Steve is an exceptional educational leader, teacher, colleague, and friend.

My family has always been a source of inspiration and encouragement in this project. My mother and father consistently modeled civic involvement. While my father and I never agreed about many political issues, he did pass on to me his commitment to public engagement and his belief in the importance of community life. Rob, Maddy, and Sam have been patient and supportive companions as I wrote this book, helping me carve out the time and space I needed. The quiet, solitary work of scholarship is made more tolerable and perhaps more soulful in the context of a loving and noisy household. I am grateful for their interruptions and inspirations, as well as their love.

Introduction

It is increasingly fuzzy, in our day and age, what we mean by a "public school." Magnet and charter schools receive state funding, but most have selective admissions. In a handful of states and cities, private parochial school tuitions may now be paid with tax-funded school vouchers. Virtual home schools chartered as public schools, in my home state of Ohio, mean that children can be schooled entirely at home, at state expense. In the twenty-first century, the meaning of "public education" is seemingly up for grabs, and perhaps going the way of the dinosaur. Never has there been so much speculation about what makes a public school public.

In this book, instead of asking what a public school *is,* I ask, how should public schools *be governed,* and in particular, how can citizens, parents, and civic leaders be *engaged in* the process. I invite the reader to consider the "public" description not just as an adjective, but as a verb. How do we *achieve* public schools, not simply through how such schools are funded or regulated (although these are important questions), but through how they are governed and led?

This book aims to articulate a path for leading a renewed conception of—and commitment to—the public dimensions of public schooling. The leadership that this requires is not only explicitly public in its orientation, but also must be taken up by various sorts of citizens, and not just the parents of school-age children or the most privileged parents in a district. Schools do not educate alone; multiple actors from family life and civil society serve as teachers, counselors, and guides for young people. Thus, this book is written for any reader who has an interest in "educational leadership" in its broadest and most inclusive meanings of the term. I hope to inspire energy and enthusiasm for all kinds of community work on behalf of public schooling through this short book.

By a "renewed" conception of the public dimensions of schooling, I mean a conception created for our current times and contexts. I do not use this term to refer to the reclamation of a long-lost civic utopia, in which all students were educated in excellent schools that were unfailingly supported by an energetic, inclusive, participatory public citizenry of equal social standing. There is no evidence such a society ever existed, and democratic life is not a fairy tale. There is no golden age of either democracy or public schooling. Democratic societies are rife with exclusions and conflicts, and their public institutions often engage in struggles of various sorts. The whole notion of a "public school" is one only invented less than two centuries ago, and is always in process, always evolving. It is in this sense that I use the term "renew," for democratic forms of shared governance should be adapted and reconceived in every age, to respond to the particular conditions and problems of each unique era.

This book is a work of educational theory, primarily utilizing works of philosophy and philosophy of education to build a set of responses to the question, "What is the public of public schooling today?" While I draw from a variety of fields relevant to this question—educational policy and governance, and educational leadership, among others—this book primarily uses philosophical ideas and arguments related to democratic theory as applied to the question at hand. Philosophical thinking in education broadly deals with questions of logic, aims, values, and meanings related to education, learning, and schooling. By questions of "meanings," I refer to the work of clarifying the use of common-sense concepts so that our use of these terms becomes more precise, less contradictory, and ultimately more meaningful (literally, full of meaning and thus better able to guide our action). Thus, my hope for this book about the public of public schools is that the term *public,* as a result of this exploration, acquires more meaning and thus becomes better able to guide practice in local contexts by educational leaders. While I will discuss practices and examples of public-building among educational leaders in real communities, I purposefully shy away from overly specific practical recommendations or technical prescriptions, for I write primarily here as a philosopher and theorist of education. The details of application are so sensitive to context, place, and personality that attempting to give instructions to educational leaders would be worse than useless; it would be presumptuous. However, in addition to plenty of examples and empirical support for my arguments, I have compiled an appendix where readers can find a list of promising contemporary resources to assist with the application of these ideas in real school-community settings.

As I write this book I am influenced by the many different roles I live out in my past and present lives as student, parent, citizen, and teacher. These roles shape the words and arguments that I form on these pages. I am a product of elementary and secondary public schools. In the fall of 1969 I headed off to my kindergarten classroom in a public school district in rural Virginia that had only recently been racially desegregated. My teachers, coaches, principals, and schoolmates helped to form some of my impressions, critiques, and ultimately hopes for public schooling. I am now a mother of two children enrolled in public schools; I experience public schooling anew as I see them navigating a system that is in some ways quite different from that which I attended over thirty years ago. I have been a citizen of many places, but my primary context for local citizenship these days is an Ohio town. It is here that I participate not only in general civic affairs but also in issues related specifically to the public schools.

Finally, I am a teacher, advisor, and critical friend to educational leaders—people who work in and with the public and private schools in localities surrounding the university at which I teach, and who have taught me many lessons over the years. These leaders are superintendents, activists, teachers, principals, school board members, and parents. They have in common an involvement with schools and children, and they all seek to make schools better places in which youth can become educated, however diversely they may define this term. They have little patience for formalist, abstract philosophy, yet they often yearn for theoretical writing that speaks intelligently and clearly to the challenging questions of value, meaning, and purpose that confront them in their work. It is this yearning I kept in mind through my writing process. I hope the arguments here can inspire leaders such as these toward critical thinking, dialogue, and experimentation with new forms of democratic governance in education.

—*Kathleen Knight Abowitz*

Chapter 1
Where Is the Public in Public Schooling?

What does it mean to say that in the United States, we have "public" schools? The term *public* calls to mind tax-supported, compulsory schools for all children, managed by the state. To most of us, "public" is associated with what are now mundane realities: taxpayer-funded schools, charged with admitting and educating any legal minor in a catchment area such as a neighborhood, city, town, county, or regional district. But public life is far more substantive and meaningful than these formalities communicate.

This book explores the meanings and purposes of public schools today. From their origination in the nineteenth century in the United States and many other Western democratic countries, public schools have evolved in size, structure, and in the expectations that citizens hold for them. The locally supported New England common school of the 1840s has changed dramatically, as has the public sphere to which the school is responsible. Educators and educational leaders are often in the middle of negotiating this "public" evolution, as they stand toe-to-toe (literally and virtually speaking) with both the government officials who sponsor these schools and the citizens that fund, support, and populate them. In these negotiations, political and moral meanings of public schooling have sometimes become lost, as the title of this chapter suggests.[1]

This study of the *public* and *publics* of state-funded schooling is much needed today. The very idea that schools have a public, and are responsible to it, can be a challenging one for many educational leaders (a broad term I will use in this book to mean anyone in a formal or informal leadership role related to education or schooling). Educators hear a great deal from the public, who as individual citizens are sometimes behaving more like (often unhappy) customers. David's mom is angry about the discipline sanction he received from a principal and wants the sanction revoked; Teresa's dad wants her history teacher to overlook her plagiarism; and Maya's mom is threatening a lawsuit unless her daughter is admitted to the Honors program. These parents often seem to believe that the job of school is to please the customer-parents, taxpayers in an economic exchange of taxes for schooling. Professionals in education tend to see things differently. To many educational leaders, the public *is* the problem with public education. There is an overabundance of public involvement in public schools, if by "involvement" we mean the self-interested lobbying and threats of parents for the special treatment and individual achievement of their own children. To other educational leaders and parents, the public represents not complaining parents, but an unwieldy bureaucracy believed to be part and parcel of any government institution.

Yet the public is not the government. The *public* refers broadly to *the people,* the population of a society whose political system is governed by democratic norms and procedures. The *government* or *state* is the institutional apparatus that should carry out the will and aims of the public, or people. Thus, while the term *public* is not synonymous with government or state, public institutions in Constitution-governed democratic states are organized and managed by governmental entities that are, in theory, accountable to the views and wishes of the citizenry within the bounds of their own Constitutions.

A public school today is responsible to complex layers of local, state, and federal governing bodies. These layers translate into rules, regulations, testing, and content standards that are part of the territory of present-day public schooling. The view that public schools are unnecessarily bureaucratic—and more responsive to the regulations of governance than to the concerns of local citizens, students, and educators themselves—is a popular refrain.[2] This view has heightened the appeal for school choice policies for many parents and teachers, who may seek escape from the bureaucratic aspects of government-run schooling. The bureaucratic sides of government-run schooling can be especially hard on educators, who can experience burnout brought on by the nonteaching, administrative aspects of the job and the increasingly narrow focus on standardized testing to meet state and federal mandates. For these educators, the difficulties of navigating cumbersome and sometimes inane regulations bog down the interesting and occasionally inspiring work of educating young people.

The public, then, is not necessarily a positive term for many people today. Calling to mind complaining parents or an unwieldy bureaucracy, many school leaders find *public* to be a troubling descriptor. The solution, for many districts, has been to adopt the logic, language, and strategies of the private sphere. The *private sphere* refers to aspects of our lives that are not subject to Constitutional principles, government scrutiny, or requirements of transparency; our homes, our religious worship, private schools and clubs, and the business, for-profit sectors are all considered the private sphere. As schools seek to manage the troublesome aspects of the public sector, they increasingly turn for alternatives to the private sphere of business and commerce. A 2007 incident in Pittsburgh, Pennsylvania, shows us how this kind of private approach works. It serves as a good example of how the idea of the public school has evolved into a moniker that does not always inspire confidence and loyalty, but doubt and uncertainty.

"Pittsburgh schools drop public name to boost image," read the headline in the *Pittsburgh Post Gazette*.[3] The new policy stated that schools in the district would have "public" dropped from their formal names, and have more standardized names in a rebranding effort. Under the new policy, the Pittsburgh Public Schools would now be called simply Pittsburgh Schools, an attempt to avoid the apparently negative connotations of the public moniker. "School board members offered little reaction to the policy, which does not require board approval," the reporter noted. One school board member stated, by way of explanation, "by dropping 'public' from its name, the district might be able to avoid the negative attitude often associated with public schools." The article continues:

> [One district staff member] noted that suburban districts don't have "public" in their names, and a marketing consultant who helped develop the policy, Meade Johnson, said the district is less interested in the "public" tag than in linking its identity to the "Excellence for All" agenda. By adding Pittsburgh to the identity of each school, Ms. Fischetti hopes the public will come to associate a level of quality with every school in the district.... Also, the district last night announced plans to upgrade its parent hotline into a "customer service center," another initiative aimed at boosting the district's image.[4]

The attempt to remove the name *public* from these urban public schools is telling. One marketing expert notes that public education's major problem today is its very name. "The perception out there is that anything run by the government is lousy. That may not be the way it is, but anything that is government-run is seen as big, inefficient, many times ineffective, and not as well run as the private sector."[5] As one blogger wrote of the incident, "public is now a four-letter word."[6]

Granted, it is rare that schools actually attempt to formally remove the "public" designation, but in many other ways public schools attempt to shed their problematic "public" label by acting like private corporations or businesses. Superintendents in large cities are often called CEOs, chief education officers. Marketers and public relations experts are regularly employed to shape perceptions about public schools—what is known as *branding* in the public relations business—as they were in Pittsburgh. Slogans and image campaigns, such as the "Excellence for All" tag, are sought to equate the public's schools with contemporary calls for "achievement" and "equality" and "high standards." Central office personnel can make such changes without public debate or discussion. In Pittsburgh, the change of name was not subject to school board, teacher, or citizen scrutiny before it was adopted, at least as far as the article tells us. The imprint of the marketer's logic and language is also seen in the new-and-improved "customer service center"—formerly a parent hotline—where the parent/customer can be served.

Turning to marketers and worrying about the public image of public schools is one outcome of what some call "the war on public schooling." It is commonplace for news media to carry negative reports on public schools. Gerald Bracey, a researcher who built a career of regularly dispelling many of these myths using data and good evidence, provides examples of these negative campaigns. Bracey argues that the "schools-are-awful bloc" regularly uses "misinformation, distorted information, deliberate attempts at obfuscation, [and] sloppy thinking" to break public support for government-run schools.[7] Many in this so-called bloc are from business and corporate ranks, leaders in private industry who have national clout and good resources to make their opinions heard.

So while it makes sense that school officials are worried about public image, why do schools turn to the corporate or business model, when it is business leaders who are often most vocally critical of what the schools are doing? In a capitalist society, the gut-level appeal of market logic and language is undeniable, particularly as business's reputation for efficiency contrasts with the public school's renowned bureaucracy. And the privatization of public institutions—prisons, military, and public utilities, among other sectors—has been a trend in recent decades. The contentious battles over a public health care system in 2009–2010, and the election of many Tea Party candidates in 2010, show more examples of the fear and loathing of government involvement, and the strong faith in the superiority of the private sphere of business, among a vocal and growing group of American citizens.

Yet the private sphere of business—always run ultimately in the interest of stockholders—is distinct in important ways from the public sphere. Moreover, the public sphere—where "the people's" interests are to be served—has a unique and critical place in a society that claims to be democratic. What is lost when we simply import private-sphere logic, language and management principles into the public arena of schooling? What is fundamental and worth retaining—or perhaps rebuilding—in the idea of a "public" school?

Thus, we arrive back to the original question: what do we mean by "public" schools? In the chapters that follow, I will systematically examine this question, looking at questions of legitimacy and leadership to argue for the distinct importance of *public schooling*. These arguments will clarify the concept of the public for educational leaders of all kinds, and will discuss leadership habits, skills, and strategies designed to help schools become more sensitive to and skillful in working with their public constituencies.

As it turns out, the effort to remove the "public" label from public schools in Pittsburgh failed. "The proposed removal of the word 'public' from a school district deeply identified with the city caught many residents by surprise. There are many who wear their association with Pittsburgh Public Schools like a badge of honor."[8] After a week of criticism, the superintendent responded to the public outcry by reversing the decision, after which he was commended on the local paper's editorial page. "The response to Mr. Roosevelt's ideas haven't always been to his liking, but he should be encouraged by the depth of the community's response to his ideas. His constituents take him seriously because he takes their input seriously. We hope this passionate give-and-take continues."[9] Clearly, there remains some positive meaning for citizens in the idea of "public" schooling—a meaning that has roots in over 150 years of common schooling in the United States. The following brief account of this history sets the stage for the book's purpose: reconstructing and fostering some of the substantive meanings of *public* schooling.

"Our" Schools: *Demos* and the Making of Public Schooling

Public schools are institutions uniquely associated with states that claim to be democratic, defined here as a state ruled by and for the people, its citizens.[10] (*State* here refers to government in general, not more narrowly an individual state's government, unless otherwise indicated.) *Demos,* a Greek term meaning "the people," refers to the citizens who enjoy the means to participate, in a variety of ways, in shaping the laws that govern them. As Pittsburgh citizens ultimately indicated to their superintendent, these are *our* schools. Although run by the state, they are understood to belong, in some way, to the citizens.

Public schools are historically and philosophically linked to the ideals and structure of a democratic state. In the United States, the democratic state grows out of a complex combination of two systems of political thinking. One is *liberalism,* which provides foundations for individual liberties and rights encoded in our Constitution. The other is *republicanism,* which is based on civic participation and individual involvement in governance through activities such as voting, lobbying, or expressing political opinions. So in the United States, *democracy* refers to a government structure in which individual liberties are protected and in which the people or citizens play a role through electing representatives and participating in various other ways in the governance of the state and its institutions. Particularly because they educate our children, public schools are seen to belong and be accountable to the people in unique and significant ways not always shared by other public institutions in a democratic society. Thus, people should play a role in shaping their schools, in participating in the governance of these institutions. While quickly rejecting simplistic formulations of this idea—citizens cannot run their schools without the help of professional educators, as one obvious example—it is important to note how democratic ideals are central to the public school institution, both historically and today.

Public schools were born as common schools, an idea that began to take hold in US society around 1830 in New England. The origins of common and public schooling are found not in consensus and easy implementation, but in debate and struggle. The idea of free, universal, and common schools represents an institution that was hard-won, long fought, and remains controversial to this day among some sectors of our society. Prior to the early nineteenth century, formal schooling was only for those who had the financial means, an arena reserved primarily for families of white propertied males. Education in general was seen as the domain of the family, not the society or the state. Communities and public figures advocating for common schools in the 1800s were concerned with basic literacy, nation-building, and the moral character of the citizenry.

Common schools of the early 1800s were firmly rooted in localities; white citizens who were formally educated attended neighborhood or town schools.

Local committees of citizens were responsible for raising the funds for school buildings, teacher salaries, books, and supplies. But common-school reformers of the nineteenth century sought to challenge local authorities as the singular providers and authorities of schools. Horace Mann's 1848 appointment in Massachusetts as the first head of a state's board of education shows that while the origins of the common school are local, the state's presence as equalizer and legitimate evaluator of common-school education gained an early political foothold during the common-school era.

Why common schools? Beyond basic literacy and numeracy were goals of socialization for nation-building, creating workers for an industrializing society, providing moral education, and equal opportunity. Federalist views of a school system that would morally educate as well as integrate students into a free-market society strengthened popular arguments for winning support of state-funded schools. The goals of building a cohesive, patriotic nationalist identity and a strong Protestant work ethic among young Americans, as Noah Webster made clear in his extensive writings, were powerful reasons offered to convince citizens to part with hard-earned tax dollars to educate all students. Common schools were seen as a primary means for realizing our national motto, *E pluribus unum*; out of the many, one. Equalizing educational opportunities among regions and social classes was another important purpose. Mann documented the wide range of schooling conditions and the often very poor condition of schoolhouses and educational resources in communities across Massachusetts. His early school inspections provided early evidence of the inequality of educational resources and opportunities when schooling was solely a local affair.

Common schooling communicated a shared political and moral ideology for those children deemed educable during the nineteenth century. "Within the context of political education, the common in common school meant the teaching of a common political creed," one combining moral and political beliefs aiming toward a consensus among citizens.[11] Or as William Reese more bluntly puts it, "The whole point of common schools, after all, was to teach the same things to every white child of a neighborhood or area, in the same classroom, with the same teacher."[12] "Common schooling" is an idea rooted in goals of cohesion and equality, but it was most powerfully understood well into its second century of existence to mean cohesion and equality of resources for children considered ethnically white.

After the Civil War, the idea of common education for freed blacks, while abhorrent to southern whites, spurred much social action for education among former slave communities. As W. E. B. Du Bois noted, "public education for all at public expense was, in the South, a Negro idea."[13] The idea of levying taxes against the people to pay for a universal school system in the southern United States came out of the experience of ex-slaves who understood the essential value of literacy and education. Black communities in the South worked independently as well as with missionary groups, private foundations, and governmental agencies to construct schools for their children and themselves. Due to white resistance and Jim Crow laws, these common schools promised schooling for a group long denied formal education, a shared space where black children might legally learn literacy, numeracy, and other basic subjects. Like most others of the period throughout the nation, these schools were racially segregated by law, a condition that would characterize (and belie the name of) most common schools, whether by law or by custom, for the better part of another century.

As the nineteenth century drew to a close, the common-school name slowly gave way to "public school," the name that became popular beginning in the Progressive Era, which lasted from roughly 1890 to 1920. "Public" replaced "common" in this period of major social change, as schools became more ethnically diverse as well as more accountable to governing bodies beyond the local school board or town council. The Progressive Era was a period of massive immigration, urbanization, industrialization, and social reform (a period whose levels of immigration were only rivaled in the United States by those at the end of the twentieth century). Southern blacks fled the rural south for new opportunities in urban centers in the north but struggled to find equal educational opportunities there. The Irish escaped famine in their homeland in cities like Boston, New York, and Chicago. Southern and Eastern Europeans came to the eastern United States for economic opportunity as well as political and religious freedoms. Opportunity was thought to begin, for children of immigrants, in the public school, and these early schools sought to make all ethnically white children into Americans.

It was in the Progressive Era that social reformers and state government officials began to more assertively challenge the localism of common schools and to assert the authority of educational expertise. Progressive reformers viewed local governance as parochial and subject to corruption; larger systems run on principles of efficiency and scientific learning were thought to be superior. In response, Progressive Era reformers created the large, more centralized school systems that came to define the twentieth-century public schools. During the Progressive Era, schools were shaped by the assumption that educational experts, operating as social engineers, are primarily charged with educating in efficient ways, for the betterment of society. Progressive reformers worked to standardize the number of hours and days children were in school each year in all localities; they established credentials for teachers and administrators across districts. As Stephen Macedo characterizes this era: "The reforms shifted the emphasis of the public system away from neighborhoods and lay control, away from localistic pluralism, away from what Teddy Roosevelt called 'the patriotism of the village,' and toward that of the great community, represented by autonomous professionals and impartial experts."[14] By 1918, all states had compulsory schooling laws, so powerful was the idea that systematic education, fueled by the power of state authority, equated to social progress.

Common schools became public schools not only in the move away from localism but also as population centers grew, and as curricula in these schools emphasized more differentiation—differing tracks of study for different kinds of students. The numbers of students in schools greatly increased during this era due to population growth, mandatory schooling laws, and the gradual increase in the average years of schooling attained. Partly as a result of many more young people in school for longer periods of time, and partly out of many Progressives' social efficiency concerns, schools became less common or similar in their curricula and purposes, and more differentiated. Often these differentiations fell along social class and racial lines. The early twentieth century saw the development of overtly racist educational institutions, with the rise of state-sanctioned segregation by race and ethnicity, enabled by the birth of IQ testing and the segregation of pupils by perceived ability into academic tracks. This period also witnessed the emphasis on vocational schooling as a distinct course of study.

In addition, the distinctions between "private" (tuition-charging) and "public" (free) schools became more distinct during this time. In the earlier common schooling era, these distinctions were much more fluid; schools that charged tuition but would enroll any tuition-paying student regardless of religion, race, ethnic background, or social class were sometimes called common or public, in that they were performing a public function.[15] The Progressive Era witnessed the clearer distinction between the terms *private* (tuition-paying, selective enrollment) and *public* (free, universal enrollment) schools that we now use today. It was in the Progressive Era that public schooling came to mean free and universal schools that were managed and controlled by government authorities. In a very early appearance of the mention of the term *public school,* George Boutwell of Massachusetts in 1873 offered this definition: "A *public school* I understand to be a school established by the public—supported chiefly or entirely by the public, controlled by the public, and accessible to the public under terms of equality, without special charge for tuition."[16] Boutwell's definition encompassed state authority and funding, under the terms of full accessibility for all children "under terms of equality." Schools were understood to be "public" in this period when they were (1) funded using tax revenues, (2) governed according to rules and funds supported by legislation and policies passed by elected officials, and (3) providing admittance to all children (most often only "all" white children) in a catchment area. Public schools were schools run by the government, according to principles of representative democracy, where people elect fellow citizens to represent their interests. This was a more distanced form of civic engagement with schools than in the common era, where local control meant that white parents and community members could, depending on their status in the locality, have much more direct involvement with shaping their community's school. While the local control of schools would not so easily be shaken, public schooling beginning in the Progressive Era took on a systematized and bureaucratic form that would distinguish it from its common-school forerunner.

The more complex forms of twentieth- and twenty-first-century schooling would come, in a sense, from adding more publics to the mix, which would help work against the racism and other exclusions built into the institution of schooling. In early common schools, the local citizenry constituted the *demos*; they were wholly accountable for starting, running, and evaluating their local schools. As the country grew, the *demos* of the local community expanded into what John Dewey called the "Great Community" of communities, states, and nation. Adding more and more publics meant additional layers of governance—increasing state and then federal control—from the Progressive Era right up through our current No Child Left Behind (NCLB) age. This is not to say reform efforts like NCLB are simply the consequence of a growing society; rather, it is to say that NCLB signifies one type of formalized and dramatic expansion of public school accountability in our era. Schools are no longer viewed as simply accountable to local civic leaders or board members but are now accountable to the state and nation, and increasingly, to global standards of learning.

These multiple layers of governance, today comprising a major part of our educational bureaucracy, are caused by—but also help to generate—even more of the negative impressions of public schools that seem to be so prevalent today. These complex layers of governance can be readily defended by the belief that additional forms of state accountability were required for achieving increasing degrees of equality. The democratic promise of full access and equality in school-ing seems to have required the intervention of government at multiple levels, particularly after the nineteenth century. So, in a sense, the struggle for truly public schools—which promised by their name to be accessible and educational for all students—led to very bureaucratic structures that cause such disdain for all things public today.

From Public Schooling Expansion to the Reign of Private Purposes

In the twentieth century, public schooling grew in the number of students en-rolled, school buildings, and the degree of access for many constituencies. Civil rights battles gradually expanded both the numbers and the diversity of students who could attend public schools. The idea of tax-payer–funded schooling was no longer as much of a controversial issue by the twentieth century; the question of who controlled these schools, however, and whose interests they primarily served, was sharply and directly challenged. Most twentieth-century school reformers viewed centralization and increased state and federal involvement in schools as an improvement over "the sectional and local interests" that had dominated the common schools.[17]

During the post–World War II era, federal involvement in education dra-matically increased. US leaders interpreted the 1957 Sputnik launch as a sign that schools were not fulfilling their duties to math and science disciplines, the primary engines of the defense industry. Federal agencies sought initiatives com-pelling districts to focus more attention on teaching subjects aligned with these national goals. During the Civil Rights Era, the federal government was called in to compel districts to both admit *and* educate all students—blacks, Latinos, women, disabled students—in free and equal environments. Local and state districts in southern states doggedly fought racial integration, requiring federal agencies and funding to ultimately, if not entirely successfully or permanently, achieve racial integration in public schools. While these desegregation battles helped public schools to begin to live up to the values of equality implied in their name, they also served to expand state and federal governmental involvement in school policy. Whereas the federal government's presence in public schooling was almost entirely absent before the twentieth century, it had dramatically increased by the end of it. Nothing could be more symbolic of this fact than the No Child Left Behind Act passed in 2001 to federally mandate school accountability as measured by standardized test scores. This law asserts a historically unprecedented federal role in US public school governance.

Increased federal and state involvement is not the only hallmark of the contemporary era of schooling. If we think of our present era of school reform as beginning with the publication of *A Nation at Risk* in 1983—a document that launched a flurry of new reforms in education in the late twentieth century—we see the growth in popularity of what David Labaree calls the "social efficiency" aims of public schooling. *Social efficiency* refers to the aim to "make schools a mechanism for adapting students to the requirements of a hierarchical social structure and the demands of the occupational marketplace."[18]

Vocationalism or careerism has been a powerful influence on modern thinking regarding the purposes of public schools. Careerism, however, was not an invention of the modern era but represented a philosophical shift that began at the end of the nineteenth century. After the 1870s, when the United States experienced a severe economic recession, general and liberal education curricula were increasingly seen by many to be impractical and irrelevant to the concerns of most people.[19] As one school board member in Muncie, Indiana, famously stated in 1929, "For a long time all boys were trained to be President.... Now we are training them to get jobs."[20] Labaree explains:

> More important than the inclusion of typing classes alongside those in history was this fundamental change in the purposes of schooling—from a lofty political goal (training students to be citizens in a democratic society, perhaps to be president) to a practical economic goal (getting students ready to enter the workforce, preparing them to adapt to the social structure). This change affected students who were going to college as much as those in the auto shop. The social efficiency argument for education is found at the heart of nearly every educational address delivered by a governor or president, every school board's campaign for a millage increase or bond issue, every educational reform document.[21]

The rise of the social efficiency argument is nearly complete in our era; contemporary rhetoric about public schooling focuses primarily on economic purposes. The social efficiency purposes of education aim at both national economic prominence and individual competitiveness and career success. A strong sense of consumerism shapes many families' views on schooling.[22]

Achieving national economic strength and individual economic success has positive public effects for citizens in many ways, yet a strong economy and a prosperous citizenry is only one part of a healthy democratic society. In addition, education aimed exclusively at economic competitiveness often equates to a strongly privatized objective of schooling in the minds of students and parents. The purpose of school, according to many, is to get a good job or career. This aim, while important, is essentially private—aimed at promoting economic gain for individuals, families, companies, and, by default, the nation. As Mike Rose laments, "we've lost hope in the public sphere and grab at private solutions, which undercut the sharing of obligation and risk and keep us scrambling for individual advantage."[23] Jim Giarelli writes of how in the nominally public sphere, we as individuals and families seek mostly private aims. He describes a public school in his suburban Northeast town widely thought to be a "good school system … considered effective because it prepares children for successful competition in the private economy." As measured by this school's substance and aims, it is essentially private schooling, operating for the advancement of individuals in the market-based economy.[24]

Public schooling deserving of its name would never ignore economic aims of education but would promote equally important civic and social aims as well—and it would do so in a manner that was consistent with principles of collective self-governance, of public scrutiny and participation, and of liberty and equality, promised by the US Constitution. When the central administration of the Pittsburgh Public Schools tried to remove the label *public* from its schools, in many ways it was merely acknowledging what Labaree, Rose, Giarelli, and many others assert: that the public purposes of schooling are today greatly diminished and confused. Tensions between local, state, and national layers of accountability—added over the course of the past century—further muddle the situation, contributing to the complexity of public education governance. Clearly, part of the work of reconstructing a more substantive notion of *public* schooling involves thinking through these governance tensions, as well as the diverse views of what should constitute a good public education.

Whose Schools Are These Schools? This Book's Response and Plan

Public education is part of a democratic promise of self-rule or, as we might conceive it today, of participatory governance. The *demos* of democracy symbolizes forms of collective self-rule, or the shared participation in determining the scope, direction, and substance of our shared political life and culture. It is from this shared participation in governance that public schools achieve legitimacy, or the collective belief that government-run institutions are using their power in the interests of the people. In a real sense, legitimacy provides public schools with the earned authority to educate the children of a district.

For a school to be legitimate in a democratic society, its governance should be guided by democratic principles. Citizens can become involved in this type of governance when schools meet two important requirements. The first is that all people should be *prepared* to participate equally in this self-rule through the education provided them in public schools. This principle requires a substantive education in citizenship, in which students learn the knowledge, skills, and values that prepare them for life in a democratic, pluralistic society in a globalized world.

The second is that all citizens of a particular ward or district should be able to become involved with the governance and direction of schooling itself. This does not mean all citizens *will* become involved, but all will be able to do so and actively solicited toward that end. Public schools are at their most public, in this sense, when they are morally and politically *legitimate*; when they provide a quality education to all students—an education whose purposes the public, through its participation in shared governance, has helped to shape and guide.

Self-governance is only democratic when it is widely shared by many diverse citizens, for government by a few select groups or an elite class is more accurately called plutocracy. Legitimacy is secured not by meeting the narrow interests or aims of the few but of the wider populace itself. Public schools are called upon to educate all students who walk through their doors. This call is particularly critical for those millions of students who exclusively rely on the public schools as a place of opportunity, class mobility, and full citizenship. Providing this opportunity is vitally important today, in an age of unparalleled inequality in wealth among social classes in the United States. The journey from common schools of villages to the public school systems of today can be read as a struggle to realize this call.

Ironically, as schools were pushed to achieve more equal outcomes across different races, abilities, and the like, they became accountable to an expansion of "publics," even as the size and layers of governance of modern public schools have eroded their public responsiveness in other ways. Whose schools *are* these public schools? There is increasing doubt and cynicism that "public" schools are anything more than government schools, as we lose sight of the *demos* of democracy and the possibilities of public life in an age of extreme political divisiveness and privatization.

This book articulates a path for a renewed conception of and commitment to the public dimensions of public schooling. This path requires us to examine three concepts essential to this renewal project: legitimacy, public life, and public leadership.

The controversy over the "public" moniker in Pittsburgh Public Schools signals the legitimacy problems that public schools today face. Their ability to provide an excellent education is in doubt in many places, and this is a view often held irrespective of how well a school may actually perform, how well its teachers may do their jobs. As a result, public schooling's ability to inspire political trust and confidence among citizens is also depleted. Legitimate political institutions enjoy the consent, if only often implied consent, of the citizens of the public. Legitimate political institutions thus are rewarded with the confidence and support of their citizenry. This does not mean that principals in schools enjoying a high degree of legitimacy never hear from angry parents, or that superintendents in such districts count on every bond levy passing easily. But legitimacy is a condition that helps educators and educational leaders build capacity for educating all children in their communities. In Chapter 2 I examine the notion of legitimacy, exploring its power for institutions of a democratic society, and the US public schools' legitimacy problems today. I aim to clarify the complex nature of earning and keeping the citizenry's consent and trust of its state-supported public institutions in an age of media attacks, divisive politics, punitive accountability plans, and litigious parents.

In Chapters 3 and 4 I turn to the central concept animating this study: the public, and public life. While US citizens oftentimes equate "public" to "government run," I separate the roles of the government in state-funded education from the roles of the citizenry, operating in civil society, with regard to its public schools. The *demos* or people of a democracy elect legislators and, in most districts in the United States, school board members to represent them in shaping their schools. These representatives govern; they help guide the apparatus of the state with regard to schooling and youth. But while such forms of democratic governance are still necessary, they are insufficient today. Schools are also public insofar as they demonstrate responsiveness to and reciprocity with associations of civil society, the "third" sphere beyond government and markets. The *demos,* through civil society networks, collectively participates in public schooling in ways that can benefit both the public schools' capacities to educate and their legitimacy in the eyes of its citizens. Citizens engage in this work through their participation in publics.

In Chapter 3 I argue that the "publics" of public schooling are not just awaiting us, not simply ready-made, not consisting in merely the tally of votes for school board members or the masses of people that enroll their children in public schools each year. As I make more clear in Chapter 4, publics for schools are achievements, formed of problems, existing in conflict, developing in deliberation. Yet the work of achieving publics requires a particular view of public life and a particular approach to leadership.

Achieving publics requires a bifocal view of politics and public life. On the one hand, the idea and name of a *public* institution usually suggests notions of a universal, symbolic sphere of individuals bearing rights and responsibilities, a sphere where political decisions are guided by constitutional principles discussed in Chapter 2. "The people," in this notion of the public, have little actual political power in real terms but much symbolic power through the derivation of constitutional principles used to make school governance decisions. These principles are based on values of individual liberty, equality of opportunity, civic education, and participatory governance.[25] These values, symbolic of constitutional commitments, achieve political power when used to guide leadership and decision making in public schools. This is a typical interpretation of the label *public* when used to describe public schooling. It is the public with a capital P, the most dominant meaning of the term.

Yet there is a second, often forgotten but essential meaning of the public idea as it relates to schooling. Contrasting with a universal Public sphere of rights-bearing individuals and constitutional principles are the more organic and episodic manifestations of public will and social movement forming in response to shared problems in schools. There is a universal Public within the context of nation-state borders, but there are also multiple publics. In a world inhabited by diverse ideologies, religions, ethnicities, and nationalities, a social universe characterized by pernicious inequality of educational resources and outcomes, our political society noisily brims with multiple, episodic, and occasionally chaotic emergences of "the people."

A *bifocal* conception of public life is used in this book to frame an argument that educational leaders do not work with "the public," as is commonly assumed, as much as they help to *achieve* publics for public schooling. "The people," in the case of school politics, mobilize around particular problems related to young people and their schools, and they are best understood not as *the* public but as multiple public*s*. These mobilizations, when they mature beyond embryonic formations, come to understand their shared educational problems and potential solutions through political practices and shared work. Educational leaders work with these publics bifocally; at the local level in particular contexts, but also with a longer view toward constitutional principles and the (shifting and contested) ideals of a unitary Public domain. These multiple publics need to be engaged in the governance of schools; their energies and motivations must be harnessed, when possible, to build greater capacities for teaching and learning in schools. But such harnessing is not necessarily inevitable. Most publics, as John Dewey noted, do not move beyond initial, embryonic formative stages.[26]

As I explain in Chapter 4, educational and civic leaders of all types can become more adept in seeing the dual nature of the public and in harnessing the potential of multiple publics through specific skills and habits, guided by the unitary constitutional ideals. I argue here for a bifocal understanding of the public idea as it relates to schooling, and I assert that educational leaders must help *achieve* publics for public schools—that public schools are, in effect, *more* than the sum of their parts, more than merely schools run with tax dollars and elected school boards. The universal Public is achieved through decisions guided by constitutional principles; the multiple publics achieved through engagement, conflict, and collaborations with nascent publics that arise in relation to shared problems in their schools or districts.

A bifocal vision of public achievement leads to particular ways of governing education, leading schools, and engaging citizens. Public schools are achieved when the individual political freedoms constructed by constitutional principles are joined with a broader understanding of school governance: governance as enabling the development and channeling of the political authority created by the mobilization of actual publics. Rights-bearing individuals constitute the universal Public, but public life is simultaneously inhabited by radical pluralism; and schools earn legitimacy neither by avoiding or managing this pluralism through a simplistic, individualist constitutional logic nor through playing the game of public relations. Public schools are achievements, moments when citizens focusing on the problems of school or youth can build forms of communication, leadership, and political influence to enhance the capacities of educators in public schools.

In Chapters 5 and 6 I examine concrete ways that schools achieve publics. In these chapters I offer two different examples of public formation and development, showing how these formations can productively engage and foster the growth of these publics to improve the quality of public education. The first example, explored in Chapter 5, concerns community organizing. Social action or community organizing for education creates associations of community members—particularly parents—who work to build power for improving the quality of their public schools. Long associated with class-based social movements of progressive politics in the United States, community organizing has inspired fear and loathing among many an urban superintendent, as organizers' activities can garner negative attention to schools through news media. Yet in recent decades, interest in this work has been renewed for those who wish to reform public schools, particularly in urban centers. Social action or community organizing can build publics for schools in ways that build educational capacities, and it does not have to be a threatening practice for educational leaders. As I argue in Chapter 5, it can be an approach to building publics that makes great strides in empowering families, building social service networks across multiple institutional sectors, and enhancing teachers' capacities to educate all students. It is also a practice that, when successfully implemented, puts leadership development at the center of its work, realizing that community organizing requires skilled community leaders.

Chapter 6 takes up the second example of deliberative politics in school decision making and governance. Formal deliberative processes are inclusive community forums that enable citizens to think together about particular problems they face in their schools. Deliberative forums are diverse in design and purpose, and they can be messy. Yet they enable educational leaders in schools to help the publics of their district become more informed, more reflective, and often more united on some basic desires for educational outcomes. However, a deliberation is not a failure if consensus is not reached; far from it. Deliberation enables parents and community members, who often act like consumers, to begin to see themselves as interdependent citizens who share accountability for their school systems and whose voice in education governance matters. I discuss examples of public schools that have employed deliberative strategies to illustrate how deliberation can not only improve a school's focus and its capacity for educating all students but also build legitimacy for the school.

The final concept anchoring this exploration of public schooling is leadership, treated in Chapter 7 with Steve Thompson, first author of the chapter. The discussion of leadership is everywhere in our society, but it is most heavily influenced by writings and thinkers of the business and corporate worlds of private enterprise. The dominance of business-oriented leadership rhetoric and practices is the very reason we take up the term *leadership* here; to describe the particular meanings of leadership that *public* roles and work require for public schooling work. "In the conventional view, the purpose of leadership is to define and present a policy agenda for the community and to motivate people to support that agenda."[27] This conventional view of leadership can be misplaced in public realms. Instead, good public leadership works to "improve the public's ability to understand the hard choices confronting it and to contribute to its ability and readiness to form a public perspective on the problem" and to then enable publics to reach judgments that all can live with.[28] For citizens to organize themselves into publics capable of reflecting, acting, and guiding political institutions such as public schools, they need leadership, but not the typical forms of leadership that are most lauded or touted in popular culture narratives and by the private-sphere oriented leadership literature. Public leaders work strategically across sectors, they collaborate, they convene citizens, and they enable citizens to make decisions about shared problems. This final chapter offers rationale and suggestions for forms of leadership that are essential for achieving publics for public schools.

CHAPTER 2
THE PROBLEM OF LEGITIMACY

- Michael Smith, in his blog "The Principal's Page," issues a warning to anyone thinking of becoming a public school principal today: Prepare to be sued. "You need to prepare yourself, not just for your impending legal trouble but also for the noise. Parents seldom say they are going to sue you in a nice quiet inside voice. They scream it."[1]
- In Ohio's 2009 "off-year" election cycle, just over 40 percent of the eligible electorate, on average, turned out to elect school board members and weigh in on levy issues in districts around the state. The turnout rate was up from 31 percent in the 2007 cycle, but down from the presidential race a year before, when 70 percent of the electorate cast votes.[2]
- Conservative pundit Jonah Goldberg, in "Do Away with Public Schools," argues that "Americans want universal education, just as they want universally safe food. But nobody believes that the government should run 90% of the restaurants, farms and supermarkets. Why should it run 90% of the schools—particularly when it gets terrible results? . . . Private, parochial and charter schools get better results," Goldberg asserts. "Parents know this. Applications for vouchers in the [District of Columbia] dwarf the available supply, and home schooling has exploded."[3]

Public schools today are said to be in "a legitimacy crisis."[4] While crisis language should only be used with caution, there is evidence for such a dramatic claim. The previous examples are just the tip of the iceberg, as anyone who follows educational issues in the media knows. There are, in abundance, negative interactions with litigious parents, poor political engagement in traditional forms of participation such as school board elections, and many across-the-board attacks on the institution of public education itself. I am not suggesting these criticisms, apathy, and attacks are necessarily unwarranted, as each case or each particular claim or issue is distinct and should be considered on its own merits. However, important here is what all this adds up to: a diminishment of normative legitimacy of public schools. In this chapter I explain the concept of legitimacy, and why it matters for all educational institutions but particularly for public schools. Legitimacy is a precious, intangible, but significant "good" for public schools. As I will argue, it is of particular concern to government-run institutions in democratic societies. Understanding legitimacy as a cultural and political good is an important first step in our inquiry of examining meanings of the public for public schooling.

Defining Legitimacy

As organizational theorists Meyer and Scott state, "organization is in part a matter of shared opinion." They offer a broad definition of legitimacy: "Organizational legitimacy refers to the degree of cultural support for an organization—the extent to which an array of established cultural accounts provide explanations for its existence, functioning, and jurisdiction, and lack or deny alternatives."[5] Opinions and perceptions about public schools are everywhere in our society, perhaps because schools are one of a few public institutions with which a vast majority of US citizens are regularly and significantly involved. Most of us have attended a public school for at least several years, if not our entire school careers, and know many others who also have significant public school experience. Thus, the idea that organization is partly a matter of opinion is exceedingly relevant for public schools, an institution about which many of us can express firsthand knowledge. It is irrelevant that my firsthand experience is incomplete or partial at best, in that it is probably based on my own experience or perhaps those of friends or family members. My opinion about public schools, and that of my neighbors, can be a particularly strong force. These opinions are powerful, in addition, because they are not simply composed of (often subjective) facts and evidence but, like most of our opinions, involve feeling and emotion. Schools often evoke strong emotional responses in students, teachers, and parents alike that linger far beyond our years in school. Belonging, fear, pride, joy, shame, and anger are but a few of the feelings that shape our subjective perceptions of public school legitimacy. These feelings are with us as we go to the polls (for those of us who bother) to elect school board officials, to vote on school funding issues, or in our various interactions with schools and educators.

Perceptions are not just shaped by our subjective experiences, feelings, and individual opinions, however. We exist in a culture wherein educational commentary, information, and research are widely available. Most of us, if we want to gather information about public schools, seek sources that confirm our own views and suspicions rather than challenging them (a phenomenon called confirmation bias[6]). Nevertheless, more than at any other time in our nation's history, today there is a plethora of published viewpoints about the state of public education. The Internet, Web 2.0, and social media have exponentially multiplied not only the number of these perspectives available to readers and viewers but also the number of people able to author or express these opinions. Pundits, education think tanks, news stories, research reports, blogs, editorials, popular books, magazines, and websites are all widely available sources of information and opinion for any citizen who can read, turn on a computer or a social media device, do a simple web search, or find a talk radio station.[7]

Much of what we can hear or read about public schools from these sources is "bad news," critical in some way or form. Critics of public education would say that this is due to the poor state and outcomes of public schools. Neutral observers might simply point out that "bad news sells." A third reason might be that, as Parker puts it, "there is a great appetite in this nation for bad news about schools."[8] Supporters of public schools would argue, among other things, that this "bad news" is enabled by a number of well-funded groups who generate opinion and biased research against schools, for ideological rather than educational reasons. What matters is not which of these claims is true; there is some truth in all these accounts. The quality or lack thereof in any school must be judged by good evidence (not headlines or hearsay), and the quality of public schooling varies enormously by context, often very closely reflecting the patterns of socioeconomic status of families within the district. What matters here is how easily anyone can seek out and find information and opinion about public schools today, and indeed, how *available* are so many, and so many negative viewpoints on public schooling—part of what Parker calls the "discourse of derision" that now represents the common sense opinion of public schooling.[9] If legitimacy represents a cultural accounting of an organization, then there is much material, and much of it negative in nature, for citizens to use in judging their public schools. Again, not all that material is true, relevant, or unbiased (hardly any of it is that), but there is more of it now than there has ever been in the history of public schooling.

Abundant information about a public institution ought to be a boon for collective forms of self-rule wherein an informed citizenry is better equipped to share governance. But more available information and opinions about public schooling obviously do not equate to more legitimacy for the institution, particularly of the political type. While organizational theorists look at cultural dimensions of legitimacy, *political legitimacy* is a particular form that we are concerned with here. Political legitimacy gives "an account of the justice of political arrangements," on the moral defensibility of the school's authority to educate. Public schools are indeed political arrangements: state-supported institutions subject to collective governance of the citizenry and the will of the representative bodies that shape its rules and regulations, acting on their interpretation of constitutional boundaries.[10] Political legitimacy is an invisible but invaluable good for public schools, and there are signs that it is diminishing.

Political Legitimacy for Public Schools

Democratic governments can be thought of as covenants, or agreements. In exchange for a citizen's obedience to law and share of income in the form of taxes, the government promises to provide for the safety, constitutional liberties, and basic means for promoting "happiness" for all citizens. State-supported institutions such as schools, in a political society claiming to follow principles of democracy, are given contingent authority based on this covenant. Citizens agree (mostly by implied consent) to be taxed, and most of us who have school-aged children send them to these schools for seven or eight hours a day. In exchange, schools are to prepare these children for the future roles they will occupy in the society. In a democratic society,

> stable governments and their institutions require citizens who respect and can function within the established political order. If government is to be stable without being repressive, it must be legitimate in the eyes of its citizens. If it is to be seen as legitimate without manipulating citizens to accept an unjust regime, citizens must see it as legitimate because it meets appropriate normative criteria of legitimacy.[11]

Legitimacy is a political good in a democratic state, one acquired by schools when they meet criteria asserted by those to whom they are responsible: the people and their elected representatives of the state. Normative criteria are the broad measures of evaluation that people use to judge the quality and worth of the school system. Simply put, if (most) people believe schools are meeting these normative criteria, (most) people willingly enroll their students in schools and support the schools in various ways. Government institutions that lack legitimacy are in danger of governing using unethical means, including coercion and force.

There are two kinds of criteria that a school must achieve in the eyes of the people to whom it is accountable. The first are criteria for properly meeting its basic aims and purposes, "which should aim at the good of those they serve." The second set of criteria concerns how to meet these purposes specifically under conditions of a liberal democratic form of governance.[12]

The first kind of legitimacy criteria for public schools is a standard based on meeting the institution's basic organizational goals and objectives. As defined by government legislation, discipline-based content standards, and local school boards, as well as numerous popular and scholarly perspectives, these goals and purposes are neither stable nor the product of complete consensus. These goals are, however, broadly concerned with literacy, numeracy, critical thinking, and knowledge of US and world history, science, current affairs, government, foreign language, geography, mathematics, economics, technology, health/ safety, and the arts. These goals also include and reflect some generally shared public views on behavioral and moral standards for youth. I do not wish to overstate the extent of our agreement on any of these goals, but evidence suggests that US citizens broadly share some common aims for public schools. The actual curriculum and conduct standards of any school or district are always the product of ongoing argument, reflective of a combination of educators' beliefs and values, local politics, and voters' desires, as well as state, national, and international trends. While the goals for public schools are diverse and wide-ranging, all are often subservient to the dominant vocational view of the broader purposes of education today in US society. Yet the larger point here is that any school's legitimacy can be judged by how well it meets these broad educational goals. This type of legitimacy criteria is simply, but importantly, a standard of how well a school is helping all students learn about knowledge that is socially valued. While this sense of legitimacy is not explicitly discussed in this book, it is obviously of central importance in establishing the public good of legitimacy for public schools.

The second kind of legitimacy criteria is explicitly political and democratic; we will refer to this second type as *political legitimacy*. Why is a second set of criteria for legitimacy necessary? Whereas the first criteria are largely appropriate for school organizations in any type of political society—totalitarian, socialist, or communist, for example—constitutional democracies have requirements that impose additional legitimacy standards for its state-sponsored schools. Kenneth Strike lists the following normative or moral principles of political legitimacy for public schools in such societies: (1) fair participation—all must be able to participate in the shared governance of the school; (2) liberty and pluralism—public schools must respect constitutional freedoms of religion, free association, speech, and the press, and they must respect cultural, religious, and human diversity; (3) equal opportunity—equal protection of the laws and a level playing field for all students and families; (4) political education—producing good citizens who can function well in a liberal democratic society; (5) professionalism—ensuring that decisions requiring expertise are made by those with appropriate expert knowledge and authority.[13] It is important to examine each of these in turn, as all play a role in the current problems schools face with regard to political legitimacy.

Principle 1: Fair Participation in Shared Governance

The principle of fair participation traces its legacy to the strong tradition of local governance in US public schooling as well as the basic principle of democratic collective self-governance. All citizens, and not just parents, should have the ability and opportunity to participate in how their state-sponsored schools are run, and help shape what aims their schools pursue. Most districts, as well as local, state, and national governments, rely on formalized electoral forms of participation to satisfy this principle. These forms are usually *representative, aggregate* modes of voter preference—voting for school board representatives or proposed funding increases. Such forms of participation are necessary but increasingly inadequate, by themselves, to sustain legitimacy for public schools, as I will argue in later chapters.

Representative democracy concerns the work of officials elected to represent our views and diverse interests. This model of governance in a large and complex society like ours works as an "aggregative democracy," a "process of aggregating the preferences of citizens in choosing public officials and policies."[14] Representative democracy shapes and legitimizes public schooling at several levels. The first is at the national level, in the form of federal legislation passed by elected officials, to which state-supported schools are legally bound. The No Child Left Behind Act is the most obvious, recent, and far-reaching national law to influence many aspects of public schooling. Similarly, we elect representatives for our state legislatures who pass laws and allocate funding for public schooling programs and initiatives. The historical overview of the public school system in Chapter 1 shows how federal and state legislative bodies, and their appointed government agencies, have come to assert more authority over public schooling in the post–World War II period, with local authority on the wane.

Over the past one hundred years, the role and scope of school board governance has changed dramatically. The administrative centralization prominent in urban schools in the early twentieth century—when municipal and state authorities began to regulate schools more heavily—did not impact rural schools as significantly. Yet rural boards were dramatically altered by school consolidations that began in the late 1940s with the aim of cutting educational costs and enabling wider curricular options possible through larger school systems and schools. "The 89,000 districts of 1948 became 55,000 five years later, 31,000 by 1961, and less than 14,000 in 2007."[15] This meant that an average board member now represents the interests of many more citizens—who are, in turn, more diverse—than she or he did fifty years ago. And while many Americans are still loyal to the idea of a "locally controlled" public school, contemporary school boards work without much understanding or support from most citizens.

> A basic paradox exists: Support for the idea of the school board is coupled with widespread public ignorance of specific board roles and functions. Deep public apathy and indifference are common, as the tiny turnout for board elections in many communities demonstrates. This civic ignorance bodes even greater trouble for the future, when student populations become more diverse and creative leadership is even more necessary.[16]

These trends suggest that there are only very limited ways that citizens can become more involved in public school governance today. Enacting the principle of fair participation in the governance of public schools represents a serious challenge in this era. This challenge calls for creative exploration of new forms of democratic governance that might supplement and shape the dominant representative, aggregate forms currently in use. Participation in the formal channels of representative aggregate democracy is weakening, particularly as related to school governance, by measures of voting rates during school board elections.

People's trust in representative bodies tends to run quite low as well: a 2009 survey in Ohio found that only 6 percent of respondents expressed a great deal of confidence in the US Congress, and a national survey reported similarly low confidence numbers.[17] Further, mayoral takeovers of school boards in many cities signal that the legitimacy of the school board itself, as an institution, may be eroding in urban regions. There is disenchantment, to say the least, with representative forms of governance generally and with regard to formal channels of political representation in particular.

Public schools do not have to exclusively rely on representative and aggregative democratic means of governance. While school leaders must follow the laws of the land and respect the authority of the legislatures, they can "also attempt to create deliberative and participatory institutions within their schools [or districts]" for teachers, parents, older students, and other community members.[18] Such attempts represent the infusion of *associative* or *associational democracy* into our current representative democratic structure, models in which "key importance is attached to the individual participation taking place in the context of self-governing interest groups or associations, which in turn have some sort of democratic structure, ... [and which] can also directly or indirectly provide the society with additional means of representation, ... regulation, [and] governance."[19]

Creating new institutional avenues for citizen participation in school governance is an important theme of this book. Chapters 5 and 6 specifically explore some of the promising associative democratic practices that can revitalize, shape, and complement representative and aggregate forms of citizen participation in school governance. Continuing to rely exclusively on representative aggregative forms of democratic authority, as they currently exist, will not enable educational leaders to fulfill the spirit or substance of the principle of fair participation in shared governance.

Principle 2: Respecting Liberty and Pluralism

The second principle of political legitimacy is respect for liberty and pluralism, describing the moral and political goods that public schools must both observe and protect in educating students. State-sponsored public institutions are charged with upholding the Constitution, and schools are obligated to observe constitutional principles as understood to apply to students (legal minors in the eyes of the state), teachers, and diverse families. School leaders face the difficult task of ascertaining the particulars of how to protect constitutional rights as well as interpreting the confusing and shifting court opinions regarding those rights, as law inevitably evolves over time.

In addition, the task of upholding rights to constitutional freedoms often bumps up against respect for pluralism, as well as against local control and governance of schools. What the Constitution or the courts seems to guarantee for students in schools may directly clash with local norms and values regarding child rearing, religious expression, or the origins of human life, for example. And as our country has become much more diverse, these clashes seem to become more numerous as they are certainly more widely publicized. Immigration to the United States exploded from the 1980s through the end of the twentieth century, and the religious, national, linguistic, and cultural pluralism in our classrooms has become more visible. In addition, as a gay, lesbian, and transgendered civil rights movement builds in many states as well as globally, people of diverse gender and sexual identities work to find safety and respect in US public schools. As diverse students and families attempt to establish a legitimate place in public schools, educational leaders find themselves caught up in powerful political battles in their communities and in the courts.

In Ponce de Leon High School in Florida, a student who complained to her principal about harassment based on her sexual orientation was told by him that "it isn't right" to be homosexual, and he threatened to inform her parents about her sexual orientation. After a false rumor circulated that this student had been expelled for her sexual orientation, a group of students expressed support for her by writing "GP" or "Gay Pride" on their bodies, wearing gay pride T-shirts, circulating petitions, and displaying signs and messages in support of gay people. Many of the students engaging in these activities were later sanctioned and/or suspended, based in part on the principal's belief that they had disrupted school activities and learning. The school board supported the principal's actions, and a lawsuit followed.[20] A US district court in Florida found in 2008 that the students' speech in school on behalf of gay rights was protected speech. Judge Smoak of the federal court wrote:

> The Holmes County School Board has imposed an outright ban on speech by students that is not vulgar, lewd, obscene, plainly offensive, or violent, but which is pure, political, and expresses tolerance, acceptance, fairness, and support for not only a marginalized group, but more importantly, for a fellow student at Ponce de Leon. The student, Jane Doe, had been victimized by the

school principal solely because of her sexual orientation. Principal David Davis responded to Jane Doe's complaints of harassment by other students, not by consoling her, but by shaming her.[21]

This principal and the school board in this case were facing a complex problem. The local majoritarian values of the community in which they lived (and likely themselves held, to at least some degree) were seen by the court not only to conflict with constitutional rights to protected political expression, but also to go against the value of respect for the pluralistic student body they were charged with educating. Local majoritarian values and resistance against these values about what constitutes an appropriate moral code are part of a larger national "culture war" where many battles are waged over the rights and dignity of nonheterosexual and nongender-conforming persons.[22] Young people with gay or alternative gender identities in schools seek respect and safety in schools, where peers as well as teachers and administrators may harass, intimidate, or threaten them. They and their supporters (including gay teachers and administrators working in schools) wish to speak up on behalf of this cause. Others in their community, and often their own parents, wish all this would just go away. Principals and school boards are caught in the middle of these wars, and the Ponce de Leon High School case shows us how the criteria for political legitimacy provide difficult standards that often seemingly conflict with local "common sense" as well as what a majority of vocal parents might wish.

Achieving political legitimacy is not just "following the rules," nor is it bending to the wishes of the most powerful parents in a locality; it often demands negotiating dilemmas and can sometimes mean going against the grain of local values. It demands seeing through a bifocal lens, as we will more carefully explore in the following chapters. A bifocal view of school governances uses the guides of constitutional principles of capital-P Public life, but also navigates the competing demands of local citizens and their value orientations in lowercase-p publics. Working in accordance with principles of liberty and pluralism, in the face of "the demands of an increasingly diverse society divided by 'culture wars,'" poses enormous difficulties for the political legitimacy of public schools today, requiring careful political analysis and navigation by educational leaders.[23] This is not simply a matter of following the will of "the people" locally, but enabling school leaders to interpret local problems with a broader bifocal lens. The difficult fact is that respecting the liberty and pluralism of citizens and youth in a school district may sometimes go against the will of the local majority.

Principle 3: Equal Opportunity

The third principle of political legitimacy for public schools is that of equal opportunity. This principle concerns equal protection of the law for all students, as well as equal opportunity for all students—of all social class, racial, ethnic, and other backgrounds—to have a level playing field through their public schooling experience. Horace Mann helped popularize the idea of common schooling across Massachusetts as well as the nation when he called attention to radical inequities among schooling opportunities and resources in the early nineteenth century. In the early twenty-first century, we are still facing inequalities of various kinds and enormous proportions, and public schools remain a central arena for confronting the problems that inequality brings to a democratic society.

While twentieth-century civil rights battles went a long way toward enabling public institutions to confront and eradicate some of the legacies of slavery and ethnic-based discrimination, sustained progress on equalizing educational outcomes has been evasive. Massive popular (and court-enabled) resistances to integration and to other efforts to equalize opportunities have challenged progress on this principle. As supporters of the original *Brown v. Board of Education of Topeka* decision marked its fifty-year anniversary in 2004, many lamented its only partially fulfilled promises. In fact, as David Kirp commented in the *New York Times* in May 2012, desegregation as an educational policy is "effectively dead." This despite its success as a policy that helped to dramatically equalize education for African American children.[24]

In addition, the increasing socioeconomic inequalities between families in the United States today have serious implications for the school's efforts to "level the playing field."

> When one looks at where the population growth is occurring in the United States, it is mainly among non-Whites. Because of the inequalities in our society, this means that children are increasingly from poor, disadvantaged families, which presents a big challenge to the public schools. At the same time, the middle class has become more affluent, better educated, and more quality-conscious consumers. With the increasing importance of education for the future success of their children, their expectation for quality and choice in services and goods has created the basis for a "politics of excellence and choice in education."[25]

In an era in which legislators have increasingly moved away from a welfare-state ideal of governance, legislative responses to increased inequality do not involve increased funding that might be used for social welfare programs or to enable schools to hire more qualified teachers. Instead, tackling the problem of inequality in schooling during this political era has largely relied on either market approaches (ostensibly giving some parents more "school choice") or top-down accountability measures (holding each school accountable for equalizing test score outcomes among all groups). Thus the principle of equal opportunity, so critical for the political legitimacy of state-sponsored institutions in democratic societies, becomes widely though inadequately translated into school choice policies in many states, and into high-stakes standardized testing dictating the curriculum in too many public schools.

While the debates about the outcomes of both NCLB and school choice policies rage on, these responses to unequal educational opportunity have created at least as many problems as they attempt to solve—and they are often simply inadequate for the task. Many educators and parents believe so strongly that the high-stakes testing requirements of NCLB are destroying the teaching and learning environments in schools that they are organizing politically to change or eradicate the law. Others take a more academic but nonetheless critical viewpoint. Larry Cuban argues that while NCLB doesn't necessarily do much harm to top or second-tier schools, at the schools with the highest concentrations of children from poor and working-class families, these broad-brush policies can do the most damage. Policies like NCLB have, in these schools, drained "attention and resources from where they are most needed," in that NCLB has led to a heavy emphasis on instructional practices designed to boost test scores to the neglect of other kinds of teaching and learning resources and reforms. Since "poor academic performance stems from an entangled blend of in-school and out-of-school factors," this shift in emphasis has been particularly harmful in poorer urban schools, where an array of complex conditions in the home, community, and school help produce poor school achievement. Schools in any community, but especially in poor communities, cannot just focus narrowly on producing passing test scores, or even on what happens inside the classroom or inside the school, as "schools cannot do it alone."[26]

Schools are but one institution that must battle against inequality, but today they are often shouldering the heaviest collective burdens when it comes to leveling the playing field. Those burdens are very large, partly due to our firm cultural beliefs in the Horatio Alger, rags-to-riches legends that fuel our beliefs in unlimited social class mobility. Recent educational reform discourse at the national level echoes these cultural beliefs. In an "Educational Reform

Manifesto," national reformers such as Joel Klein, Michelle Rhee, and Paul Vallas assert, along with prominent members of the Obama administration, that "the single most important factor determining whether students succeed in school is not the color of their skin or their ZIP code or even their parents' income—it is the quality of their teacher."[27] This assertion, while literally true, suggests a simple answer to a very complicated problem, and it flies in the face of persistent evidence of the relationship between skin color, family social class status, and educational opportunity. Two different reports published in 2012 about public school outcomes clearly point to such evidence. *A Rotting Apple,* issued by the Schotte Foundation for public education, asserts the apartheid-like nature of public schools in New York City:

> Most, if not all, students in majority middle class Asian and White, non-Latino Queens Community School Districts 25 and 26 ... have an opportunity to learn in a high-performing school, where most students are able to achieve at high levels. None of the students in Harlem, Bronx and Brooklyn Community School Districts 5, 7, 12, 13, 16 and 19 ... have the opportunity to learn in a high-performing school. The latter districts serve some of the poorest children in the city.[28]

Similar findings from the national context are documented in a different report, issued by the Brookings Institute. *Housing Costs, Zoning, and Access to High-Scoring Schools* examines city zoning practices across the United States and analyzes how these exacerbate unequal access to quality schooling. The report points to the significant differences in access for low-income populations to high-quality schools in many US cities. For example, "Northeastern metro areas with relatively high levels of economic segregation exhibit the highest school test-score gaps between low-income students and other students." The report also documents that "across the 100 largest metropolitan areas, housing costs an average of 2.4 times as much, or nearly $11,000 more per year, near a high-scoring public school than near a low-scoring public school."[29]

Increasing opportunity and achievement gaps are the consequence of a shift in educational policy making. Political-economic trends in recent decades have been dominated by neoliberal governance policies. Neoliberal political ideologies reject a strong government, preferring instead market-based, privatizing solutions to those supporting traditional government institutions (such as, in educational policy, school choice plans like vouchers and tuition credits for private schooling). Neoliberal government policies, popular since the 1980s, reduce tax burdens on middle-class and wealthy Americans, and these in part have helped lead, in the United States, to some of the largest gaps in wealth and access to resources that any modern western democratic state has faced.

This expanding gap in wealth as well as educational opportunity has set up an extremely difficult situation for public schools and their political legitimacy, particularly in districts with high concentrations of impoverished households. The failure of many public institutions of education to eradicate gaps in achievement is based on a ludicrous but widespread belief among many citizens and even many educators: that schooling is *the* social institution primarily responsible for eliminating differentials in outcomes among populations that are wildly divergent in their access to living-wage employment, healthcare provision, adequate housing, nutrition, and social supports.[30] The child poverty rate in the United States, according to the 2009 Census, was 21 percent; and "among all children, the poverty rate was three times higher for Black children and nearly three times higher for Hispanic children compared with the poverty rate for White, non-Hispanic children."[31] In a 2005 comparison among industrialized wealthy nations of the world, the United States fared terribly: "At the top of the child poverty league are Denmark and Finland with child poverty rates of less than 3 per cent. At the bottom are the United States and Mexico, with child poverty rates of more than 20 per cent."[32] This poverty problem is not one that educators can solve alone, despite much educational and political rhetoric to the contrary.

Problems of growing poverty, vast wealth differentials, and continued biases against racial-ethnic groups in schools serve to make the proposition of realizing the principle of equal opportunity elusive. More ominously, growing poverty and vast wealth differentials can have very destabilizing effects on societies in general and on societies claiming to be democratic in particular, where principles of equality that underlie democratic foundations of government are seen as a core value by citizens. Thus, schools face a very serious challenge to their political legitimacy when it comes to the principle of equal opportunity, despite centuries of grappling with this problem and the fact that these poverty rates and wealth gaps are not problems of their own making.

Principle 4: Political Education for Democratic Life

The principle of political education is one that, like equal opportunity, has been a persistent theme in the historical rhetoric and movements for common and public schools in the United States. *Political education* refers to forms of learning (at home, in schools, and elsewhere) that prepare students for the future roles they will occupy within political systems of shared democratic governance. One of the primary justifications for nineteenth-century common schools was political education and socialization, and in early American schooling this idea was largely associated with Anglo-American assimilation, unquestioning patriotism and national loyalty, and knowledge of American history. Through recent decades, while the battles over multiculturalism have shifted the ways many educators regard the task of political education, most US public schools continue to include this principle among its objectives.[33]

Schools provide two critical functions with regard to political education, and their performance of these functions helps build their political legitimacy.

> First, in complex societies [public schools] advance public safety and development by socializing children into the general rules of the society, by establishing in them a commitment to the safety and well-being of their fellow members, and by providing them with the skills to advance both their individual and the social interest. Second, schools are critical instruments for reproducing the basic values of liberal [free] society itself and of assuring its continuation across different generations.[34]

To live in a liberal democracy, citizens must understand how to live not only with a relatively large degree of social freedom (for *liberal* here means "free") but also under certain kinds of rules and with specific kinds of responsibilities. These include understanding the rule of law, of the importance of respect for individual freedom, intercultural capacities for life in a multicultural society, and tolerance of human difference. Citizens must also possess the knowledge and abilities to participate in forms of collective self-governance—including those that express dissent[35]—so as to shape government to the will of the people and to the changing contexts of democratic life. Such knowledge and skills, central to citizenship in a democracy, also ensure the reproduction of democratic forms of life and governance in the future, important to political legitimacy.

As citizens, students are expected to have knowledge and capacities to participate in the collective self-governance thought to be the driving engine of democratic societies. Yet, too many schools are not properly educating for political citizenship. Two different concerns about contemporary political education are important to highlight, for they reflect the diverse (and sometimes conflicting) political perspectives that citizens bring to the project of educating for political life in a liberal democratic society. The first concern is best expressed in a 2003 report, *The Civic Mission of Schools,* authored by an impressive group of political scientists, scholars, school leaders, and activists. This report outlines goals for civic education, makes a case for the importance of schools as a primary venue for this type of education, and argues that civic education reform is much needed now. Despite the fact that many more young people are volunteering in communities than in the past, there are a number of signs of civic disengagement in today's generations that demand attention and reform.

> Most modern political campaigns, for example, increasingly do not interest or engage young people in government and voting.... Confidence that government officials listen to "people like me" has eroded over the past half-century, especially among young people.... Popular culture, a powerful influence on the attitudes and behaviors of young people, may have exacerbated disinterest in and cynicism about civic engagement through anti-civic messages that celebrate materialism, selfishness, and even violence and lawlessness.[36]

In the midst of all these factors, "school-based civic education is in decline" in the United States, with fewer required and offered courses than were common in schools until the 1960s.[37] Even worse are the disproportionate trends of political disengagement among poor and minority students and adults.[38] The same report contains substantive recommendations for more engaged teaching and learning of civics, government, and the active participation in community and political life, noting that stereotypical civics classes are part of the problem and not the solution to the current ills of civic disengagement.

The Civic Mission of Schools represents a point of view shared by groups of teachers, parents, and political and educational leaders: that schools are not meeting the goals of political education for creating informed, active citizens. But another criticism of public school performance related to political socialization concerns the degree to which this education should stress patriotism, or love of country, and loyalty to the United States people and government.

Pressure to educate for overtly patriotic citizenship increases during periods of wartime. In the wake of wars and conflicts spawned by the September 11, 2001, terrorist attacks, such pressures for patriotic political socialization have mounted for schools. Laws mandating the school recitation of the Pledge of Allegiance, calls for increased focus on US history in social studies curriculum, and the call to teach with historical narratives that inspire admiration and devotion have all proliferated in the past decade. One commentator argues that "patriotic sentiment is likely to develop if we tell America's dramatic story in a way that engages young people's imagination, excites their gratitude, and reveals what is at stake in the American experiment."[39] Yet some civics educators find such "dramatic stories" to be impediments to helping students develop critical thinking skills as well as a full accounting of American history. Such laudatory narratives also may do nothing to help develop students' ability to act in dissent of one's government, when political events may be deemed to warrant such actions. As is predictable, defining "political education" is politicized terrain, subject to ideological variations. Achieving political legitimacy through the principle of high quality, effective political education appropriate for democratic citizenship can thus be a challenge for educators.

Principle 5: Professionalism

The fifth principle of political legitimacy is professionalism. This principle's status as last on this list belies the powerful and nuanced part it plays in helping public schools be viewed as authoritative political institutions, worthy of citizen respect and support. *Profession* usually designates white-collar work requiring intensive training, specialized knowledge, and vocation, or a calling to a certain kind of work that one is particularly qualified or drawn to do. The "professionalization of teaching" movement has deep roots in a field dominated by women, as the teaching profession since the common schooling era has struggled to achieve adequate pay and respect in a society long plagued with patriarchal norms. Teacher professionalization movements were revitalized in the late twentieth century. In 1986, two important reports helped usher in a series of reform initiatives that continue to exert influence today.

Tomorrow's Teachers by the Holmes Group and *A Nation Prepared: Teachers for the 21st Century* by the Carnegie Task Force both argue that "the quality of public education can only improve if school teaching is transformed into a full-fledged profession."[40] Both reports urge enhanced professional education for teachers, recommending graduate education as the new entry-level credential for teachers. According to the Holmes report, teachers would learn the "science of teaching" in graduate programs and in extended clinical internships. More professional certification systems were created, including the National Board for the Professionalization of Teaching Standards (NBPTS), which has now launched a professionalization certification for principals. According to the

NBPTS website, since 1987 over 74,000 teachers have received National Board certification. The site extols the rigors of this process: "Like board-certified doctors and accountants, teachers who achieve National Board Certification have met rigorous standards through intensive study, expert evaluation, self-assessment and peer review. NBPTS offers 25 certificates that cover a variety of subject areas and student developmental levels."[41] As is made plain in this excerpt, "the explicit model for these reforms comes from medical education, because medicine provides the best available example of a successful effort at professionalization."[42]

Professionalism does indeed enhance legitimacy in all its forms, including political legitimacy. The central norms of professionalism are two: "that authority is warranted primarily by expertise, and ... an ethic of client welfare."[43] No one would dispute that expert authority is requisite for the complex task of managing and facilitating the growth of diverse young people through engagement with content knowledge across multiple disciplines of study. And the latest efforts to professionalize the teaching profession are in many ways understandable for a profession that feels as demoralized and disrespected as the ranks of US public school teachers today. The attacks on teachers in public discourse in recent years—full of accusations that teachers are overpaid, that teacher unions only pursue their narrow self-interests, and the like—has resulted in much demoralization and is likely turning many young people away from the profession entirely. American educators need more "professional capital" for many reasons, but the primary one is that it is required for a good educational system. The world's top school systems have all cultivated highly professionalized, committed, well-respected and well-paid corps of teachers, and this should be an essential educational reform in the United States as well.[44]

Professionalization, and the authority of committed, respected teachers and principals, must be balanced with community voice in governance. The push for professionalization, in itself, can at times have negative side-effects; it can lead to a shutting out of community perspectives, among other dangers. Just as a doctor might very well examine you and prescribe medicine without fully discussing with you your overall health, illness, and treatment plan, so can education become a closed process of expert authority wielded to help schools reach annual yearly progress (AYP) as mandated under NCLB. While many citizens may support the overall aims of NCLB, not many equate the passing of tests with the process of becoming a well-educated person. Even most parents supportive of standardized testing wouldn't simplistically conflate those two aims. Parents and community members know education is a broader affair, just as patients know that managing their health involves more than "take two aspirin and call me in the morning."

Public schools share authority of children with parents and, indeed, with other citizens of the state, for the welfare of our collective future as a society is caught up in the education of our public school students. Yet it is extremely important to delineate *how* teachers and other school leaders are to share this authority. Because parents do not have to send their children to public schools—private and home schooling are popular options for 10 to 15 percent of the population these days—parents still hold the ultimate authority over their child's education. Once they choose to send their children to public schools, however, they share the authority of their children with professional educators, fellow community members, and the state through legislative, school board, and other governing bodies.

But in an age where middle-class parents often act like "consumers," school leaders feel tremendous pressure from powerful parents who seek to micromanage and shape schools to the benefit of middle-class children. This, in part, is driven by an era of "school choice" where increasingly, (urban and suburban) parents may have a choice of both public and private options to consider in lieu of a neighborhood school. It is also due to the realities of political power; middle-class parents can more easily access leverage in policy making, curriculum, or hiring through personal and professional networks, and forceful communications with elected and appointed officials.

The overrepresentation of more powerful voices in shaping public education, however common-place, is antidemocratic—for "government by and for the people" does not imply "by and for the powerful people." Listening to parents and community members from all walks of life is very important; teaching is a profession with a significant civic dimension, demanding that as professionals teachers "learn to work *with* other citizens, rather than *on* them or *for* them."[45] Professional authority, the knowledge of expert educators, should be balanced with what Strike calls "democratic localism," the idea that inclusive deliberations among local players (parents, students, citizens) are legitimate forms of power and authority for shaping educational aims and goals.[46]

Following the principle of professionalism, therefore, represents a delicate balancing act in this era. Educational leaders must discern, or judge, how to balance the demands of democratic localism—the power of local voices, including but certainly not limited to those most vocal parents—with their obligations to teachers/employees, the Constitution, the state (in the form of its law-making bodies), and its educational agencies that may govern public schools. Underlying these multiple obligations is professional knowledge, which teachers and other educational leaders should consistently use as a central guiding rudder in navigating these multiple authorities. But education is far from purely a "scientific" endeavor, and professional knowledge and judgment is but one (albeit important) factor among many that should influence decision making.

Legitimacy Problems in a Diminishing State

Political legitimacy for public schools is a matter of earning organizational authority through the consent of citizens. Earning this authority comes from successfully meeting organizational goals, which are not only numerous for public schools but, in some cases, also quite ambitious. Earning political authority also comes from meeting criteria that are part of governance in a society that proclaims to be a constitutional democratic republic. Principles of liberty and pluralism, civic participation in schooling, equal opportunity, and political education all have to do with the ways public schools hold unique and important obligations as democratic institutions. The principle of professionalism, while not unique to a democratic institution, is one that must be carefully negotiated with the power of legislatures and local citizen input.

This chapter focuses on the problem of political legitimacy for a simple reason: the lack of it is diminishing the abilities and capacities needed for public schools to function well and to fulfill their obligations as public entities. While there are aspects of this legitimacy problem that are unique to education, many public institutions now face similar problems. The idea of "democracy" may enjoy worldwide legitimacy today, but ironically, the primary agent of delivering democracy in the nineteenth and twentieth centuries—the state, or government—does not. The twentieth century was an era when government authority significantly expanded, as the modern-nation state witnessed an apex of power prior to and after World Wars I and II. The political legitimacy of schools was sought through this expansion, as principles of equal opportunity, liberty and pluralism, and professionalism were all movements supported and legislated through increasing and centralized forms of governmental power.

But after World War II, a new era slowly emerged, and by the 1980s we saw a new set of political-economic forces that changed the landscape of political legitimacy. Mark Warren observes that

Politics today is exceeding the state, owing to forces of globalization, complexity, differentiation, culture shifts, and deterritorialization of issues. Democracy is a response to politics; it is one way among many that collectivities can organize conflict and make political decisions. *If politics exceeds the state, so too should democracy exceed its state-centric forms—an argument found in the traditions of anarchist, associational, and participatory democracy that contemporary circumstances have instilled with a new relevance.*[47]

The power of the state, and state-supported institutions, is no longer total, nor is it uncontested. We can certainly see how the authority of government-run public schooling is now challenged in multiple ways, and how state authority wanes in the eyes of the citizenry, even as federal and state authority has increased over public schools, and as the power of private corporations has grown through (for example) the landmark US Supreme Court ruling *Citizens United v. Federal Election Commission* (2010). As public schools have been subject to more centralized and more diverse forms of control over the past several decades, they have witnessed a decline in political legitimacy. "The legitimacy of a given organization is negatively affected by the number of different authorities sovereign over it and by the diversity or inconsistency of their accounts of how it is to function."[48] This quote explains a lot about the crisis of legitimacy in US public schools today.

All too often, the political legitimacy of public schools is seen by educational leaders to be a marketing or a branding problem. This view holds that the reputation of public schools can, if correctly packaged and sold, be improved, and with that improvement, the consent of the citizenry follows. Such a view relies on the logic of markets. But consent cannot be bought and sold: "legitimating consent must be earned, not manufactured."[49] While trying to come up with a good "brand" or slogan for a public school system may appeal to many, such quick fixes do nothing in themselves to enable schools to meet the criteria of political legitimacy, and may, through distortion or lies of omission, be simply unethical. They may ultimately harm the legitimacy of schools, as Americans are particularly apt at "sniffing out" slick marketing attempts, insofar as we are exposed to so much marketing throughout our entire lives.

Instead of always looking to the private sphere for solutions to our legitimacy problems, we might look back to the public sphere, as Warren suggests above. He draws our attention to new forms of democracy—and we will pay particular attention to the associational and participatory forms in this book—that can shape, complement, and enrich the state-centrist forms we find in the largely representative, aggregative school governance procedures that govern schools today. These new forms of democracy, emerging with the energy and evolution of civil society reforms around the world, can help educational leaders achieve publics for public schools. In sites around the United States, localities are experimenting with these new forms through community organizing, deliberative forums, and participatory experiments in school governance that require new forms of public leadership.

Political legitimacy is not a simple outcome of experimenting with new forms of democracy. Neither is it automatically gleaned when school administrators follow the constitutional principles relevant to education in a lock-step fashion. Political legitimacy is one of the goals that can be achieved when educational leaders see governance challenges in a *bifocal* way; when they can focus on the local democratic possibilities in developing publics, as well as on the constitutional demands and guidelines that shape their work. This idea, as illustrated in Figure 2.1, requires that educational leaders acquire a dual vision, viewing small-p local publics simultaneously in the context of the capital-P Public requirements of a constitutional democratic state.

Complementing the constitutional (capital-P Public) principles of normative political legitimacy discussed in this chapter, therefore, should be the generation of new models of democratic governance for public schooling that enable the development of small-p publics with the capacity to address complex school problems. Such new models are already under construction through creative experimentation in sites around the United States and abroad. These governance models create pathways for building the publics of public schools, as discussed more explicitly in later chapters. These new governance models also represent "post-statist" solutions to current problems of legitimacy, wherein alternative forms of democratic participation and governance are used to help us rebuild political legitimacy of democratic institutions. The "post-statist view" holds that democratic governance involves multiple actors—not merely government officials and elected representatives, but a wider array of civil society associations and

Figure 2.1 A Bifocal View of Public Life

citizens who engage in communication and contestation about issues in public life. The task of rebuilding political legitimacy for schools requires such an array of democratic engagements with citizens, parents, students, and educational leaders in schools. It requires engagement and collaboration with associations and citizen groups in neighborhoods, towns, and cities. As I have argued in this chapter, such rebuilding is necessary for today's public schools. The regenerative project of political legitimacy for public schools hinges not merely upon school actors using the criterion of legitimacy to guide their actions, however. It also requires locating and facilitating the development of publics *for* public schools.

CHAPTER 3
THE PUBLICS OF PUBLIC SCHOOLS

Publics are queer creatures. You cannot point to them, count them, or look them in the eye. You also cannot easily avoid them. They have become an almost natural feature of the social landscape, like pavement.[1]

The central concept of this book is *public*. Philosopher Michael Warner expresses the slippery nature of the term in the quotation above. Publics are everywhere, cannot be avoided, but we often cannot see or point to them. They are plural—publics—but so often we refer to the idea in the universal singular: *the* public, and what *the* public wants from its schools. In addition, the public concept is both real (descriptive and tangible) and ideal (referring to normative ethical, political principles that should guide our actions). Being accountable and responsive to the public represents a democratic ideal hinged to the political legitimacy of the institution of public schooling, but "the public" is also an imperfect, lived reality in our political existence.

This chapter and the one that follows take apart the notion of public as it is relevant for public schools today. In this chapter, I lay philosophical groundwork for understanding the nature of public life and interaction, and I use this to analyze the current form and function of contemporary public schools. I argue in this chapter that too many public schools today are formally but not functionally public. In Chapter 4 I offer a conceptual remedy: a notion of public life as pluralist, contested, and deliberative. This is not a "remedy" in the sense that public interactions become necessarily easier to navigate. Yet a different description of contemporary public life may more fruitfully guide educational leaders in their engagement with publics. These two chapters then, taken together, make a queer concept more plain, as Warner describes; less like the indiscernible pavement we take for granted, and more of a guiding orientation for those working in and with public schools.

Public and Publics: The Bifocal Vision

A unitary public, *the* public, refers to an inclusive totality of persons in a political society. I am a citizen in the public domain of US society, which provides access to its freedoms and subjects me to its laws. The US Constitution is our primary symbol of this unitary public, as discussed in the previous chapter. The unitary public refers to this general, conceptual domain of democratic freedom and law. In addition, the Public often refers to the totality of citizens in a nation-state, those constituting "the people," the *demos* of democracy. All governmental institutions, supported by tax dollars and subject to legislative and judicial mandates, are accountable to *the* public, or the mass public of the total citizenry of the nation-state.

However, today that public is constituted by over 300 million people, organized into states and regions, affiliating with multiple ethnic, religious, and other diverse identity-based groups, associated with wide ranges of wealth levels and lifestyle affiliations. All citizens are indeed part of the universal public of the entire nation-state, but whenever citizens are undergoing or experiencing similar consequences of a particular problem or situation, they constitute *a* public. *Publics* form around issues, and in reaction to perceived needs, clashes of values, or shared problems, and come in and out of existence depending on circumstance and context.

To meaningfully talk about public life, it is helpful to become more pluralist in our speech. While any local school is responsible to the total *demos* or mass Public of the nation-state—students must be prepared for political, civic, and economic life whether they end up living in Nebraska or Alaska—schools also have *publics*, often locally or regionally based, to which they must respond, to which they are responsible. Responsibility does not equate to servanthood or a simplistic bending to the requests of any and all groups of citizens, but to being attentive to the cultivated interests and expressed needs of publics. These publics may be purely local in nature, or they may be interconnected with broader issues, and with regional, state, national, or global movements, associations, or networks.

Schools are thus responsible to both the unitary Public and the multiple publics that emerge or develop in response to educational problems and issues. The *Public,* singular, is more a symbol of universal citizenship and political membership than it is a political association of real persons engaged in participatory work on behalf of shared interests. As discussed in Chapter 2, schools are Public when they are governed by the constitutionally derived principles that represent the shared agreement of democratic citizens. Yet schools are accountable to local, emergent publics as well, associations of citizens who come together out of shared concern or shared frustration over educational issues or problems. We thus ought to distinguish, in our language, between the Public ideal of school governance, and the more organic emergence of the multiple and diverse public formations that represent civic energy and possibility. A bifocal view of public life enables educational leaders to see both the unitary Public of the nation-state and the multiple publics that can emerge in localities in the face of problems and issues in schools.

The Necessity of Politics, but Not Politics-as-Usual

In laying out some initial thinking about the Public and publics of schooling, I have already brought up a word that will make many readers shudder: politics. Indeed, in the United States, politics is an activity that is not admired and seemingly often avoided. In popular parlance, *politics* refers to the pursuit of self-interests in a sphere rife with controversy, corruption, and extremism, and is an activity that seems to reward narrowly self-interested behavior and interests. The "I Hate Politics" Facebook page has 33,949 "Likes" as of this writing; a *Washington Post* and Pew Research Center poll taken during the 2011 budget talks revealed that when asked for a single-word characterization of the budget negotiations, the top three responses were "ridiculous," "disgusting," and "stupid."[2] The generalization that "Americans hate politics" is culturally rampant; certainly many school leaders must be among that number.

Yet schooling is inescapably a political endeavor. All schools are political institutions because education is a value-oriented process, thus requiring that decisions be made regarding which moral and political values and ideas should shape or dominate the common curriculum and educational programming. There is no escaping the fact that all education and all schooling is value-laden. All schools are political institutions in a second sense, in that they are human organizations where people and groups vie for voice and control over various domains—curriculum, staffing decisions, and resource allocation to name just three.

A school district in my state recently faced a controversy over the movie *American Beauty*[3] being shown in some eleventh- and twelfth-grade English classes as part of a unit on the American Dream. One group of parents thought the schools should prohibit all movies that are R-rated, in order to protect high school students from the sexual and violent themes of films like *American Beauty*. Many teachers believed they had justifiable pedagogical reasons for using this movie in the curriculum. And many students and parents spoke for and against the issue, from all sides. This controversy was political because it involved different constituencies vying for power and influence over the decision of a curriculum that would affect many different students. Public schools are inherently political institutions because, like all schools, they deal with issues of value and with organizational governance.

Public schooling is necessarily political, though not in the narrowly self-interested popular understanding of that term. The very name *public* in public schooling implies a political and ethical relation of responsiveness to the citizenry. Because the citizenry is diverse and has pluralistic ideas related to the value-imbued project of education, and because public educators have a duty to be responsive to the publics they serve, public education is inescapably political.

Throughout this book, I use the term *political* in a different way than the common-sense notion of politics as the narrowly self-interested pursuit of power and influence. By *political* I mean related to and partly determined by activities associated with noncoercive means of making collective decisions that, in a democratic society of pluralism and substantial inequality, should serve a wide range of interests. Such political activities typically include debate, deliberation, dissent, voting, lobbying, protest, and coalition building. The political is inescapably a terrain of conflict, but it also entails practices that invite collaboration and degrees of trust over time. With regard to the *American Beauty* controversy, formal leaders in the school district could have wielded a decision behind closed doors, but they could not make a legitimate and politically defensible decision in such a manner, which would seemingly ignore citizens' various views and reactions to the use of the film.

Politics, in short, refers to the "negotiation and compromise among diverse views and interests, the alternative to violence in complex, modern societies of great heterogeneity."[4] Politics, for educators and educational leaders in public schools, describes the activities associated with the governance of these institutions, and to the processes that citizens can use to form, assert, and communicate their educational interests with each other and with schooling officials. Political activity in schools, then, includes ways of involving citizens in processes that shape school aims and policies.

The formal rules of our political society tell us how political activities related to public schooling must be governed and facilitated. The United States is a liberal democratic state that, as described in Chapter 2, brings together two different and sometimes incompatible political ideals. The liberal tradition focuses on individual rights, especially on human freedom, and on independence from the tyranny of government. "Liberals insist that democratic self-government requires a fair and neutral political framework in which individuals can enjoy freedom and be treated as equals."[5] The republican strand focuses on the promise of popular sovereignty and the ideas of equality, and the role of the people in governing. Small-r republicans insist that citizens play a valuable role in constituting the state, in helping to guarantee its freedoms, shape its common ends and purposes, and become, or choose, its political leadership. Liberal and republican philosophical strands can stand in tension with one another, as individual freedoms and civic equality at times bump up against what is thought to constitute a "common good." For conservative parents in the school district facing the *American Beauty* controversy, the common good for schools entails a curriculum that is free of—and positions itself against—the harsh language, violence, and sexual innuendo they see in popular culture and beheld in *American Beauty*. For other parents, the journey to becoming a critical thinker, a person who can govern oneself as an autonomous citizen, requires schooling that provokes thought and inquiry about serious social themes, a task both teachers and students testified that the *American Beauty* curriculum accomplished. Public schools regularly grapple with such clashes.

Liberal and republican democratic traditions have not become reconciled in the several centuries of US nationhood but constitute a "democratic paradox" that structures the political lives of all US citizens.[6] Paradoxes are living, breathing contradictions in our political lives and work. Leaders in schools, towns, or neighborhoods cannot avoid these democratic paradoxes. They are contradictions inherent in the structure of our political system. In addition, many of these contradictions are often uniquely and emotionally confronted in public schools. Publics of public schools thus emerge out of a political system characterized by a paradoxical situation wherein two imperfectly compatible political ideologies must coexist. It is out of this paradox that a notion of publics for public schools is forged.

Publics of public schooling are constituted within the realm of political activities designed to express and weigh shared interests and concerns, for the purposes of (1) influencing the decision making of elected representatives and appointed school officials, and (2) building greater educational capacity in schools and communities through collaborative work. Publics for schooling are born of education-related issues or problems of particular concern to a group of people. Those people become "a public" for schools not in their agreement or their perfect convergence of viewpoints but when citizens engage in public work related to the educational issues or problems they face. This public work is fed and enriched by the associational life of our society—civil society sectors that enhance the new forms of democracy that are shaping public school governance today. Community organizing and democratic deliberation are two forms of associational politics discussed explicitly in this book, as they have both proven successful in helping educational publics form, mature, and achieve their goals related to school improvement. The work of achieving publics for public schools enables citizens to form and sharpen their viewpoints on salient issues, communicate their views to those holding positions of power and authority over state-sponsored schools, and build capacity for higher quality teaching, learning, and development to occur in those schools and their surrounding communities.[7] This idea of the public is not new, but reflects a strain of pragmatic thinking that is quite old in democratic political life as well as in American culture.

Before elaborating further on this definition, however, it will be helpful to discuss what a public is *not*, in order to help dispel some of our common-sense thinking on the topic that can get in the way of a deeper understanding of public life. Most citizens think of public life using three basic metaphors: publics as markets, publics as audiences, and publics as communities. These are, however, diminished and often misleading ways of understanding public life today. After describing and critiquing these metaphors, I conclude the chapter by discussing the importance of new forms of democracy in public school governance, and the role civil society associations play in these new forms. New forms of democracy enable public schools to achieve publics for their schools.

Inadequate Metaphors (or, How Not to Think about Public Life)

Public life is widely conceived of as a marketplace. In an age where school su-perintendents are called chief executive officers and a customer-service mentality and language pervades school management, the citizen is increasingly thought of and treated as consumer. "Schools are now taking on the structures and the aims of business; schooling is becoming the education business, and students [and their parents] are becoming education consumers."[8]

> We have come to think of ourselves, not as citizens, but as *consumers* of what government can deliver. Hence the readiness and frequency with which we describe ourselves as "taxpayers." Taxpayers are persons whose chief concern is how much money they are spending for the goods and services their tax dollars buy. Taxpayers are the consummate political consumers. Political consumers expect public officials to do things for them. They see their own role as confined to alerting officials to their desires and opinions, and advocating actions and policies they believe will benefit them.[9]

Publics as consumers participate in educational governance and decision mak-ing by very narrow and individualistic means. In decentralized organizations like American public schools, there are two fundamental methods of influence as an individual consumer: voice and exit.[10] Some consumers of schooling, particularly in urban districts, increasingly are empowered to "participate," not by having voice in the life of the school but by the act of exit. These parents, as consumers, can remove their children from traditional public schools into charter schools or private schools using tuition vouchers. Advocates of school choice, powerful and diverse groups of paid lobbyists as well as citizens influencing educational policy and rhetoric in recent decades, have often promoted the idea of the public as a market, with parents as consumers in that marketplace.

Beyond the act of leaving the public school system, consumers of public schools are primarily provided access to political voice through the individual act of voting every two or four years. While the majority of the over 14,000 school districts in the United States are run by elected school boards, school board elections are "low-key affairs": "Participation is usually minimal, turnout low, and the content of the campaign trivial unless the public is particularly dissatisfied by a recent policy decision. Candidates often run unopposed and unaffiliated with political parties."[11] School leaders understandably draw the conclusion that their public/ customer base is content to let the expert school managers run their schools for them. School leaders who conceive of themselves as business managers in this sense do not realize that an engaged public requires an altogether distinct sort of structure, culture, and leadership, a point addressed in later chapters.

Publics are also popularly conceived as audiences. Typically, audiences watch performances on a stage or screen. Audiences are formed of people who are often strangers to one another. The individual audience member's role is to be silent and listen, observe, to take in the performance, and react through prescribed means (applause, silence, boos). The notion of public as audience is a popular one in contemporary representative forms of government, where much government work is left to elected officials and appointed experts. As public schools have come under more control of state and federal government regulation, and school districts have grown larger, the audience metaphor has grown in power, as more individual citizens watch elected officials shape the direction of their schools in the halls of power. Moreover, state-government institutions are usually aware of the ethical demands of transparency—the notion that the reasoning, evidence, and results of decision making on most matters should be open to the public. As a result, many people working in public schools conceive of the public as an audience that watches what they do, and, if they're lucky, passively or enthusiastically supports what they see happening in the school. While applause may not be necessary, many educators hope that their audiences will demonstrate their approval through volunteering, supporting school fund-raisers, or voting "yes" on school funding issues.

Finally, public life is sometimes described as synonymous with community, or even in familial-like terms. In these attempts, a public school or district is being discussed in a way that communicates elements of sameness, harmony, and homogeneity. While many communities are quite diverse, communities are usually characterized by and known for commonalities, where individual interests are communicated and joined together in shared aims, goals, and practices. A district official may describe relations in a district as "like family," and schools engage in community-building activities in ways that are quite positive for student learning and growth.

The metaphors of consumer, audience, and community, while perhaps expressing relevant ideas for particular aspects of public schooling, all miss the mark of capturing the meaning of public life and the creation of publics for public schools. Each metaphor may convey some particular elements of public life, but all three fall short of adequately expressing the notions of interdependence, pluralism, and everyday politics that are part of public life and work. None of these metaphors communicates the social activity or the lively, sometimes difficult confrontations that characterize public life today in its fullest and often most productive forms.

Metaphors of consumer and audience rely on an individualistic notion of citizen, whose participatory agency in political life is diminished to small, paltry roles. In modern political life,

> individuals have been relegated to two minor roles, neither of which meets the requirements of a functioning democracy. One is to be part of the faceless claque present at staged political debates or invoked as scarecrows or totems on behalf of someone else's argument.... The other niche is as special pleaders, either as consumers or petitioners for special benefits or as victims of particular abuses.[12]

The consumer's power is usually only in affecting her own situation, because her political power is quite narrow. She can buy more of the product or not buy it at all; she can intervene in public schooling to advance her own child's situation and standing, or—*if* she has the financial means—she can leave the school by changing residence, home-schooling, or pursuing private schooling. Her power over her own school situation is governed by her own resources and can affect—as consumer—usually only her own (her child's) situation. The audience's power is even weaker: as audience, we can whistle, or boo, or applaud, but all of our actions are *re*actions, in response to the actions of the performers. If citizens do not like what's going on in the school, they can leave (again, if resources permit); if they like the school performance, they can stay—and maybe even throw a rose. Audience members cannot truly affect the script, choreography, storyline, or performances of the actors. Curriculum theorist Walter Parker calls such conceptions of citizenship "civic voyeurism," where citizens' role is limited to watching other people—elected representatives, and their appointed officials—enact citizenship and make political decisions.[13]

Moreover, an individualistic and relatively passive notion of citizenship, as conveyed by the audience and consumer models, serves only one form of democratic governance, and it is a form that is increasingly inadequate in capturing democratic work and decision making. As described in Chapter 2, there are two types of democracy that are prominent in western thinking: aggregative and associative. Aggregative democracy sees governing as a process of adding up or aggregating the preferences of citizens in order to choose public officials or policies. The goal is to "decide what leaders, rules, and policies will best correspond to the most widely and strongly held preferences," and a well-run aggregative democracy allows for the expression and competition among those preferences.[14]

A main distinction between aggregative and associative democracy is that to be a member of an aggregative democracy requires far less of us as citizens; it asks that we keep track of events through news or media outlets and occasionally communicate with elected officials. As citizens in this kind of public school governance, we might respond to surveys or questionnaires about our views on our schools or school issues, which are used by educational experts to shape schooling policy and direction.

In the representative, aggregative model of democracy that dominates our political systems today, citizens' views are heard in very narrow and prescribed ways. As a member of the aggregative public, one is asked prepared questions and expected to answer from a particular narrow range of answers. Citizens do not organize, debate, and deliberate together but, at best, "register" their current opinions, usually from a list of prescribed choices or alternatives. The idea of public as an audience understands the public role of schools to aggregate and create policies based on the total sum of people's interests, wishes, and opinions; democracy in this sense is a competition among interests, held by individuals and, sometimes, their interest groups. Polls and surveys are often used to "hear from" the citizens so that board members or state legislators can form schooling policies that meet the (singular form) public's expectations.

Associative forms of democracy, dependent upon the rich array of political associations and movements within the sphere of civil society, are distinct from aggregative forms in some important ways.[15] More associative forms of democracy, such as deliberative and participatory democratic models, are those in which citizens are not simply individual citizens with predetermined, fixed interests, but wherein citizens are envisioned as people who can become more informed, enlarged, and expanded, as well as shift and change over time. The associative models of democracy also assume that a good decision made about a shared, complex problem cannot usually be found through the mathematics of adding up individual preferences. Aggregative democracy contrasts with associative democracy in the same way that a poll compares with a good conversation. Polls register what we currently think today, in all our relative ignorance or knowledge about a subject, as individuals who make up small parts of a mass society. A good conversation is usually an exchange of views, where participants learn from and with one another, and where sometimes minds can be changed in the process of chasing an idea or a question through interpersonal exchanges. A conversation, when done well, is much more than simply the sum of the words uttered within it; it often generates new ideas, shifted opinions, or enlarged thinking.

Markets, audiences, and communities as metaphors for public life fail to capture the social pluralism of public schooling and the possibilities that this pluralism brings to its governance. This pluralism can be productively channeled to enrich the commitment and sense of vision that local publics have for their schools. Channeling and utilizing the visions of publics, however, requires infusing more associational forms of democracy into public schooling governance that currently, in most districts, relies heavily on aggregative forms. Associative forms of democracy, such as participatory and deliberative processes detailed in later chapters, help schools confront the political problems we face today—particularly the idea that schools no longer are responsive to the views its citizens. Associative forms also help schools respond to the rich forms of pluralism that characterize public life. Such forms of pluralism bring difference and sometimes conflict, an uncomfortable but requisite part of democratic life. Associative democratic models can be contexts where citizens confront and communicate over those differences in viewpoint, and communicate with elected and appointed educational officials regarding their views.

Associative models assume not only pluralism but some degree of citizen interdependence as well. We participate as citizens in democratic forms of educational governance because we share fates; we share educational fates by being associated with the same tax-payer funded school system that we rely upon to help educate the next generation of our society. We share political fates in that we exist in the same political system on whose stability we rely to guarantee our continued enjoyment of basic rights and opportunities.[16] We share ecological fates in that the ways we treat resources of land, water, and air will shape our future and future generations' health and well-being. Neither consumers nor audiences share fates in this same way; there is no interdependence implied in these metaphoric descriptions of public life.

Finally, we should address another popular metaphor for public life, that of community. While a metaphor of community certainly speaks to our human connections and interdependence, rhetorically it suggests far more homogeneity and *a priori* shared purposes than can be found in public life. While communities *can* be quite diverse and full of a wide range of interactions, including conflict, the idea of community is often used as a symbol for shared aims, history, and common purposes.[17] I believe that school leaders should help facilitate the construction of certain kinds of open, diverse learning communities *in* schools that benefit learners and teachers. But publics and communities are not interchangeable kinds of groups, though both are forms of human association. Multiple communities are contained within public life. Communities can be associated with historical longevity and often linguistic, ethnic, or religious similarity. Publics are typically more fleeting, more issue- or problem-based, more prone to open disagreement, associated with less interpersonal trust, and more explicitly political in design and purpose. Community usually refers to both the commonalities found and created in these contexts among groups of people, and the communication that helps construct and maintain the relational ties that bind these groups. Public life contains complex networks of many diverse and overlapping communities, interconnected in limitless formations.

Consider the experiences of a group of New York City public school parents, students, and community organizations working against increasingly centralized, aggregate democratic governance in their schools. Mayoral control began here in 2002, shifting from a decentralized system of governance. By 2008, Mayor Michael Bloomberg had much support for his leadership, with rising test scores and a new federal secretary of education, Arne Duncan, who publicly supported Bloomberg's leadership and mayoral control. But New York City parents, students, teachers, and others who were experiencing growing dissatisfaction with this administration had little recourse.

> In place of *involvement* in setting goals and priorities, the Bloomberg-Klein approach focused on *implementation* of their policies. In place of community voice, their approach put a strong emphasis on individual exit—giving families the option to go elsewhere if they were unhappy with their assigned school. Democratic participation in setting policy was relegated to the four-year mayoral election cycle, channeled into an arena where other issues compete for priority and where most groups do not have a direct stake in public education.[18]

Yet not everyone was a fan of New York City's form of centralized governance. In 2008, despite support for the Bloomberg school policies among national educational reformers like Duncan, communities in New York began to push back on the centralized forms of control. Two groups, formed of diverse community groups networked in coalition, emerged to challenge the centralized mayoral control in 2008 in the city. One was an all-volunteer group of parents and activists calling themselves the Parent Commission, who called for an end to mayoral control. The other, Campaign for Better Schools (CBS), was a broad coalition of twenty-six groups in the city who "took the stance that mayoral control could be improved substantially through real checks and balances, greater transparency, and authentic public participation."[19] The CBS included a diverse range of groups such as the Haitian Americans United for Progress and the Metropolitan Russian-American Parent Association, as well as several prominent youth-led organizing groups such as the Urban Youth Collaborative.[20] It sustained an active online presence, developing blogs where information, views, petitions, and announcements could be circulated to interested citizens. Through an energetic mix of neighborhood, Internet-based, and state-level organizing strategies, these organizations ultimately won legislative provisions aimed at expanding parental engagement in education decision making. One of these provisions was for the creation of thirty-two Community Education Councils across the city, composed of nine elected volunteers who serve as policy advisors to their community's public schools. While not necessarily a complete or perfect outcome for these groups, these new provisions are evidence of what public work can accomplish. These parents, students, and activists brought these reforms to fruition through their actions as citizens, not as individual consumers, private citizens, members of homogenous communities, or spectators of democratic governance.

Civil Society and Publics for Public Schools

My intention is to push beyond current metaphorical thinking about the publics of public schooling. While the metaphors discussed here may contain some value, each one is wanting as a stand-alone description of the purposes and governance of public life as it relates to public schools. To get beyond the simplicity and duplicity of these metaphors, we first need to understand the context and terrain of public life in societies proclaiming to be democratic—the realm of *civil society*.

"Public" is not synonymous with the state or government; publics are distinct yet interconnected with government in design and function. This is an essential differentiation to make for people who work in state-sponsored schools that proclaim to be public. Publics are primarily located in the realms of politicized civil society. *Civil society* is a term for the relatively public sphere that exists in the spaces between state, markets, and the intimacies of domestic life. Civil society offers a public alternative to both the government and market spheres. Yet the energy of civil society, formed of the multiple political and social associations in US society, can be pressed upon the power of the state to seek binding legislative or other types of changes to state-sponsored institutions. These associations include diverse national groups like teachers' unions, the National Association for the Advancement of Colored Persons (NAACP), Boys and Girls Clubs of America,

Focus on the Family, and the Trevor Project. Also included are the hundreds of local civic organizations in locales around the country who are working on behalf of youth and school reform. These are examples of civil society groups that are particularly interested in the growth, development, and education of young people in our society. These groups develop their goals and agenda in civil society, the spaces of relative trust where people with shared concerns can formulate common goals relative to the education and the well-being of youth.

A community organizing group is an example of such an association. These groups exist in civil society and form—sometimes as sole organizations; sometimes as a coalition of various organizations—so that individuals can formulate and work toward their common interests. When leaders developed within these groups step into "the power realm of the public" sphere, when they begin to engage with state-sponsored institutions like schools, they are doing public work.[21] The civil society sphere and the public sphere are overlapping; the former constituted by relative trust and commonality, the latter constituted by less trust, and more asymmetrical, uneven relationships of authority, influence, and power. Groups formed in civil society become publics as they build coalitions across diverse groups and work to enact policy, legislative, or other reforms related to the governance or administration of state-funded public schools.

Civil society associations help build collective networks and associations within the public sphere, enabling the development of publics. These publics and the state are in relationship, though these relationships are not always easy or conflict-free. They are also not all formed in the shared interests represented in the capital-P Public principles. Schools have multiple publics; agendas emerging from these publics are not always in line with the criteria of democratic legitimacy, which include the principle of equality of opportunity. Public schools have an obligation to achieve their democratic legitimacy from publics—whether participants in civil society associations working with schools or as individual participants in the shared governance of the school. Educational and civic leaders, however, often have the special burden of sorting out which publics' agendas best forward the aims of democratic legitimacy, a point to which I will return in later chapters.

The Private Sphere—Both Feeding and Diminishing Public Work

We have now distinguished several distinct but overlapping "spheres" and institutions of social life: civil society, the public sphere, the state (in the form of institutions like public schools), and the private. Publics for public schools are born and nurtured in civil society, engage in public work in the larger public sphere, and are interconnected with both the state (often working to reform, push against, or guide the state's leaders through associational democratic forms) and with private spheres. To bring a bit more clarity to these differing spheres, let's examine the public/private contrast. What role does the private sphere play in public work?

The English word *private* is rooted in the Latin *privatus,* or "deprived," as premodern Roman and Greek societies equated privacy with suffering. People were seen to suffer, in the ancient world, when they were not allowed to enjoy the rich interchanges and debates of the public square. Those who were summarily excluded from that sphere—all women and slaves, for example—were seen as deprived of, and not capable of, participating in this rich and fulfilling public experience. The private sphere is that which is not subject to public scrutiny, legislation, or debate; it includes the domestic sphere of home and one's private life, one's religious associations and practices, and the unregulated aspects of our market-based economy. In ancient times, the private sphere was seen, among those white males who were lucky enough to be deemed citizens, to lack the vitality, depth, and importance of public life.

Today, many people and certainly most Americans see this differently. "Being private is what people want positively to be."[22] Private life is characterized by control of my own space and information, by enclosure and exclusivity—my home is invitation-only, and what I want to consume, or what religion I wish to practice, or which websites I might visit, are up to me and my own resources. The fulfillments of private life today are considerable, and they are often an escape from the challenges of what is sometimes the stressful terrain of public life.

The idea of public in the United States is often seen as sharply distinct from private life and domestic concerns. But publicity and privacy can be interconnected, and with the explosion of Internet and social media technologies, this interconnection has been greatly enhanced. Social media, for example, blur the boundaries between self and society, private and public information. "The shifting boundaries between public and private life become a new battleground in modern societies," where a "new kind of information war" is waged. Information that might be otherwise considered private, like the sexual orientation of a teacher, or the inner emotional turmoil of a bullied teenager, may now be "public" by nature of a Facebook posting. The new world of "private information" in light of new social media tools is "a terrain where established relations of power can be disrupted, lives damaged and reputations sometimes lost."[23] As the boundaries of public and private are more porous with new technologies, even as there exists much possibility for damage, there also exist many promising new opportunities for political and educational engagement among citizens. As we discuss in later chapters, these new communication technologies are shifting the ways that publics can form and communicate around shared public school issues and problems.

Public and private are also porous in other ways, too. For-profit companies not only create jobs but can also benefit their communities through philanthropy, generating tax revenues for better roads or schools, being responsible environmental stewards, or allowing employees time off for community work. Private desires and concerns can also spur dedicated public involvement among citizens; my love for my own children can translate into powerful activism and participation on behalf of the welfare of all children in my town or region. The private religious beliefs and church community ties of African American communities helped nurture and propel the public work of such organizations as the Congress for Racial Equality and the NAACP in their long fight to desegregate schools and promote equal educational opportunities. Historically and today, parents have translated their interests formed in the private spheres of intimate relationships and religious community into political work on behalf of the welfare of their own and other children in schools. Private life, in a sense, competes with public life for our attentions and time, even as it also enriches it, and is intertwined with it in creative, sometimes unsettling new ways on the Internet and through social media networks. Our private and secular interests can motivate us to become actively involved in public life and can animate the best of our most powerful political debates. Thus, while civil society is the terrain where politicized associations of citizens with common concerns can gather, communicate, and through public work engage with state institutions like schools, the terrain of civil society can overlap with our private interests and concerns as well. These spheres of our lives are not neat compartments but malleable, overlapping areas of existence.

Form and Function of Public Schooling

Publics are not domestic spaces, nor private enterprise, nor governments; they form distinct spaces and relations from those of the private and state worlds. In the formalist sense, publics refer to formations of "the people" in a democratic political society who work to constitute the will or intent of the government's actions and policies. But how do "public" schools actually function? This is a key question in an age where the concept of a "public school" is undergoing dramatic shifts. The very meaning of a "public school" today is morphing at a rapid rate. "We can no longer rely either on tautologies (public schools are those schools in the public school system) or truisms (common schools bring us together). For better or for worse, the very project of the common school is being vigorously contested and dramatically redefined."[24]

In considering the question of the "public" school, both form and function of such a school should be evaluated. Gary Miron and Christopher Nelson offer a good formalist definition of the term *public* in public schooling: "A school (or other institution) is public if it is owned or controlled by citizens or their duly elected representatives. Assessing public-ness with this definition requires an investigation of who owns the means of educational production and to what extent schools and their activities are susceptible to oversight by elected bodies."[25]

This formalist definition offers a good starting point, but what does it mean to own or control a system as vast and often as impenetrable to individuals as traditional public schools? Whereas presidential elections in recent cycles have drawn more than half of the voting-age population to the polls, local elections for school board members draw far fewer.[26] For-profit charter schools receive taxpayer subsidies, thereby sending citizens' tax dollars into institutions that may have little public accountability, no obligations to accept special needs students, and no transparency in operations. Mayoral takeovers of city schools like New York, Los Angeles, and Philadelphia and other cities have replaced elected school boards with appointed officials and have reduced citizen engagement opportunities in many of these cities. While such takeovers may improve urban schools by measures such as test scores and lower dropout rates, they surely signal the fluidity and flexibility of what it means for the public to "control" and "own" their schools, particularly at the local levels. Such takeovers often come with increased forms of privatization, as well, and diminished avenues for citizen engagement with their schools.[27] Public schools across the nation today are governed not only by elected boards, mayoral administrations, and city governments but also by legislatures at the state and national levels, who today are asserting more control over school-level teaching and assessment practices than at any point in the history of public schooling.

It is said that "function follows form." Yet a public school might be formed as a school in the interests of "the people" but not function in ways that serve the holistic purposes of the people and publics of that district. Public schools governed by the citizenry should function in the publics' interest; they should help promote the success of all students from all walks of life. Functionally public schools should promote interests related not simply to private gain or happiness, but to wider and broader sets of interests in the political and social realms of life.

Are public schools providing good public outcomes? This is the sense of public-ness that philosopher of education James Giarelli reports missing in his local public school system, widely known in the region as a "good school." This school, like many suburban high schools, seemed organized around the aim of social efficiency and vocationalism, preparing students for entering competitive universities to prepare them for their high-paying careers. Seeking an alternative, Giarelli found that the local Quaker school, while private in the formalist sense, was functionally public; in his view, he found that the school's curriculum, structure, and assessments all prepared students to be knowledgeable, engaged, cooperative citizens.[28] Many of us falsely assume that our schools function as public schools because they are formed in ways involving some small amount of citizen control, through paying their taxes and electing school boards and legislatures. Giarelli makes the crucial point that form does *not* always follow function when it comes to public schools. He points to the fact that public schooling's primary purposes revolve around employment and individual mobility up the ladder of economic opportunity, which is largely an educational aim benefiting private interests. The concerns of "the people" and of the publics of democratic life are often much broader than the private advancement of individual workers, however.

How is it, then, we have public schools that are seemingly (thought decreasingly) public in *form* yet weakly public in *function*? How is it that many public and publicly funded schools serve primarily private interests and do not operate according to the publics' interests when they are currently guided by more state and federal legislative mandates than at any other time in their institutional history?

Gaps between Publics and Public Schooling

Three factors in modern political and educational systems bear much of the blame. The first is the overinvolvement by business and corporate interests in legislative processes at state and federal levels; the second is the underinvolvement of localized publics participating in governance of public schooling; and the third is the fear, disinterest, and sometimes outright disdain that some formal educational leaders hold for such types of localized or any sort of public engagement.

While the interests of businesses and corporations have been powerful in shaping public school policy and curriculum for at least a century, recent trends show an expanding influence. "During the past two decades, the debate over American public education has been conducted through a new form of partisan rhetoric. Private sector economic motives are increasingly prominent."[29] Although economic aims of education are undeniably important, we currently live in an era where these aims, and many of the private interests that compel them, are a disproportionately powerful influence on schooling policies today.

> A strong trend is ... toward closer control of education by partisan politicians and the corporate interests that speak through them. Lobbying, once dominated by teachers' unions, is now replete with a range of voices, including school management companies, technology purveyors, investment consortiums, think tanks, textbook and test publishers, and others.[30]

This range of voices in educational lobbying includes groups like the American Legislative Exchange Council (ALEC), a political powerhouse that has successfully promoted legislation for school vouchers, tax incentives for private education, and for-profit education ventures in many states.[31] But ALEC is just one of many profit-making interests that are overly influential in educational policy making today; the privatization of many educational sectors in the United States points to the influence of profit-making, self-interested concerns over public motives. "Privatization, particularly in the form of vouchers, removes public education dollars from public governance, transferring public funds into private entities that may or may not have any responsibility to serve a public purpose."[32] There are numerous forms of privatization, including the selling of educational curricula, test preparation programs, and the powerful role that textbook companies play in shaping curricula.[33] Historian of education David Tyack also notes this trend:

> Private agencies not subject to direct public control have exerted great influence over public education. Consider the power of textbook publishers over the curriculum or of test companies over the destiny of individual students.... What happens to democratic control of education? How can conflicts of interest or indoctrination be avoided when huge corporations that sell to an educational market also take a central role in designing schools and in providing instructional technology and materials for them?[34]

While private interests are not necessarily incompatible with public motives—private commitments often helpfully inform public interests and movements—business involvement in education is often aimed at expanding the individual profits of business or the economic sector as a whole. This aim is largely if not wholly self-interested. While businesses *can* simultaneously make profits and operate in the wider public interest, too many do not. Business and corporate sectors have expanded their influence in our political system with regard to educational policy making, and this signals a diminishment of public interests represented in school decision making.

The second factor informing the gap between the publics' interests in schooling and the actual performances of public schools is the underinvolvement of localized publics participating in governance of public schooling. This is connected not only to the first factor of disproportionate involvement of business and corporate interests in education but also to the twentieth-century movement toward centralized control over public schooling. More state and federal control over education has come largely in the form of standardization "reforms" since the passage of NCLB in 2002. "Standardization, with systems of accountability based on standardized tests, is redefining education, and educational achievement, as the production of scores on standardized tests." As Linda McNeil notes, standardization undercuts community voice: "The language of accountability tends to drive out an important component of democratic education: other shared vocabularies by which communities may discuss their goals for their children's education. These include the vocabularies of child development, intellectual capacity, cognitive growth, and, in Dewey's term, preparation for participation in democracy."[35]

Standardization "reform" is one symptom of a larger problem: the diminishment of local control. Robert Franciosi blames this problem on "the 200-year assault on local control of schools." He writes, "education reform has consistently been accompanied by a relentless centripetal force, as each new plan places greater power in higher authority levels: from district to town, town to state, and state to the federal government."[36] As local officials have enjoyed less control over education policy, and more pressure to meet nationally set standards, there have been fewer opportunities for citizen participation in local governance of public schools. Americans, for their part, work long hours and enjoy many private fulfillments, and many at present do not choose to involve themselves with politics and public formation, but this situation is circular, as meaningful opportunities to become engaged in these activities have been on the wane.

School administrators often only exacerbate this tendency in school governance to limit and block public participation. Principals, superintendents, and board members have often not sought such opportunities for increased citizen involvement. Faced with increasingly narrow and intense expectations on test scores by state and federal officials, as well as parents who can be litigious and contentious, many school administrators and board members seek to avoid participatory models of governance. These leaders usually tightly control and carefully manage citizen participation, preferring to nurture "parental involvement" over "parental engagement" in the shared governance of schooling. Scholars of school-community relations have documented the significant difference between the two terms:

> Parental involvement—as practiced in most schools and reflected in the research literature—avoids issues of power and assigns parents a passive role in the maintenance of school culture. Parental engagement designates parents as citizens in the fullest sense—change agents who can transform ... schools and neighborhoods.[37]

By endorsing deeper parental engagement with and participation in school governance, I do not wish to exaggerate the capacities or abilities of citizens or to underestimate the expertise required to run schools and educate children. Most citizens have neither the interest nor ability to take over management, supervisory, or pedagogical realms of public schooling. But citizen participation in governance is critical to the work of deciding upon the broader aims, purposes, and direction of a public education in a particular area or region. Citizen participation provides much-needed political legitimacy for public schools. In addition, citizen participation helps support a more holistic and effective approach to education, because parents, schools, and civic associations cannot educate children well by operating alone or at odds with one another.

Conclusion

Education consists of more than schooling; it comprises the efforts of multiple institutions and associations (families, religious institutions, and schools, among others) in promoting the growth of society's children and youth. Associations of citizens, members of the larger Public of the nation-state, periodically come into existence in localities or regions to give voice and influence to affairs related to schooling. Associations form in civil society and are activated by shared problems or concerns. In the public sphere, these associations help citizens gain political voice and power to express their interests and agendas. Such publics for public schools can exert pressure in order to break the "habitual behavior" that is generated from the bureaucratic, centrally controlled school system that has developed since the mid-twentieth century. As philosopher of education Leonard Waks argues, "the state system, in education and other areas of public concern, … devolves into habitual behavior and bureaucracy. It requires pressures from publics, organized and active in civil society, to transform existing situations."[38] Publics represent one formation of "the people," or the *demos* of democracy—a formation that is all too rare, to the detriment of our political life and our public schools. Developing the space and capacities for publics in relation to public schooling is a much-needed expansion of the associative and participatory forms of educational governance. Understanding how to work with publics for public schools enables school leaders to venture beyond current models of centralized representational and aggregative democracy that dominate governance of public schooling today. In the next chapter, I say much more about these publics: why they are necessary in a constitutional democratic republic, why they are important to successful public schooling, and what it means for educational leaders to use a bifocal vision of public life to help develop and engage them.

Chapter 4
Publics

Formed of Problems, Existing in Conflict, Developing in Deliberation

> It may be that the authoritative "people" that haunts our political dis-
> course is indeed best thought of neither as a formally organized corporate
> body nor as an atomistic collection of individuals, but instead as an oc-
> casional mobilization through which separate individuals are temporarily
> welded into a body able to exercise political authority.[1]

"The people" often take the form of a temporary mobilization in political life.
Whereas "the Public" references a vast, distant, and often symbolic sphere of
common constitutional principles, public life often consists of the smaller, more
sporadic formations of collective will in response to concrete problems. Educational problems—such as racial/ethnic achievement gaps, inadequate financing,
disciplinary inequities, or aging facilities—call multiple and diverse publics into
existence.

Pragmatist philosopher John Dewey wrote one of the defining texts of the
twentieth century on public life. *The Public and Its Problems,* published in 1927,
explained the idea of a public in Dewey's infamous literarily dense but conceptu-
ally clear prose. "The public consists of all those who are affected by the indirect
consequences of transactions to such an extent that it is deemed necessary to

have those consequences systematically cared for."[2] Dewey reminds us that the public and state-sponsored governmental institutions (e.g., schools, courts, legislatures, parks) are not synonymous spheres, but interdependent ones. "A public articulated and operating through representative officers is the state; there is no state without a government, but also there is none without the public."[3] A state institution like a school cannot exist without publics; thus, Dewey helps us link the public's contemporary weaknesses to the public school's crisis in legitimacy and public purpose. The public school's legitimacy is tied to any public school's engagement with its numerous publics.

Publics in education are usually temporary mobilizations—though "temporary" may be a relative term—focused on issues related to schooling. And, as Dewey tells us, it is one thing for a public to begin to form in relation to schooling or educational problems. It is another, altogether more beneficial but difficult matter for a public to achieve some forms of maturity; finding common ground and political agency through practices of communication, leadership development, building power, and the co-creation of solutions and accountability provisions for carrying them out.

Publics Form in the Shared Experiences of Social Problems

A town's high school has been housed, since the 1950s, in a building increasingly deemed inadequate by teachers, administrators, and students. All students and staff in the building were undergoing the consequences of the building's age and state, and the community was suffering the consequences in different ways. The perception that the high school was not "state of the art" caused more and more families relocating to the area to buy homes in nearby districts with glossier, newer high schools. People in the district gradually became aware of having to systematically attend to the consequences of an aging high school building.

Thus began years of debates and battles, several defeated tax levies, many impassioned letters to the editor of the local newspaper, and, ultimately, a narrow margin of victory (fewer than 200 votes) for a school levy to fund a new high school facility in 2008. The school district's official state representatives, school board members and their appointee, the superintendent, were then charged with executing the wishes of the public. The wishes of this public, ascertained through the ballot after two previous failed attempts, represented some modicum of weak consensus—the outcome of primarily aggregative democratic forms of politics—built over time in the district. Yet the new school building was a highly contentious issue in the community, where conservative residents resistant to new school taxes stood against more liberal townsfolk, many of whom are associated with a regional university. "Publics are called into being by issues"; the issue, in this case, was an aging school facility and the shared but diverse consequences collectively endured by citizens in a certain kind of collectivity, which in this case was a school district.[4]

A public was called into being in this district. Citizens involving themselves with this issue constituted a nascent or embryonic public not by their agreement (for there was precious little of that) but by their shared experience of an outdated high school. "Differently situated actors create democratic publicity by acknowledging that they are together and that they must work together to try to solve collective problems."[5] Yet this public failed to fully develop into maturity—into a public capable of investigating, communicating, and applying political power to government institutions. "A public can form only if people are aware of the many ways that they are affected by events and ways in which their actions affect one another in ongoing, important, and intricate ways."[6] Such awareness develops through productive communication, ongoing investigation into the problems at hand, and wide dissemination of that information. What happens *within* a public formation, Dewey argued, *should* be good habits of reflection, open communication, and deliberation. These processes of sharing diverse perspectives in an effort to create some common ground with regard to the aging high school were lacking. Citizens in the district thus constituted an ineffective public, largely unsettled in the weak consensus that constituted the "yes" vote for the levy. Individuals could choose to vote or work for or against the levy politically, but as an association of diverse citizens faced with an aging high school building, they were unable to constitute an effective public that could inform and shape the school board's deliberations and votes. This is because school administrators relied primarily on the aggregative model of democracy to win the day, focusing tightly on strategies to win enough votes to pass the levy to build a new school.

The public that formed around the high school issue did not get beyond a weak consensus on a new building because it failed to communicate and engage the complex issues surrounding the issue. This public was not able to develop sufficiently rich and varied forms of civil communication to understand and share meanings, ideas, and differing perspectives on the state of existing facilities. In particular, like so many nascent publics in our time, its leaders could not build networks of communication and influence *across* diverse groups and institutions that hold power and resources in the district. These diverse groups were the inter-est groups and loosely affiliated networks of like-minded voters who never were able to communicate and find overlapping interests around their problem of an outdated school facility. Such groups—parents and students who supported new school facilities, antitax groups, property owners in the district, and those who object to new school taxes because of their overall disagreement with state school funding formulas—never achieved public maturity. As is symbolically illustrated in Figure 4.1 below, they could not find overlapping interests and areas of po-tential mutual agreement, and thus they remained distinct and mostly at odds.

As a result, processes of aggregative democracy were exclusively relied upon and, in this case, helped to deliver a narrow margin of victory for those supporting a new high school facility. But these aggregative processes also served to deepen the divisions and conflicts over public schools in the community, rather than helping to create more shared educational perspectives and visions. Threats of lawsuits of various kinds by those who opposed the new high school aimed to block construction in the months that followed the election.

Dewey, who died over half a century ago, worried about the state of the pub-lic, as many other small-d democrats do today. Because of a strong individualist tradition in our country, and because of industrialization and urbanization, Dewey believed that publics were only embryonic in most places, rarely advancing to politically potent forms. He pointed out the irony of the fact that the forces

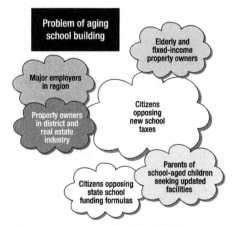

**Figure 4.1 An Immature or Nascent Public
Related to the Aging School Issue**

of individualism, industrialism, and widespread communications and technology growth expanded democratic representation and franchise even as it made "the democratic public" more diffuse and obscured. "'The new age of human relationships' has no political agencies worthy of it. The democratic public is still largely inchoate and unorganized."[7] He referred to the democratic public as "eclipsed," "bewildered," and "lost."

State institutions of schooling—what many contemptuously call the bureaucracy of public schools—are widely viewed as being solely authorized to direct public schooling's management and affairs. The publics responsible for shaping and guiding the work of these state systems often seem to be missing or are so weak as to be effectively rendered silent. A public is a group undergoing the indirect consequences of a shared circumstance. But a mature and effective public acquires the ability to have political voice and influence when its diverse members communicate in order to become more conscious of shared circumstances and purposes. "Creation and sustenance of publicity in this sense … involves the willingness on the part of participants to make claims and proposals in ways that aim to achieve understanding by others with different interests, experience, and situations and to try to persuade them of the justice of their claims."[8] Given our love affair with private fulfillments, our relative disengagement from active forms of public life, and the structure of our political systems and centrally controlled public schools, publics for schools today can often remain at the embryonic stages, their potential thereby lost to school reform efforts.

Publics Exist in Contestation as well as Ongoing Collaboration

Publics often begin in consideration of thorny problems and disagreements related to school issues of all kinds. We do well to remember that the public sphere is often "a realm of conflicts over power and resources."[9] Public education, both in the past and at present, has been fraught with such conflicts, from disagreement over whether citizens ought to support a tax levy for a new high school facility, to contentious and ongoing conflicts surrounding educational access and fairness.

The public ideal promises equality and legitimacy for all people in public life and public schools, yet the public sphere of education has historically been an exclusionist and hard-won space for nonwhites, non-Anglo citizens, the poor, sexual minorities, and persons with disabilities. Even as access was long in coming for these groups, achievement remains elusive for too many, and it falls into predictable patterns of social class and racial/ethnic classification. To offer only one example, national dropout rates for African Americans (8 percent) are higher than the rates for white students (5 percent), and Latinos drop out at rates more than three times those of whites (15.1 percent).[10] Today, in a post–*Brown v. Board of Education* era, the unfulfilled promises of public education for nonwhites and poor students are under more and more scrutiny. These gaps in achievement have roots in the gaps in income and wealth, as well as in the persistence of racial and ethnic discrimination in our society. Partly as a result of these inequalities and discriminations, democratic life can be far more contested and embattled than is often represented in deliberative models of democratic decision making. Citizens often form associations and organize in public life to help vie for power and more resources; citizens may form associations with people who are similar in social class, racial-ethnic, or religious identities. Indeed, they may experience problems with schools in ways that are uniquely tied to these identities. At times, these publics may have both oppositional and collaborative stances with other groups.

Some critics challenge such publics as "special interest" groups that impede rather than contribute to public life and problem solving. Yet calling one group's agenda a "special interest" is a way of rhetorically dismissing that group's positions; such a dismissal hides the fact that the interests of dominant groups are often misconceived as constituting the "common" interests of all citizens. Anyone with a scant understanding of the history or present of public education access and outcomes can see that this assumption is false. Citizens and publics *have* interests with regard to their children and education. All our interests are at least partially shaped by our subject positions or our social identities (white, poor, Asian, Christian, middle class, or atheist, to name but a few). These interests may begin as privately understood or articulated, but when they begin to coalesce around a public issue or problem, they are no longer private or "special," though of course they may be incomplete in terms of information and knowledge. Citizens bring their interests to public settings and educational governance processes to make appeals based on their interests. Whether or not their interests constitute "the common good" cannot be understood ahead of time; these interests must be meaningfully heard, weighed, and deliberated among citizens, leaders, and officials.[11]

In so doing, these citizens draw on their own knowledge of the problem at hand. A group of African American parents in a district discussing the integration and busing plans for a new regional high school have a particularist view on race and education, but this perspective can greatly and uniquely *inform* public problem solving rather than corrupt it. Such contributions—around sensitive issues like racial-ethnic, social class, or religious bias—add to the contested nature of public life but are essential to the striving toward a fully inclusive public school.

> It is simply not true that, when political actors articulate particularist interests and experiences and claim that public policy ought to attend to social difference, they are necessarily asserting self-regarding interests against those of others. Undoubtedly groups sometimes merely assert their own interests or preferences, but sometimes they make claims of injustice and justice. Sometimes those speaking to a wider public on behalf of labour, or women, or Muslims, or indigenous peoples make critical and normative appeals, and they are prepared to justify their criticisms and demands. When they make such appeals with such an attitude, they are not behaving in a separatist and inward-looking way, even though their focus is on their own particular situation. By criticizing the existing institutions and policies, or criticizing other groups' claims and proposals, they appeal to a wider public for inclusion, recognition, and equity. Such public expression implies that they acknowledge and affirm a political engagement with those they criticize, with whom they struggle.[12]

Easy solutions for problems facing public schools are evasive in the face of great pluralism and inequality of both educational resources and influence. From small towns to urban regions, in the United States there exist large gaps in wealth, income, and social standing of various groups and constituencies. These gaps shaped the support and opposition to building a new high school facility, discussed earlier. Some in that community—especially those associated with white-collar and professional jobs in the region—enjoy more influence on school policies and program directions. These individuals often have the networks and cultural capital to easily communicate with and lobby local school officials. In nearby urban areas, these gaps in status and influence can be even more pronounced. The terrain of much of the comprehensive public school system is highly pluralistic in terms of ideology, culture, and political influence that average citizens bring to the table. Highly pluralistic, inchoate publics often contain numerous conflicts and differences of thinking about school aims and resource allocation.

In this regard, the public terrain of public schooling can be characterized today as a space of "agonistic democracy."[13] *Agonistic* means argumentative and strained. This strain is not a modern invention but is inherent in what political theorist Chantal Mouffe calls "the paradox of liberal democracy" and is a situation that cannot be fixed. The paradox of liberal democracy consists in the tensions between liberal and democratic traditions; the former focusing on liberty of the individual, the latter focusing on achieving equality and popular sovereignty. Public schools confront such tensions regularly. Engaging in public life today means engaging this paradox and negotiating its terms in specific situations and problems.

While it is popular to regard these tensions as symptoms of the demise of democracy, we might view these tensions as signs of health. "In a democratic polity, conflicts and confrontations, far from being a sign of imperfection, indicate that democracy is alive and inhabited by pluralism."[14] This kind of democratic polity makes life more challenging for government and school leaders, and it is not one that can be eradicated through public relations. It requires a particular type of leadership and approach to governance. "Political conflict is not a problem to be overcome, but rather a force to be channeled into political and democratic commitments."[15]

A range of political activities, including community organizing, lobbying, and protest, are often necessary to express the conflicts at hand and to ensure that all interests are represented in governance processes and proceedings. Mouffe argues that all publics are thoroughly heterogeneous and formed of people with collective but shifting and multiple identities. For practical, moral, and political reasons, we must forge collective solutions to shared problems in the face of such diversity and, often, the contentious politics that can accompany it. This is true generally but especially so in public schools, where decisions must be made about how (always limited) resources are allocated and priorities are set among a diverse and unequal population of students, families, and citizens. And while organizing activities are often necessary to help raise consciousness and public accountability to the problem, particularly when those experiencing the problem are from lower socioeconomic classes, very often other forms of political work are necessary, too. The work of formal deliberation, for example, can be extremely useful as a way to further develop publics for public schooling, a way to build a sense of a diverse "we" around issues and controversies faced by a school or district. The "we" is built using a wide range of interactions and strategies, among them deliberative skills.

Publics Develop in Deliberation

In our time, then, there are multiple but often relatively weak publics. Citizens clash and do verbal battle over the myriad differences in material wealth and cultural viewpoints. How can these conflicts become generative of innovative solutions to our shared problems? How do publics become stronger, work through conflicts, and more effectively understand and communicate their interests to one another? How do these publics then effectively communicate to elected and appointed officials, and help build better capacity in schools for successful outcomes for all? Quite simply, citizens deliberate in order to develop common views and purposes.

Deliberation is the talk we regularly use to engage with an issue: to learn about it with others, to develop an opinion about it, to expand our viewpoints through listening to others' views, and to eventually come to a decision or position. Deliberation about matters relating to shared life and governance happens in many informal ways and places in our society; people talk about political life and issues at the local store, church, gym, or with friends and strangers via social media networks. The high school levy issue was discussed informally and often heatedly in offices and bars around the district. These informal discussions among (most often) like-minded citizens were not, however, ultimately the best venues for engagement with contentious issues if the goal was to find mutually agreeable solutions to the problem of an aging high school facility.

More formalized, intentionally inclusive public deliberations are facilitated forums designed to help diverse citizens talk to one another about shared problems in an attempt to find common ground and solutions. While much of our public work naturally involves informal deliberation of all kinds, and often to those with whom we tend to agree, it is usually only in more formal or organized forums that people more productively and fully exchange a range of views about a particular problem or issue. Through organized deliberative forums, people often have the right venue, structure, and incentive to work through processes of finding acceptable solutions. Deliberative democracy advocates seek to expand the number and usage of formal deliberation processes in order to widen the opportunities for, and quality of, citizen participation in shared governance. While Chapter 6 deals explicitly with deliberative forms of school governance, the idea of deliberation is introduced here to locate its importance in public life and public achievement for schooling.

Forms of deliberation are important for public creation and maturation. "The deliberative model of democracy aims to structure processes of collective deliberation conducted rationally and fairly among free and equal individuals."[16] Contemporary interest in deliberative democracy was largely sparked by the work of German philosopher Jürgen Habermas.[17] Habermas developed an ethical model of discourse to challenge the collapsing state of modern public life, and to enable conditions for good communication across divides of race, ethnicity, social class, and other differences. Discursive ethics, in the Habermasian frame, provided an early theoretical model for democratic communication designed to be inclusive, reasonable, and productive in the sense of producing good decisions for all while leveling the power differentials among participants. The goal of leveling power among diverse deliberators was and is critical to successful processes and outcomes of deliberative sessions. Formal deliberation shifts the nature of political judgment derived from aggregated individual interests to political judgments derived from peaceful but rigorous discussion:

> The public deliberation that leads to the formation of a general will has the form of a debate in which competing particular interests are given equal consideration. It requires of participants that they engage in "ideal role-taking" to try to understand the situations and perspectives of others and give them equal weight to their own.[18]

Other theorists would strongly disagree that deliberation should take the "form of debate," exploring the multitude of kinds of forums and discussion that might be more inclusive and fruitful in practice than the argumentative tendencies of debate. In other words, the Habermasian models of deliberation have given way, in more recent generations, to new theories and practical applications of deliberative work. Heavy emphasis in these later generations has been on the inclusion of diverse voices and styles of communication as a way to combat the monocultural, middle-class perception of too much deliberative experimentation and practice in deliberative forums.[19] The promising new digital tools and forums for deliberation now further the emphasis on diversity, as scholars and practitioners experiment with a new proliferation of apps, programs, and online forums now available to help engage citizens in deliberative activity.[20] "The democratic promises of social media are primarily centered around two key elements: dissemination of knowledge and new forms of participation that allow for greater inclusion and access to public decision making."[21] Deliberative democratic practices are, in many ways, experiencing a great deal of development and expansion today, which is a promising source of support for public achievement for public schooling.

Deliberations can occur in many places and forms, and a growing number of advocates are promoting the use of formal deliberations to shape school governance according to the views and interests of parents, students, and local citizens. Formal deliberations over educational issues are forums in which trained moderators provide facilitation and a process to enable diverse citizens to come together, share ideas, enlarge their own opinions, and shape policies and decisions in their schools. Some deliberations are designed to help citizens arrive at a consensus and a mandate for a particular decision; others are aimed to inform the thinking and conclusions of the elected or appointed decision-makers, both on the part of the citizens and on the part of school board or administrative team members. A number of organizations in public sector and public schooling reform efforts advocate greater use of formal and informal deliberations in school-based decisions and controversies.[22] Deliberation assumes that democracy is not a process of aggregating opinions but of helping citizens struggle to find common ground about their shared problems.

Recall the town's problem of an outdated high school building. The school district's administrative team, including its public relations personnel, tried in successive campaigns to "sell" a new levy to the voters of the district, finally beating the odds by getting enough yes-voters to the polls in a heavily Democratic turn-out election in 2008. But what if these administrators had not focused exclusively on the aims of aggregate democracy—winning more votes for the levy than against—and considered deliberative democratic processes as part of a broader solution? What if citizens on all sides of the issue had been invited to think together, trying to understand the problem from multiple perspectives, and work on mutually agreeable solutions? Public engagement is distinct from gaining "public support" on decisions already made, or securing public relations tactics or firms to help enlist votes.[23] While nascent publics can and do emerge in political life, engaging citizens in deliberation over "hot issues" can also help call a public into existence. Calling a "public" into being is enabling "a diverse array of citizens . . . (albeit in temporary and ever-shifting alliances) to decide on and advance their shared interests, the interests of the community as a whole."[24] Discovering shared interests and moving toward mutually agreed-upon solutions, as illustrated in Figure 4.2, is what mature publics are often able to do, given the right leadership, tools, and strategies.

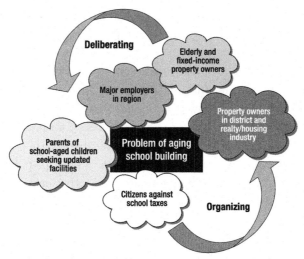

Figure 4.2 A Mature Public Called into Creation through Deliberation and Organizing Strategies

Publics in public education, when they are able to mature and grow, are diverse in population as well as in their respective orientations. They can also be highly contentious in their relations, due in part to the fact that many public formations today originate in problems of fairness and equity in schools. This is why, for educational leaders, deliberative strategies for public development must be married to strong notions of pluralism and participation, and to multiple strategies for working within groups organizing amid conflict and contestation. In Chapter 6 we will take a much closer look at multiple forms of deliberation, and how educational leaders in schools and communities can use deliberative processes to create more legitimate forms of school governance.

Achieving Publics in an Agonistic Public Sphere

Because the public sphere is a place of conflict, uneven power relations, and limited resources, it can be characterized as agonistic. An agonistic public is one where issues and agreements are fought over among disputants who recognize one another not as friends but adversaries. As Mouffe explains, "An adversary is an enemy, but a legitimate enemy, one with whom we have some common ground because we have a shared adhesion to the ethico-political principles of liberal democracy: liberty and equality."[25] Adversaries are not to be eradicated, and there is no single nor ultimate rational solution to adversarial disagreement. "Compromises are, of course, always possible; they are part and parcel of politics; but they should be seen as temporary respites in an ongoing confrontation."[26] What makes compromises possible are political practices and discourses that "domestic hostility," or tame it temporarily.

Once more, let us visit the example of the aging public high school building, to illustrate the agonistic public. The factions in this district are based on multiple and deep-seated conflicts. Forty years ago, nationwide consolidations closed neighboring village school systems and created the current district, composed of a university town and several of these former village and rural school systems. Citizens living in villages whose community schools were closed in consolidation felt these closures as a deep loss, and this loss built pockets of genuine political resentment to the consolidated school system. Today, in election after election, votes for school levies are often split along these lines: to broadly generalize, majorities in the villages vote against levies, and most voters in the town support them. While not always consistent, this split is an enduring reminder that this public school system, like most, is formed of factions. Those in this district may be somewhat unique but fall into some familiar patterns of American life. Other factions in the region fall along social class lines; still others fall along racial-ethnic differences, and others focus on religious differences, as the region is home to multiple fundamental and evangelical Christian citizens groups, nonreligious citizens, and small populations practicing Jewish, Hindu, and Islamic religions. Ongoing disputes around school issues cannot erase these factions; they are historicized, cultural realities that are part and parcel of social life in the United States.

We should not reduce our choices to simplistic either-or constructs. The choices for educational leaders cannot be reduced to either peaceful rationality or agonistic protests; these are false choices. To describe public life as agonistic does not mean that deliberation is impossible; it means that public work, deliberation, and decision making will always contain varying degrees of difference and contention, and public leaders (including but never limited to school leaders) must be prepared and skilled at working through these contentions. Agonistic public life emphasizes the pluralism, as well as the growing problems of inequality, that characterize modern western liberal democracies like the United States. This description of public life urges us to avoid false consensus achieved through excluding diverse others or silencing their perspectives and interests in public life.[27] It is a model that demands the empowered participation of diverse groups and individuals.

How can associational forms of democracy, such as participatory and deliberative governance models, help foster new publics for public schools in our agonistic democracy? Can new leadership practices help citizens create spaces of deliberation and working agreement among these factions? How can all groups of citizens be brought to the political table? Mouffe suggests that even more important than deliberative forums featuring rational arguments and counterarguments are practices that help us construct the "we" of public decision making. Schools construct such "we" moments in various ways; for example, sports teams and other competitions often bring a sense of school spirit that collectively animates diverse citizens. Yet in the political sphere, practices that enable people to find that common loyalty to principles of liberal democracy are almost nonexistent. How can we create political moments of public solidarity in the midst of contentious pluralism and inequality?

The balance of this book poses two different but related answers to these important questions. In Chapter 5 we learn about the possibilities that community organizing holds for achieving publics for public schools. In Chapter 6 we turn to the practices of democratic deliberation. Each of these public-building practices can contribute to the political legitimacy of public schools, but each draws on slightly different though complementary democratic theoretical traditions.

In Chapter 5 I examine the potential of social action or community organizing for school reform as a public-building strategy. Community organizing draws upon participatory democratic theory, which promotes forms of direct democracy in which citizens are helping to determine or shape policy and laws, particularly in pursuit of greater social, political, and legal equality in institutions.[28] In the case of schooling, community organizers have used forms of participatory politics to pursue greater equality in resources and outcomes for poor and working-class children. In the past decade, educational researchers and scholars have turned new attention to the rhetoric, theory, and practice of community organizing as a framework for addressing public schooling reform. Community organizing or social action for educational change has become increasingly popular in this era of top-down, high-stakes accountability in schools. It clearly envisions the terrain of public schooling as conflicted and political. "In a nutshell, social action represents an engagement in the struggle for social change through organizing people to pressure government or private bodies."[29]

The most documented and earliest social action efforts for educational reform have been associated with the Texas Industrial Areas Foundation (IAF). The IAF is an organization created by Saul Alinsky, whose pioneering organizing work serves as one prominent model for helping organize community groups to mobilize and strategically work on behalf of their own interests in political arenas, including those of public schooling.[30] While Alinsky is best known for his brash organizing style, Texas IAF sites "combined confrontational tactics with strategic efforts at collaboration and institutional development," working in this manner since the late 1980s to organize in predominantly black and Latino neighborhoods in multiple urban sites.[31] Organizing for schools "uses direct action tactics to apply pressure on decision-makers ... [aiming to] transform power relations that produce failing schools in low- and moderate income neighborhoods and communities of color."[32] This model of public development and involvement with schools has proven to be an effective way to make schools more responsive to and successful in educating children of low-income neighborhoods.

In Chapter 6 I explore how deliberative democracy can help build publics for public education. While the condition of agonistic democracy and practices of community organizing are often cast in opposition to processes of deliberation among citizens, I find these oppositions to be overdrawn.[33] Democratic public life today is full of conflict and power disparities, yet there are also many opportunities and examples of schools utilizing careful and inclusive deliberation work to help build increased civic and school capacity for school reform. (Good organizing, in fact, can often lead to good deliberations, as organizing can raise consciousness and understanding of school problems, and deliberations can help foster wider discussions and consensus-building toward acceptable resolutions.) Such deliberations can enable citizens to discover areas of agreement and shared purpose, as well as "foster identification with democratic values" among citizens.[34]

Today, deliberative democracy practices in multiple sectors of public life in countries around the world have arisen from a problem of democratic legitimacy. In the case of US public schools, deliberative practices can help school administrators and boards become more open and responsive to the concerns of all classes, races, and types of families.

> Deliberative democracy itself began ... as a theory for which democratic legitimacy depends upon the ability of *all* those subject to a decision to participate in authentic deliberation.... [It] implies a commitment to the maximization of

free, equal, and authentic access to debate, which should extend to individuals, interests, and groups traditionally excluded from decision-making.[35]

Deliberative forums or programs organized in school districts can—if carefully planned, facilitated by experts in this field, and utilized by school leaders—help build democratic legitimacy for schools in two ways. They can increase the shared participation of constituents, and they can help guide educators on the kinds of educational aims and purposes valued among the publics in their district, thereby increasing capacity among educators to be more successful with all students. Such processes can supplement the overreliance on aggregative forms of democracy in school governance.

Theoretically, I am suggesting a mix of democratic traditions for use in building publics for public schools. The twin strands of republican and liberal theories are wound up together in our current representative, aggregative structures of school governance. Elected and appointed officials at the local, state, and national levels are designed to represent the will of the people to make law and policy for public education within the guidelines set by our US Constitution. I am not calling for an end to that system of governance. My argument thus far has tried to show, however, how the current representative system in its aggregate forms is inadequate to the legitimacy problems our schools now face. To strengthen public schools, new forms of associational democratic practice can breathe new life into the current representative structure, and simultaneously build new educational capacities for schools and educators. In Chapter 5 I use the participatory tradition to discuss the potential of community organizing for building the legitimacy and capacity of public schools. In Chapter 6 I draw from the deliberative democracy tradition of political theory. I view these two traditions as complementary to one another as well as to the representative structure currently used to govern most US public schools.[36]

A theoretical pragmatism, as opposed to theoretical purity, therefore distinguishes my argument for achieving publics for public schools, as does my recurring emphasis on leadership. Building school capacity through responsiveness to publics—whether these publics come about through community organizing, deliberative forums, or other means—is the work of school leaders in conjunction with civic, neighborhood, religious, and other leadership in a district. When I refer to "educational leaders" in this book I refer to all such types of formal and informal leadership in schools and surrounding locales. Moreover, leadership work must be based on the principles of democratic legitimacy: guided by norms of fair, inclusive participation in shared governance; respecting constitutionally guaranteed freedoms and human diversity; ensuring equal opportunity; educating for political citizenship among young people; and using professional knowledge and standards of the education profession to guide this work. Building the capacity for publics to work on behalf of schools builds the capacity of educators to achieve better success for all students, and it simultaneously builds legitimacy for public schooling in the eyes of citizens.

Yet this public work and capacity building is neither easy nor simple. It often requires the help of multiple facilitating community organizations as well as precious resources of time, money, and human energy.[37] It requires the skills and will to engage in communications and confrontations with diverse political players, groups, and constituencies, attempting to build bridges across multiple interests and associations. The public as an agonistic space is a model of public life that holds no illusions about what it takes to achieve publics for schooling and channel their energy into forming better schools. This model of public schooling focuses on the divisions and power imbalances in our society, and it sets about using political knowledge and practices to achieve goals related to democratically legitimate schools. These goals are achieved through both confrontations and collaborations between associations in civil society and schools, wherein shared senses of purpose can lead to initiatives for concrete school reform. These moments of working consensus and common aims enable schools to achieve the promises of the public. Agonistic relations—relations among friendly and worthy adversaries—are part of public school life but are also part of the condition of shared education in a society aspiring to be democratic. Rather than ending such agonistic relations, there is ongoing negotiation of compromises and working agreements. To achieve such agreements, public leadership is needed, practiced through a multitude of democratic practices and guided by some basic principles of democratic life. Chapter 7 will explore these practices. But first let me turn to the voices of the skeptics and discuss some potential criticisms that may be lodged against the arguments I have constructed thus far.

The Critique of Utopian Irrelevance

There is much institutional distrust of associational models of democracy, and many critics find any alternatives to aggregative democracy to be utopian, or just plain wrongheaded. "Complex modern societies, this criticism goes, are too highly differentiated culturally, economically, and otherwise to be organized along these lines."[38] There are three parts to this criticism. One is the assertion by many political conservatives, popular of late, that the United States is not a "democracy" at all, but a republic. This charge asserts the lone supremacy of representative governance over other forms. The second part of the critique expresses the belief that we should not trust "the people" with richer forms of participation and engagement, as policy and governance decisions are too complex for most citizens to comprehend. The third part of this criticism is more practical in nature and points to the enormous challenges of this work in very diverse and politically contentious societies. Such conditions, this objection goes, make associational forms of governance simply beyond the ability and time constraints of citizens as well as busy educational leaders.

Many contemporary conservatives insist that the United States is not a democracy. "The fact that we are a republic needs to be reiterated over and over. We are not a democracy. It is important that we understand the difference between a republic and a democracy. This cannot be emphasized enough."[39] These statements are taken from an editorial by Nancy Salvato on the Republican Party's website in 2011, but similar sentiments are expressed frequently across multiple media forums by conservative citizens. The logic of such assertions runs like this: "Accurately defined, a democracy is a form of government in which the people decide policy matters directly—through town hall meetings or by voting on ballot initiatives and referendums. A republic, on the other hand, is a system in which the people choose representatives who, in turn, make policy decisions on their behalf."[40]

The obvious error in this thinking is to equate one very narrow form of democracy, called *direct democracy* by political theorists, to the entire spectrum of democratic forms of governance. David Held's *Models of Democracy* offers a broader definition of democracy, one widely accepted by theorists and scholars: "Democracy means a form of government in which, in contradistinction to monarchies and aristocracies, the people rule.... The history of the idea of democracy is complex and is marked by conflicting conceptions."[41] But what counts as rule by the people? There has been debate and disagreement since democracy's inception. The range of possible positions includes, on the most direct end of the spectrum, the idea that all citizens should be involved in legislating and deciding on policy and law, to the most distant and passive description of democracy as the idea that rulers should act in the interests of the ruled.[42] Thus, Salvato and others mislabel "democracy" to refer to only the most inclusive and perhaps most impractical of a wide range of possible meanings of the democratic definition of "rule by the people." Apart from what the framers of the US Constitution may have intended, school governance is today set largely in republican terms, where a system of representation is set to shape the policies and laws of public schools. For reasons discussed earlier—the increasing ratio of school board representatives to citizens in a reduced number of districts across the nation, the great diversity of the population, and the declining political legitimacy of public schools—an exclusive reliance on this republican form of governance is a mistake.

Democratic elitism, sometimes called democratic realism, is the name of the belief that the general citizenry lacks the capacity to share in governance. Advocates of this school of thought find "ordinary men and women irrational and participatory democracy impossible and unwise under modern conditions.... [They argue] to strictly limit government by the people and to redefine democracy as, by and large, government for the people by enlightened and responsible elites."[43] This belief is shared by many elected and appointed officials in public schooling, who, through their encounters with parents and voters, often believe citizens to be mostly self-interested, highly critical, short on the ability to reason through complex issues, and disinterested in productively engaging with schools. Citizens, in this view, do not have the intelligence or the public skills needed to govern. Most community members, they will argue, are disinterested in being on school committees or getting involved in deliberative forums.

There are two responses to this view, which itself serves to promote centralized control over schooling and diminish possible avenues for more participatory governance of public schooling. The first is that including citizens in governing is not a call for all citizens to manage or run schools. Managing most school functions and creating good educational experiences is primarily and rightly the work of educational leaders and teachers in schools. Working with publics and the citizens who constitute them, facilitating communication in and among publics in order to find common solutions and satisfactory decisions, and finding more ways to substantively engage citizens about broad goals and policies do not replace the role of teachers, administrators, or school boards. Administrators and school board members remain the local officials who were elected or appointed to govern. Participating in decision making should not constitute micromanaging, nor does it imply any one structure or organizational design (though participatory opportunities for citizens are certainly more available in some kinds of school structures than others).

Successful organizing campaigns and public deliberation processes in the United States and around the world are proving the skeptics wrong. As we will read in the following chapters, empirical studies of these practices are abundant now, and they clearly show the effectiveness and great potential of what average citizens can do in organizing for and deliberating about school issues and problems. Associational forms of deliberative and participatory forms of governance allow publics to shape the purposes and vision of their schools, and help leaders address the problems that affect students and parents most directly. Further, these forms of governance can help schools to build political legitimacy, in that these forms can result in schools that are more reflective of publics' interests and visions for schooling. Last, and perhaps most important, engaging citizens with their schools can also help build educators' capacities to create schools where all students are more successful. Given the problems public schools face with regard to legitimacy as well as unequal educational outcomes across social class and racial-ethnic groups, deliberative and participatory forms of school governance can enable schools to build much-needed public consent and increased capacity for their work.

Another response to a rejection of deliberative and participatory governance based on citizen irrationality and inability to govern lies in the question of alternatives. Has the current model of heavily centralized federal and state control over schooling resulted in expanded forms of high-quality education for all students? In more satisfaction with those in political power and in public school systems? How satisfied are we with the status quo? In examining the evidence of over fifty years of federal and state involvement with school reform initiatives, Larry Cuban finds little to justify increased state and federal involvement when it comes to student achievement.

> As a rule, reforms emanating from the states and the federal government do not improve student achievement. In other words, neither historic nor contemporary evidence has shown much of a cause-and-effect relationship between the federal government of the states mandating goals . . . [and] uniform standards, and the achievement gaps between races and social classes.[44]

NCLB supporters would say that the jury is still out on final verdicts regarding the question of the effectiveness of federal mandates. Others would point out the importance of the state and federal role in public schooling's becoming more public, more accessible to all races, ethnicities, and religious groups. As Robert Franciosi soberly reminds us, "local control has frequently meant the freedom of local communities to harass dissenters and burn witches without meddling by higher authorities."[45] There is, undeniably, a vital role for the federal and governments to play in public education.[46] Responsiveness to the interests of various publics must be guided by the principles of democratic legitimacy; local publics and school officials acting on local authority are not free to simply side-step constitutional guarantees of civil rights. This is indeed one of the points of a bifocal view of public life that I argue is so necessary for educational leadership today. The political will of publics in localities is not without bounds of larger constitutional, legislative, and judicial rulings, laws, and constraints.

There are certainly legitimate roles for states and federal authorities to play, but centralized control can accomplish some things and not others. There are irreplaceable roles for local officials and publics to play in improving schools, and some forms of centralized control can hinder this localized work from getting done. As Cuban points out, school improvement is a long, slow, laborious process that is frequently quite specific to the problems and resources contained in a particular school, community, and region. "Essentially, the well-documented, failure-studded record of state and federal implementation efforts and the repeated cases in which seeking compliance has overwhelmed the building of local capacity" compel us to search for alternatives to the current top-down reform policies that centralized authorities now too often use in governing schools.[47] "We need to radically refocus on the local."[48]

The third objection that critics might offer to my arguments has to do with the diverse and contentious nature of political life today. Public life is divided, difficult, and often characterized in the national media by extremist views. Because of the highly partisan nature of national and state politics, we often see conflict as permanent and unsolvable. The "culture wars," much publicized in journalistic and scholarly sources (even this one), can lead us to the belief that as a society, the United States is permanently locked in irresolvable conflicts of various political sorts. Yet not all conflicts are "tragic conflicts," philosopher William Caspary notes. "It is easy to slide from the restricted usage—unresolvable at present, in practice—to the a-historical notion of irreconcilable in principle." Such a slide then becomes "a rationalization for avoiding the hard work of inquiry and political action."[49] While the US population contains many "tribes," and much rich variety in religious, ethnic, political, sexual, and social class diversity, it is indeed possible for people to find sources of commonality and agreement when it comes to aims and purposes of public schooling. Models of organizing and deliberation within our agonistic public life convey this possibility and signal the ways citizens can come to forms of "we" and agreement without the necessity of communal ties, intimate friendship, or neighborly affection. Examples of organizing, deliberating, and public-building in schools, to be examined in the next two chapters, will show that conflicts and contestations can be moments of growth and learning. Conflicts can yield new habits of educating, governing, parenting, and collaboration. Shared working agreements among political adversaries and diverse publics are possible under the right cultural, organizational, and leadership contexts.

In addition, as noted earlier, we already have degrees of public participation in many schools, but usually only for the select few. Powerful parents often wield the kinds of social and cultural capital that enable them to have more regular and meaningful access to school leaders and board members. Such middle-class or even more wealthy parents may be able to devote considerable volunteer time or money to the school and district as well, thus making their voices in school vision and leadership even more powerfully heard. But selective participatory governance yields a selective vision of who and what the public schools are for, and the idea of public symbolizes the most inclusive sense of a public school: a school designed to meet the educational interests of multiple publics and all citizens in the district.

As Kenneth Strike notes, there are two criteria for democratic decision making in schools. Decisions can be considered democratic "when the interests of all citizens of the polity are fairly considered . . . [and] when all citizens of the polity have a fair chance to influence decisions via voice and/or authority."[50] Without more participatory forms of public participation and without the development of publics for schools, such decisions—and political legitimacy itself—will remain elusive in most districts.

This is not to suggest, however, that associational forms of governance are easy to implement. Nor is it to suggest that deliberative and participatory forms of democracy should be uncritically and radically implemented in wholesale fashion. But US civil society does offer, in many ways, fertile ground for these forms of school governance. As Mark E. Warren nicely sums up,

> The American case provides exceptionally rich terrain for conceptualizing the democratic possibilities of association not because it is exemplary, but because it combines a rich tapestry of associative venues for collective action with more than enough cautionary tales to give pause to anyone inclined toward uncritical celebration.[51]

CHAPTER 5
COMMUNITY ORGANIZING

CREATING PUBLICS FOR SCHOOL REFORM

> Perhaps the "public realm" is not a given, but rather a social and political achievement that allows individuals to step out of their private spheres to discover common interests in solving jointly shared problems.... [We can] benefit from learning about the diverse outcomes created by political strategies intended to revitalize schools as fulcrums of community engagement in our new context of standardizations, testing, and measurement.[1]

I have thus far argued that to achieve publics for public schools, school leaders should view their roles bifocally. That is, public schools are not simply schools responsive to the mass public of US citizens as symbolized through constitutional principles; they are schools that both engage with and respond to the educational issues raised by citizens in their district, town, or region. Citizens raise these issues through the creation of publics, political associations of will-formation and problem solving. Publics are achieved through particular political strategies, habits, and skills, described in the remaining chapters of this book. In this chapter, the political strategies of community organizing are examined.

Typically associated with dissent and contestation, community organizing has often received a bad name in our society by those who decry organizing as the work of radicals or anarchists. Yet a growing literature on the practice and success of community organizing in education in recent decades shows the practice to be a much needed, nonpartisan, and highly diversified form of political activity on behalf of school improvement. In this chapter, I discuss community organizing as one approach for achieving publics for public schooling, and I examine the necessary practices for public achievement in light of this particular approach to public creation and development. I show how community organizing can stimulate the formation of publics for public schools and discuss some of the positive outcomes as well as challenges for school leaders in this kind of public creation.

Community Organizing as a Tool for Achieving Publics for Schools

- The Northwest Bronx Clergy and Community Coalition (NWBCCC), Mothers on the Move (MOM), Sistas and Brothas United (SBU), and the Association of Community Organizations for Reform Now (ACORN) "all work with the same overwhelmingly poor, predominantly Latino, African American, and African populations in the Bronx. They are all fairly small, and have all been engaging in grassroots political campaigns for similar goals in local school reform and funding increases in the South Bronx. Together, these groups have garnered millions of dollars in new program funding and construction, voted in politicians and forced public officials to resign, received quite a bit of attention in the news, and struggled to maintain campaigns. They are also part of a burgeoning social movement of grassroots organizing for school reform. In the South Bronx alone, the number of such education organizing groups has tripled to more than a dozen in the last fifteen years. Over half of these groups started as or were sponsored by social service organizations."[2]

- In Oakland, California, citizens concerned about their decaying neighborhood and overcrowded schools began to organize in the early 1990s. They channeled their efforts through Oakland Community Organizations (OCO). OCO is an affiliate of the Pacific Institute for Community Organizing (PICO), a federation of thirty-one congregations and 40,000 members. Oakland citizens, with the facilitation of OCO community organizers, engaged in research concerning the issue of school overcrowding and discovered huge differentials in achievement between overcrowded schools in their neighborhoods and those in the more affluent Oakland areas. During the same time period, a nearby abandoned Montgomery Ward mail order warehouse was deteriorating and becoming a haven for criminal activity. In organizing meetings, organizers and community leaders learned about the citizens' concerns with this building as well as with school overcrowding. OCO strategized with citizens about how they might turn this warehouse property into new schools for their children. Leaders of the organization repeatedly met with school district officials, school board members, and city officials. They formed powerful partnerships with regional school reform groups and national foundations. The citizens and organizers working on this effort spent almost a decade in their quest to have the Montgomery Ward building acquired by the school district, torn down, and designated as a site for the building of new, smaller schools to serve these neighborhoods. They helped secure passage of a $300 million bond for new school facilities and a Gates Foundation grant for the implementation of small schools in the Bay region.[3]

- "Accountability sessions, parent and community engagement in schools, and careful work to build trust with educators are some of the strategies used by Austin Interfaith to reinvent and reinvigorate low-performing schools in Austin, Texas. As part of the statewide Texas Industrial Areas Foundation (IAF), Austin Interfaith organized low-performing schools on the city's east side into a local network of 'Alliance Schools.' During an eight-year period, this network grew to involve roughly a quarter of the Austin Independent School District's elementary schools and half of the district's high-poverty schools. In these schools, Austin Interfaith organizers provided leadership training to parents, teachers, and administrators and supported them in implementing reforms to improve student learning. The organization also developed an effective working relationship with Superintendent Pascal Forgione, whose leadership of the district brought a decade of stability and concentrated focus on improving low-performing schools."[4]

- "The Alliance Organizing Project (AOP) in Philadelphia has worked both with individual schools and citywide, focusing its efforts on issues of safety, student achievement, and teacher quality. Recognizing the lack of parent engagement with previous waves of reform, a new superintendent and many of the city's advocacy groups conceived of AOP in 1995 as a component of the District's reform plan. AOP's mission is to help in the 'transformation in the relationship between every school and the parents and communities which surround it.' AOP's safety campaigns are the direct result of the deteriorated school facilities and extreme conditions of blight and high crime in the declining city neighborhoods where it has been most active. The safety campaign targeted city council, which passed an ordinance to increase funding for crossing guards. AOP also raised funds from local non-profits and the District for after-school programs, providing children with a safe place after school hours as well as with academic enrichment."[5]

Community organizing for public school reform, often called education organizing, is a strategy for school improvement that relies on political activity and public work to achieve better schools. While some US politicians and pundits have cast it as a "left-wing" activity, community organizing is a political approach used all across the political spectrum. Groups as diverse as the Christian Coalition, labor unions, and the Moral Majority have used organizing strategies consistently and with success. Universities like Harvard, Occidental College, and the University of Wisconsin–Milwaukee offer courses or programs in community organizing. As it becomes further mainstreamed, organizing is becoming more widely recognized as work that merges the values often stereotyped as either liberal or conservative in US political culture.[6] Community organizing groups working on behalf of school reform regularly emerge out of faith-based as well as secular coalitions, rely upon strong familial involvement and parental support, and promote educational achievement and success for those usually "left behind" in schools.

Community-based organizations (CBOs) typically attempt to rebuild civic infrastructure in low-income communities to work on a range of issues including housing, health care, crime, and economic development. Starting in the 1990s, CBOs have increasingly turned to education as an issue, as more parents and other community members demand relief from the poor quality of schooling in too many working-class and low-income communities. Some of these, like the Logan Square Neighborhood Association in Chicago or the Jamaica Plain Parent Organizing Project in Boston, are local in their base and membership. Other groups, like the OCO in Oakland or Austin Interfaith in Texas, have affiliations with long-standing national organizing groups like the Industrial Areas Foundation (IAF) or faith-based groups such as the People's Institute for Community Organizing (PICO). Currently, school-related community organizing is used in American cities to "disrupt long-standing power relationships that produce failing schools in low- and moderate-income neighborhoods and communities of color."[7]

Education organizing comes out of the tradition of neighborhood organizing done by Saul Alinsky beginning in the 1930s, but it also traces its roots to civil rights, labor, immigrant, and poor people's movements throughout the twentieth century. Dennis Shirley, an expert on education organizing, connects community organizing to participatory models of democratic governance. Simply defined as a form of "political decision making and action in which citizens are prime movers rather than passive observers," participatory democracy models have a long history in education reform and experimentation.[8] However, the historical record for participatory democracy in education, starting in the 1960s and impacting large urban systems in New York and Chicago, has not always been stellar in terms of real, lasting impacts on school improvement. Participatory democratic governance in and of itself has no magical, automatic, or lasting impact on school quality.[9] However, the force of these organizing movements has always been the degree to which they harness and amplify the power of political voice and participation among a school community's poorest and most disenfranchised citizens. This harnessing can help ignite, push, and sustain school improvement efforts (though greater understanding of how these efforts can be sustained over the long haul is still needed). Participatory democratic movements like community organizing for education thus represent an important foundation for building publics for public schools.

Education organizing today comprises a divergent set of strategies and groups working to achieve political power to help citizen groups leverage needed reforms in their schools. This power is particularly necessary for working-class and poor families who, unlike their middle-class counterparts, do not always possess the kinds of cultural and political capital that enable them to gain access and voice within processes of school decision making.[10]

Education organizing is the work of bringing together "public school parents, youth and community residents, and/or institutions to engage in collective dialogue and action for change" and "building grassroots leadership" by training parents, youth, and other neighborhood residents in "skills of organizing and civic engagement."[11] This leadership in turn develops political agency for these groups by building membership and helping members develop a clear agenda for school change marked by tangible goals. Political agency is realized through a variety of means: lobbying, direct action, negotiation, and collaboration with those in positions of influence in schools and governments. Ultimately, organizing works "to strengthen public institutions to make them more equitable and accountable to low- and moderate-income communities."[12]

While organizing campaigns achieve social change through grassroots citizen participation, community organizers are usually key agents in this process. An organizer can be paid or unpaid, and affiliated or unaffiliated with a national organizing group; the term usually refers to professional organizers who are frequently part of organizing efforts. Organizers are typically paid staff members who are instrumental to much organizing work for several reasons. They often help disparate groups come together to work more cohesively and powerfully on common interests. They can help local citizens learn to think more politically and more strategically about the problems they face. They help develop citizens into civic leaders, educating them on important knowledge and skills needed to organize communities. They usually bring personal and organizational experience to the often-isolated efforts in individual communities, enabling leaders to benefit from hard-earned wisdom gleaned from similar organizing campaigns in other regions or states. Organizers are said to be like tutors, working "to share insights, to teach methods of analysis and to provide tools of research, to challenge citizens to sharpen their public skills, [and] to develop their ability to reflect and to act."[13]

The United States is experiencing growth in community organizing for school improvement. "One leading scholar's best estimate . . . is that roughly 500 of over 800 community organizing groups are now working in the area of educational change in the US."[14] Shirley cites multiple factors that have led to this increase. Organizing for public school reform has benefited from more widely available informational technologies, the rise of more precise ways to disseminate data on schools, and the development of entrepreneurial opportunities such as charter schools, enabling organizations to pursue educational goals outside traditional public school channels.

And the positive results of this organizing are available in the emergent research on school-based organizing outcomes. In *Community Organizing for Stronger Schools,* researchers evaluated eight diverse study sites with mature education organizing—that is, where there had been at least five years of organizing experience prior to the study. They document clear evidence of improved outcomes in school districts that have been sites of sustained organizing efforts. "In sites where intensive and sustained school-level organizing was carried out for at least five years, we found evidence of improved capacity in the climate, professional culture, and instructional core of schools."[15] As the researchers summarize,

> The evidence suggests that organizing efforts are helping increase equity, capacity, and outcomes in urban school districts. The high degree of convergence

across our data—teacher surveys, district and school administrator interviews, and school-level administrative records—is remarkable, pointing to a positive relationship between education organizing and educational change.[16]

While these results are early and tenuous, and more assessment of organizing outcomes are clearly needed, research suggests the diverse positive impacts of this work on school improvement.

Community organizing can initiate healthy and more diverse publics to strengthen communities and the schools within them. Community organizing can also occasionally work against productive school reform efforts as well; as will be discussed, organizing is altogether human and imperfect political work. But to begin, let us examine community organizing as a force for creating and developing publics for public schools. How do these publics form, take shape, and become politically effective with regard to creating change in schools, neighborhoods, and families?

In this chapter and the two that follow, I discuss four important requisite habits or skills of public creation and development (the last three chapters of the book explore practical applications of the arguments developed in the first four). Habits are developed dispositions for established forms of action and thought; "a habit is a form of executive skill, an efficiency in doing," as Dewey noted.[17] Alison Kadlec argues that habits are "acquisitions that require the use of reason and active preference; in a basic sense, habits are *skills*." More than mechanical and thoughtless forms of action, Kadlec states, "it is possible to view the acquisition of habits as a matter of 'thought, invention, and initiative in applying capacities to new aims.'"[18] Building habits or skills (I will use these terms interchangeably) of public development is necessary for educational leaders who seek to achieve publics for public schools. Some of these habits are in stark opposition to the typical types of managerial and administrative habits of today's educational leaders. As discussed in this chapter and Chapter 7, the status quo of educational leadership as practiced in too many public schools is characterized purely as top-down management, however well-intended. In contrast, achieving publics takes a different set of leadership frames, dispositions, and habits. I argue here that habits and skills of *communication, building power, leadership development,* and *collaborative creation* are necessary for achieving publics for public schooling. These habits or skills, as illustrated specifically for community organizing work in Figure 5.1, broadly represent the work of educational leadership for public education.

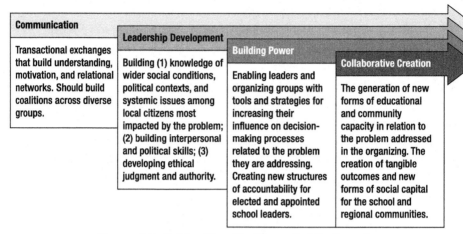

**Figure 5.1 Habits That Facilitate Public Creation,
as Used in Community Organizing**

In this chapter I discuss these skills as they relate to community organizing's contribution to publics for public schooling. Citizens gain more political consciousness and build more collective political power for advancing school reform agendas through these activities. Educational leaders in schools and in communities use these habits to facilitate and channel public formation, so that new publics can enhance the capacities of schools, expanding the knowledge and resources necessary to help all children succeed.

Habits and Skills of Communication

> To be a recipient of a communication is to have an enlarged and changed experience. One shares in what another has thought and felt and in so far, meagerly or amply, has his own attitude modified. Nor is the one who communicates left unaffected.[19]

Publics begin and are achieved with human communication; here, the term has a particular meaning. Communication changes both those who deliver a message or idea and those who receive it. If you and I are talking, this activity is not simply an exchange of information wherein each party delivers and receives ideas like so many e-mails in our "in" and "out" boxes. Communications change, if only subtly, all parties involved; the act of sharing and receiving information, ideas, feelings, and nuances from another person or persons is thus labeled "transactional." A transactional understanding views communication as more than a causal exchange of information between two or more people or groups, more than the stimulus and response reactions between human beings. The idea of transaction signals how communicative actions change actors undergoing a communicative experience. Transactionalist accounts of communication thus emphasize the continuing evolution and growth of people through these processes.[20] In addition, a transactional view of communication does not see the process as "pure" but as constantly moving through and in subjective interpretations and cultural contexts. In other words, what we express and hear in communication is always shaped and filtered by our social positions, our cultural lenses, and our identities as people. Despite this, people can come to build shared understandings and goals through communication. Communication is thus a complex and crucial ongoing process in the development of functioning publics for public schooling, in which citizens are engaging in community organizing on behalf of school reform.

Communication practices take on multiple forms in community organizing, and in a very real sense the development of an organizing campaign is fundamentally a communicative endeavor. Communication designed to help people become active within the realm of everyday politics is an ongoing, contextual process. It cannot be cleanly separated from the people, problems, and cultural contexts in which organizing is taking place. For this reason, communication for education organizing is subject to the cultural norms and styles of a group, culture, and region. How one might recruit leadership in a small Mississippi town might be different from how similar education organizing might work in a southern Californian city. Communication also takes on different forms depending upon the purpose and "stage" of the organizing work.

Education organizing typically begins in the acts of people discussing the problems and issues related to youth and schools. In the neighborhoods of Austin, Texas, where IAF school-based organizing was focused, these initial and intentional acts of communication were the important groundwork for school-based organizing. "What the IAF will sometimes do is spend up to a full year just having one-on-one conversations! Teachers talk with parents and clergy. Parents talk with small business owners and police officers. Clergy talk with bus drivers, barbers, and janitors."[21] Organizers call such intentional, preliminary conversations *one-on-ones*. "In a nutshell, a one-on-one is a structured conversation with a twofold purpose: to surface community issues that are foremost in the mind of citizens, and to establish a relationship with one's interlocutor."[22] These conversations help create the relationships and relational networks that are crucial to organizing work. Such dialogue opens up intentional conversational space for the youth and school-related issues on the minds of citizens.

At times, education organizing grows more organically, such as when parents come together for a particular project only to find they have many broader concerns in common. In Montgomery County, Mississippi, a group of parents "began collaborating with the principal and teachers at a local elementary school to implement a cultural enrichment program." Through this work, "parents began sharing their concerns about the school system, which ultimately led to the formation of the Concerned Citizens of Montgomery County [CCMC]," an organizing group that has gone on to develop a mission centered on fighting racial inequality.[23] The CCMC "holds school officials, teachers and public officials accountable to educating African American children in the same way that white students are educated."[24]

It is important to recognize that this process of communication, in initial organizing stages, is not simply a matter of people expressing their already formed and logical complaints about schools, education, or youth. Communication is transaction; it transforms us and our situations. While some citizens may have a very clear sense of their views about their district schools, people's understanding of their interests are often not so fixed or easily articulated. Frances Polletta, who has studied processes of community organizing, notes that "both individual and common interests may emerge from discussion and deliberation—not through a process of negotiation (which assumes that interests are fixed) but through a process of self- and collective discovery."[25] This would seem particularly true for peoples' views and interests as they relate to organizations as complex as most public school districts. It is through the act of discussing our observations and perspectives about schooling and youth with others than we can learn and understand more about the problem, comparing our perspective and views with those of others.

Successful organizing relies on this initial work of discovering what school- or youth-related problems are important to people in a district or neighborhood, and whether or not there is enough collective energy and motivation to work for change. These early communications can *build* that energy and motivation, as people share their understandings of the situation with one another—as communications transform people, often toward positive momentum for community action. "In IAF parlance, organizers use 'one-on-ones' to build relational capital," or the accumulated energy, wisdom, and capacity generated by networks forged in human relationships.[26] One-on-ones, in IAF work, are followed by house meetings, where neighbors come together to discuss their common concerns and what they might do about them. "House meetings enable organizers to identify natural leaders in a given community and to begin parent training in such issues as preparing an agenda; opening, leading and concluding a meeting punctually; and evaluation."[27]

These initial communication strategies begin tapping into citizens' ideas, feelings, and perceptions about their schools. Often, parents who have experienced their own individual struggles with their schools gain insight that it isn't simply their child who has a problem. Emma Paulino was one of those parents, struggling to help her son who had been passed into third grade "even though he could barely spell his own name. His teachers assured her 'he was fine,' Paulino recalls," but she suspected otherwise. "When Paulino saw the Oakland Community Organization's (OCO) analysis of school size and student achievement, the district's stark inequities became clear" to her, and she became involved with the organizing work.[28]

Organizational momentum builds as these communications motivate individuals, form relationships, and reveal leadership potential among citizens. These relational bonds, built through communication habits and skills within neighborhoods, religious organizations, or parental networks, constitute a powerful force for educational organizing, although not always a purely democratic one. As Polletta notes from her observations of community organizing, these relational bonds help grease the wheels of organizing but can also undermine it:

> Friendship, tutelage, and religious fellowship provided the microinteractional norms—the rules behind the rules—that enabled people to make decisions without constant negotiation over the terms of engagement. The problem ... was that, along with caring, cooperation, and a complex equality that made for mutual learning, those relationships also came with norms that undermined democratic projects; variously, exclusivity, deference, conflict, avoidance, and an antipathy to the rules that might have made for more accountability.[29]

In other words, the bonds forged by communications among citizens organizing for school reform can be forces for mutual learning and the achievement of organizational goals, but they can also bring about less desirable outcomes as well. For example, relational bonds are facilitated by preexisting bonds formed in friendships, neighborhood associations, and shared religious membership, enabling diverse citizens to identify and organize around common goals—yet such bonds can also lead to problems that can undermine the group's ability to engage in democratic decision making for the purpose of sustainable school reform. Bonds of friendship, for example, can lead to cliques and exclusionary decision making. Cultural deference to the authority of a respected community leader might inhibit dissent within the organizing group. Thus, relational bonds built through communication are best guided by clear organizational rules and guidelines to ensure healthy, inclusive organizational work.[30]

Another significant type of communication in educational organizing relates to bridging differences across diverse stakeholders and cultural groups. As seen in the OCO effort in Oakland, successful organizing includes communication strategies designed to bridge cultural, ethnic, and linguistic divides.

> Through public actions and evaluation meetings, OCO leaders and organizers brought together principals, teachers, and diverse community residents—all stakeholders in public education—who do not usually associate with each other because of ethnic/racial or linguistic differences or differences in roles and positions. This "bridging" social capital—across diverse groups within the community and across groups with different roles, status, and authority—is especially important in moving organizing campaigns forward because it creates accountable relationships that build the political will to override private interests.[31]

Communications designed to bridge differences—whether through public meetings, assemblies, targeted outreach to particular groups, or other means—can help to build relations between relatively powerless, poorer citizens and school district and government leaders. This bridging communication can happen between different groups, or within groups. As an organizer with the Los Angeles Youth Organizing Committee notes, multiracial, multilingual organizing takes real commitment. "We try to make space for all experiences and cultures.... We really try to make it bilingual and make that positive. That helps expand and build our base."[32]

Coalitions between diverse organizations require bridging communication but result in a stronger political voice; for example, over thirty grassroots and advocacy groups campaigned successfully in Los Angeles to give all high school students a college preparatory curriculum.[33] Mark Warren notes the importance of such bridging communication, particularly across racial boundaries. "We simply do not have very many institutions in which Americans from different racial groups cooperate with each other," and segregation across class boundaries is also extremely common.[34] In the face of such race and class isolation, bridging communications are vitally important for creating publics that enable sustainable school reform.

Bridging communications can enable citizens to locate common ground across cultural and linguistic difference and can also be used to create strategic alliances with professional educators and administrators. "Community organizing is perceived to be threatening to many educators. Some teachers also show distrust of organizing activities and distance themselves from these activities."[35] Organizing groups have found many ways to help build common ground and agendas with educators. The Logan Square Neighborhood Association (LSNA) in Chicago, as part of its educational organizing effort, collaborated with teachers and principals to create a Parent Mentor program that has now trained over 800 parents to provide extra academic and social help in classrooms. Most of these parents are poor and working-class Latino women, who felt alienated from their children's schools. The LSNA raises money to pay these mentors to work two hours a day to support classroom teachers. Such mutual support not only improves school climate and increases student achievement but also creates greater respect and understanding between teachers and local parents.[36] These types of interactions between educators and parents are distinct from the typical "accommodationist" forms of parental involvement where parents are encouraged to support the already existing educator-led initiatives and programs through fundraising and volunteering. Bridging communications enable greater trust, mutuality, and reciprocity between educators and citizens in low-income neighborhoods.

Communication is a key, complex transactional practice for building a democratic "we," or a political will among a group of people organized for particular changes in a public institution. This formation of relationships and political will among an association of diverse citizens is not simply a function of logical argument or intellectualized discourse. While we can point to the functions of different types of communication in educational organizing, it is important to note the importance of the emotional, embodied dimensions of public creation and development. These dimensions refer to the ways that communications are not purely cognitive exercises of argument but rather practices engaging our bodies, emotions, and intellect simultaneously. The use of symbols, slogans, and other types of unifying rhetoric to create cohesion and unity of purpose among a group, for example, acknowledges the power of emotion in organizing. Such rhetoric and use of symbols is a necessary part of individual citizens becoming part of a larger public association. While emotionalized rhetoric can be used in manipulative ways designed to squander critical thinking and decision making, we cannot ignore the fact that embodied, emotional interaction is part of human communication, including political communication. The history of African American organizing illustrates this fact; the power of collectivizing, sermonic styles of oratory in this and other movements is legend.[37] Politics, Dewey said, has to be "emotionalized; it must appeal to the social imagination."[38]

Stressing the importance of the embodied, emotional dimensions of public-building activities should not be read as downplaying the role of virtual communication in this work. Much of the writing about educational organizing examples and exemplars—in the form of scholarly case studies and empirical accounts of organizing work—does not yet describe extensive use of new social media in organizing. As online activism increasingly plays a role in education organizing, this is rapidly changing. The Internet and social media allow CBOs to communicate with members, conduct research, create their own media outlets, and quickly organize actions. The power of these new media is quickly becoming evident. Take the case of Michelle Ryan Lauto, a student in Bergan County, New Jersey, who was angry about proposed deep cuts to the state's education budget in the spring of 2010. "The youth who will be affected by all these cuts need to rise up and do something," Michelle wrote on Facebook, where she posted an event announcement: a mass student walkout, protesting the budget cuts, on April 27. "By April 24, RSVPs had grown from a few hundred to over 5,000. Just two days later, sign-ups surged past 16,000. Nervous school officials tried to intimidate the students, threatening suspension, criminal charges and the banning of students from graduation."[39] Summing up the Internet's power, reporter Ben Brandzel metaphorically suggests that

> the Internet functions very much like a hydrant. Its only promise is a powerful flow of information that enables learning and collaboration. This resource stream can lead to either revolutionary change or recreational noise. When properly understood and deployed, online organizing allows modern activists to employ time-honored strategies while aiming for the big changes our times require.[40]

Clearly, organizing tactics and strategies will continue to evolve and flourish as activists learn to effectively use social media to reach their goals. The use and potential power of social media for education organizing does not diminish the need for embodied social interaction but provides another enabling medium or tool for the dialogue, interaction, and alliance-building required of public creation and development.

Education organizing depends upon the power of communication as a transactional practice, and this practice is cognitive, virtual, and embodied in the real bodies and emotional lives of citizens. Communication practices are fundamental to the enterprise of public creation and development; while I present communication as one of the four habits and skills of public creation and development, it is the basis of all of the practices that will be discussed in this chapter and the next. Communication helps citizens more clearly label and identify their educational and schooling issues, become cognizant of which issues they have in common, and solidify their own interests, motivations, and leadership potential to address them.

Habits and Skills of Leadership Development

Throughout this text I attempt to use "leadership" in the broadest possible way, intentionally expanding the term *educational leaders* to mean all those adults in communities, organizations, and institutions who are actively working to solve problems and challenges related to schools. This expansive use is both to challenge the popular uses of the word *leader* and to make an explicit point about achieving publics for public schools.

Leadership, while widely thought of as an innate capacity related to personal charisma or positional authority, is best conceived not as a position or an innate power but as a practice. As leadership scholar Ron Heifetz writes, "rather than define leadership either as a position of authority in a social structure or as a personal set of characteristics, we may find it a great deal more useful to define leadership as an *activity*" (emphasis in original).[41] Leadership is understood here as an activity for both the experts of schooling—the administrators, school board members, and teachers—and the concerned and interested citizens (though the final chapter of this book addresses leadership particularly as practiced by school administrators).

CBOs have long placed leadership development at the center of their organizing work. Aaron Schutz, who participates in and studies education organizing in Milwaukee, notes that "a core aspect of organizing is providing opportunities for people impacted by injustice and inequality to acquire the skills to fight for themselves and to build their own power."[42] Mark Warren puts it this way: "Local communities represent the first-order places where leadership can emerge and develop, because, here, citizens can gain strength and support from each other as they attempt to rattle the dry bones of their communities and become leaders of American society."[43] Developing leadership among citizens is a key practice in the simultaneous rebuilding of schools and the local towns, neighborhoods, or places where those schools exist. Rattling the dry bones of places diminished by poverty, neglect, crime, racism, or unemployment requires leadership, as Warren suggests. Leaders are those who facilitate organized action to improve the conditions of people, particularly in low-income or disenfranchised communities.[44]

Leadership, conceived as a practice or activity rather than (simply) as a role or position, can take different paths, but successful organizing efforts feature leadership development as an important focus in the work. The development of citizen leaders in educational organizing is characterized by, at minimum, the acquisition of three types of knowledge. The first is an understanding of the wider social conditions, political contexts, and larger systemic issues of the problems at hand. The second concerns the appropriate interpersonal and political skills needed to move a group forward. The third is knowledge of how to wield democratic authority and judgment that is inclusive and accountable to the broader group. Each of these is discussed in turn.

Leadership in community-based organizations requires the ability to help others come to political judgment, that is, to weigh alternatives and decide on a course of action together.[45] To help others come to judgment about an organizing group's goals and strategies, citizens working in leadership must achieve a deeper understanding of the context of schooling. They must particularly become more versed in the political, economic, and pedagogical factors that shape how schools function. Schools often feel closed off to citizens, particularly in low-income communities. Like proverbial black boxes, many in these communities do not know how to access reliable information about their school's or district's resources, procedures, or outcomes, despite the efforts of some school administrators who may have good intentions in opening their schools up to all sorts of families. Organizers often help citizens engage in inquiry about schooling, enabling them to build the power of knowledge about their schools, as well as enhancing their analytical abilities.[46] Organizers will provide instruction on some of the political and social realities of schooling and political life, sometimes painting a grim though realistic picture of how poor schooling will impact their children's futures.

Shirley, who studied Texas IAF organizers in Austin, discussed this aspect of leadership development with organizer Ernie Cortés. Following neighborhood IAF house meetings, organizers hold leadership training sessions that are, Cortés notes, "a fairly didactic phase" of their work. Cortés admits that these sessions are designed to "rub the parents' noses in some ugly realities—about globalization, wages, and their kids' prospects."[47] Other groups aim at similar types of leadership development with methods such as "reviewing performance statistics that compare schools in their neighborhoods with other schools, taking tours of well-appointed schools in better off sections of the city, [and] touring schools that are successfully educating low-income children of color."[48]

Approaches to leadership development vary widely, depending on the style of organizing used, the cultural norms of the region and neighborhood, and the particular ways leadership practice might be envisioned.[49] While some organizing groups utilize leadership training opportunities sponsored by national organizing groups with successful histories, other groups create their own programs. Within the Parent Mentoring Program developed by the Logan Square Neighborhood Association in Chicago, organizers do not envision leadership as a "club" but as a ladder of opportunities available to everyone in the organization. Parents, usually mothers from the neighborhood, can begin with volunteering to be mentors in the school, but the LSNA offers more avenues for motivated parents to become more involved. This ladder not only builds different layers of learning for citizens but also recognizes that not all parents aspire to the same levels of involvement and leadership in school organizing and engagement. Parent mentors work for two hours a week in classrooms. They attend weekly workshops on a "range of educational and social issues designed to enhance their ability to be school *and* community leaders."[50]

Leadership development often combines knowledge of educational issues and systems with the technical skills of public work.

> To develop knowledge and skills, parent leaders participate in trainings, mentoring sessions, small group meetings, and public actions. From these experiences parents and community members expand their understanding of educational matters. They learn how the school system works, including issues related to curriculum and budget. They acquire an understanding of school data and how to use it to leverage change. Moreover, parents and communities become skilled at public speaking, researching issues, leading meetings, and negotiating with public officials.[51]

Leadership not only helps organizing groups come to judgment about goals and strategies through enhanced knowledge about schooling but also helps guide the group's "collective efforts in the political arena."[52] Guiding these efforts requires technical skills and capacities of political work: "leading meetings, interviewing public officials, representing the community at public events and with the media, and negotiating with those in power."[53] Such skill building is crucial to much of the leadership development work that happens in education organizing.

Warren argues, however, that at times organizing groups place too much emphasis on this aspect of leadership development—skills of running a meeting, conducting research, producing a leaflet—at the expense of other types of requisite leadership knowledge. "Technical skills are important. But, to the extent politics requires a collective action, attention must be paid to the substance of leadership offered to organizations and communities."[54] While political and interpersonal skills are crucial for leaders in educational organizing, the practice of leadership development is not to be simplistically equated with technical skills. That said, many citizens in contemporary political life, perhaps most particularly those from poor and low-income neighborhoods, may lack these necessary skills for successful education organizing.

The third and last aspect of leadership development discussed here relates to authority and how to wield it responsibly and effectively. Here, *responsibly* means in accordance with democratic norms of equality and transparency, and *effectively* means the ability to help organizing groups achieve most or all of their goals with regard to school reform. Leaders of educational organizing, being human, are not always responsible in the sense of behaving democratically in their wielding of authority; and organizations that use democratic processes of participatory leadership, as one example, may not always be effective in accomplishing their desired school reforms. Both responsibility and effectiveness are important in leadership for educational organizing. Leading responsibly, in the democratic sense of the term, is characterized by inclusiveness and accountability. To promote inclusive processes and an inclusive organization, organizing leaders devise ways to hear the input and ideas of membership, to seek out diverse viewpoints about strategy, and to constantly develop new leadership from all corners of the organizing group, wherever there is potential. Leaders in community organizing efforts best promote accountability through shared norms and rules that keep decision-making processes open and transparent.

Leading responsibly is not synonymous with eliminating the authority or power of leaders. Some democracy advocates and activists eschew authority in all forms, aiming for leadership paradigms and flat organizational structures where everyone is viewed as a leader and shared authority is the ideal. While egalitarian processes of leadership can be very successful, some observers of community organizing remind us that patterns of authority can and should be used in organizing work:

> Most advocates of participatory democracy have become uncomfortable with discussions of authority. But utopian preferences for pure egalitarian relationships are unrealistic for developing effective power for communities. Social relations that are characterized entirely by hierarchy, of course, are oppressive and lend little to democratic action. Yet most communities contain some pattern of authority. Political leadership in collective processes, in fact, requires the development of authority. The question is whether authority is legitimate, inclusive, and accountable to the broader community.[55]

IAF leadership in Texas has a tradition of never referring to the people who come to meetings or assemblies as "volunteers," preferring instead to refer to all participants as "leaders" as part of its inclusive leadership development program. But by leadership, IAF organizers mean something quite powerful and simple: "men and women who have a following and who can consistently deliver that following." A "following" indicates quality and reliability, and mutual accountability between leader and followers, according to Ed Chambers of the IAF.[56] These leaders understand that "leadership is not by nature a form of individual aggrandizement, but rather a means of continuing to expand the number of their fellow-leaders in the interest of collective power."[57]

Habits and Skills of Building Power

Power is defined here simply as the ability to authentically participate and exercise influence in decision-making processes.[58] Building power for disenfranchised groups of citizens is a fundamental goal of all community organizing. Practices that build power and influence on behalf of organizing groups in low-income neighborhoods or regions are, in a sense, the raison d'être—or entire purpose— of these groups. Comprised of individuals who, as solitary citizens, have been able to exercise little influence in school decision making, these groups see real problems in the ways that their schools work. Without practices that enable these groups to have a legitimate and respected voice in decision making about their own local schools, organizing groups fail in their most basic goals.

Skeptics may ask, why do these groups of citizens need extra influence on decision making, if they have helped to elect school board leadership in fair democratic elections? Are CBOs the kind of "special interest groups" that seek power to simply promote their own political agendas? Organizing groups may at times assert narrow interests that do not meet the criteria of *public* and shared interests. A group seeking to teach the Bible as the literal word of God in public schools would have a hard time convincing Muslim, atheist, and Hindu citizens and associations that such a goal represents a shared and public interest. Interests or agendas asserted as *public* interests must be debated and judged by citizens and leaders according to the merits of each particular agenda. These interests must be judged to be politically legitimate for public schools in a constitutional democracy.

Educational organizing as it is seen in the United States today, however, is typically seeking goals associated with the principle of equal opportunity. Michael Fabricant asserts that "parent-led campaigns, although differing in strategies, tactics, and agenda, almost always cohere around one common issue: the inadequate funding of public education in the poorest neighborhoods."[59] Citizens are using organizing to seek greater equity in the processes, facilities, and outcomes of their children's schools. On the broad level, such a set of interests are clearly public and widely shared, though it can be tremendously difficult to convince some citizens and groups of this fact as the micropolitics of school governance play out. The bipartisan No Child Left Behind Act, while in many ways a terrible piece of legislation, is at least a very clear symbol of some national consensus on education inequality. NCLB represents a fairly abstract national agreement that educational inequalities based on wealth, income, race, or ethnic identity are intolerable and incompatible with a society aligning with democratic ideals. Gaps in graduation rates, college matriculation, and academic achievement persist along racial, ethnic, and social class lines, and such unequal conditions and outcomes are antithetical to one of the primary democratic principles of equal opportunity. Such gaps erode the political legitimacy of public schools, and institutional legitimacy is an enabling factor for the success of all public schools. Attacking these gaps is clearly part of the work of education organizing groups, whose influence helps focus attention on these gaps and hold officials accountable for remedying them. As Fabricant notes, "a central challenge for poor communities is to create new structures of accountability for public education officials," yet the work to increase local resources for poor and working-class students meets frequent and powerful resistance on the part of more privileged citizens in a school or district.[60] The challenge for CBOs is to build the social and political capital needed to combat this resistance.

Despite efforts in some districts to introduce more participatory forms of decision making that are inclusive of all kinds of families, some parents and citizens exercise more influence than others, and this influence is directly related to social class and race in the United States. Inclusive and fair participation in shared governance is one of the principles of democratic legitimacy for public schools in a constitutional democratic state, as argued in Chapter 2. Yet it is no secret that powerful middle-class parents and families tend to have weightier influence in decision making at all levels, from the Parent–Teachers Association, to curriculum advisory groups, to school board deliberations. Even in school districts where participatory reforms have been introduced, the interests of the poor and working class tend to be neglected. As educational leadership scholar Gary Anderson notes, "ostensibly, participation in decision making is intended to provide more opportunities for disenfranchised groups to have a greater voice in organizational life, but too often the opposite occurs."[61] Anderson reviewed a wealth of research demonstrating that participatory reforms such as local site-based decision-making teams lead to unequal participation. Often in spite of good intentions, the participation of poorer and disenfranchised citizens is limited and co-opted by already powerful parents and school officials. Authentic opportunities to participate in shared governance of public schooling are difficult to achieve, even when administrators are well-intentioned and CBOs are well-run. It therefore stands to reason that organizing groups focus much of their time and energy on practices that build power for citizens and families whose educational interests are often neglected in school decision-making processes.

"Organizing groups mobilize parents, youth, and community members for local school improvement and district wide reform, often applying pressure from the outside to generate the political will necessary to adopt and implement reforms."[62] Building membership, circulating petitions, registering voters, writing letters to the editor, attending school board meetings in large numbers, organizing rallies, and holding meetings with school and civic officials are among the practices of building power in education organizing. The power-building practices CBOs employ with school districts vary from confrontational to collaborative, and most use a careful combination of each approach.[63] On the confrontational end of the continuum, groups can conduct mass actions and demonstrations that garner sustained media attention, subjecting schools or districts to enormous public pressure. Such actions can generate "fear and respect" on the part of school and city officials so that CBOs and their constituencies will be included in future decision-making processes.[64] The IAF in Texas regularly uses parent assemblies, for example, as part of a plan to move conversations with superintendents, principals, and school board members into public settings, where empowered leaders give prepared speeches and pose incisive questions to school officials in the eye of media. "Large public assemblies," for the IAF, "are key venues in which communities can begin the process of assertive self-governance and the nurturance of a proactive civic culture."[65] Other organizing efforts use more combative types of public action. As reported in one research study on educational organizing,

> youth-led and intergenerational groups placed a particular priority on this approach. ACORN affiliates in particular seemed to favor direct action in the form of street protests and rallies, while youth organizations had staged student strikes, walkouts, and occupations of school facilities to force administrators to the negotiating table. In Selma, Alabama, for example, student leaders organized a five-day take-over of a local school that helped bring about an end to tracking in the state.[66]

Confrontational practices make use of the idea of an adversary as a motivating force for political action. Combative practices like sit-ins or marches try to create a temporary "us versus them" mentality, but "enemies in this model are not static entities or individuals, then, but instead fluid and strategic achievements that allow a community to act as a coherent collective."[67] Combative practices of building power can be difficult to navigate when you are a principal or superintendent, but in a pluralistic society, a lively *demos* inevitably produces scenes of conflict. "A well-functioning democracy calls for a vibrant clash of democratic political positions."[68]

Contrasting with confrontational practices of building power are more collaborative forms. "Popular writings on community organizing sometimes overemphasize the combative nature of these groups." Aaron Schutz points out that "organizing groups nearly always begin their efforts on an issue with attempts at dialogue with those in authority. Only when they have been rebuffed do these groups begin to pursue more militant strategies."[69] Many successful organizing efforts have ultimately achieved positive working collaborations with school districts and leaders. CBOs have successfully tapped into the kinds of power that can be built through human relationships. Ernie Cortés, long-time organizer with the IAF in Texas, distinguishes between unilateral power and relational power. While the former is typically coercive and domineering, "the IAF teaches people to develop the power that is embedded in relationships, involving not only the capacity to act, but the reciprocal capacity to be acted upon."[70] Education organizers have used strategies for both relational and unilateral power, but their goals are usually collaborative. "These groups are willing to confront powerful institutions, but only when recalcitrant elites refuse to negotiate. They approach schools as partners, but this does not mean ignoring tensions and conflicts."[71] More collaborative forms, as Warren notes, have been more successful in "creating the civic capacity to build and sustain school reform. Taking a more relational understanding of power, parents and educators can look to their shared interest in advancing the education and well-being of children to help them work through inevitable differences and conflicts."[72]

An example of relational practices of building power may be helpful here. Alliance schools, products of IAF organizing efforts in Austin, Texas, are in predominantly black and Latino neighborhoods; IAF affiliates in this city are broad-based organizations "engaging parents, teachers, community leaders, and administrators in an effort to improve student performance and connect the local school more constructively to the surrounding community."[73] Though IAF was founded by Saul Alinsky, well-known for his confrontational tactics, the Alliance School organizing work represents the evolution that community organizing has undergone in recent decades. Alliance Schools are those entering into an agreement with a local IAF organization, which are often based in religious congregations in low-income neighborhoods. Teachers and administrators elect to enter into a relationship with an IAF organization to become an Alliance School, but from there, no prescription exists for the work to be done. IAF organizers organize parents as well as teachers, principals, staff, and students to address a range of school issues. "In this approach, public schools are not the object or target of outside community organizing; rather, organizing occurs in the school with all of its stakeholders."[74] The organizing occurs with the assistance of paid organizers, who train and empower key parent leaders; these people, in turn, work with civic, government, business, and educational leaders to leverage broad-based changes that affect student success in multiple ways.

An important part of the Alliance School story is the role of school leaders. Because principals and teachers elect to partner with an IAF organization, they are much more willing to work with these organizers instead of against them. "Principals had to be interested in moving away from traditional, hierarchical

notions of management toward a collaborative model, to see their role as fostering this new style of leadership that is congruent with organizing."[75]

Practices of building power are, in effect, efforts that build relationships and
relational networks between education organizing groups, school and civic officials, educators, and other civic and community-based organizations, including
national organizations.[76] These relationships are not without conflict, antago-
nisms, and difficult confrontation; thus we should not understand the term
relational to be a description of easy collegiality or immediate understanding
among groups whose differences can be quite substantial. Building power is the
work of achieving the right balance between pushing for accountability outside
of the educational system and working with administrators and educators inside
the system, to achieve goals for improvement. Fabricant argues that CBOs in the
South Bronx found success in part because of their ability to delicately balance
their "insider" and "outsider" status, gaining enough trust to build relationships
and collaborative efforts, but keeping enough organizational boundaries and
distance to put pressure on district or school leaders when required.[77]

The work of building power for disenfranchised citizens and groups requires
relational skill but yields incredible opportunities for educational leaders in districts serving poor communities. Developing relationships between groups who
may have very distinct ethnic, racial, social-class, or linguistic identities requires
time, patience, and a sensitivity to the obvious and not-so-obvious ways in which
the powerful among us can co-opt and silence the voices of the disenfranchised.
Developing relational networks among all these groups and interests is enabled
when school administrators, civic officials, and educators do not see practices
of building power as simply threatening or confrontational, but as unique opportunities for building the civic capacity necessary for better-quality schooling.

Habits and Skills of Collaborative Creation

Education organizing is a creative act; through political work, organizing can
result in new forms of educational possibility and opportunity. It can have these
results because organizing can catalyze educational publics. Publics, in turn,
help to collaboratively create myriad changes in schools: increased funding and
resources for a variety of programs, including after-school programs, mentoring
networks, facility improvement/construction, and programs that enhance college
readiness for poor or working-class students are all examples. These outcomes

happen through the practices of creating educational partnerships, programs, and policies, as well as the accountability expectations, shared agreements, and leadership resources to sustain them. Practices of collaborative creation also develop intangible goods for the schools and the neighborhoods, towns, and regions; resources such as trust, political capital, and political legitimacy are examples of such intangible outcomes. "Given the relationship between schooling outcomes and community conditions, truly transformative change in the educational futures of young people is unlikely to result from strategies focused on improving schools in isolation from communities."[78]

This chapter began with examples of education organizing around the country, and among these was the story of the OCO in Oakland, which struggled with the civic leaders, realtors, and owners of an abandoned Montgomery Ward building in their city. Their goal was to have the site bought by the school district and turned into an additional high school, as they understood the problems and liabilities associated with their overcrowded schools. Their communications, leadership development, and building power in their Montgomery Ward building campaign gradually led to a number of amazing partnerships and initiatives working on behalf of their goals:

> During the 8 years of the Montgomery Ward struggle, OCO made a number of significant accomplishments to further its small-schools initiative. OCO and the Bay Area Coalition of Equitable Schools (BayCES), a local school reform group, joined together in a powerful partnership. Together they hired an organizer to work directly with teachers around the idea of small schools. As a result of the partnership, the support of hundreds of teachers, and the systematic one-to-one meetings OCO leaders had with school board members and other elected leaders, the district adopted in May 2000 a small-schools policy that BayCES had drafted.... A new superintendent created a school reform office charged to work in partnership with OCO and BayCES to implement the new policy. OCO helped to win passage of a $300 million city bond for new school facilities targeted to low- to moderate-income neighborhoods.[79]

Education organizing in Oakland has resulted in not only new resources for facilities, but increased capacities among educators to use smaller school settings to students' best advantage. Organizing both created a new policy for the district around smaller schools and developed the citizen leadership necessary to continue to implement the policy, helping the central office to "budget, hire, and in other ways provide support to small schools and building the capacity of parents and teachers to work collaboratively in the design and implementation of small schools."[80]

Organizing helps create human and organizational capacity to better educate students, particularly those students whose current abilities and potential are not being tapped and reached by current schooling arrangements. *Capacity* describes our ability or power to do, experience, or understand something. Capacity also describes a container's ability to hold; a baseball stadium's capacity is an example. In a sense, organizing helps shift the daily habits of educators, school leaders, citizens, and parents; it helps them create new habits that expand their capacity to educate children and youth. These new habits enable these educators, parents, and leaders to hold more; to contain and hold enhanced abilities and resources with which to effectively educate the youth of poor and working-class families.

Capacity describes not just an individual power but an organizational and social power as well. It is a kind of "social intelligence," a term Dewey used to describe the knowledge developed as a result of inquiry and democratic experimentalism as citizens deliberately set out to change a social situation and experience the consequences of those efforts. Organizing generates a particular kind of social intelligence that scholars studying organizing call *community capacity*. Community capacity is "the interaction of human capital, organizational resources, and social capital existing within a given community that can be leveraged to solve collective problems and improve or maintain the well-being of that community."[81] Such capacity is based on the assumption that schools cannot generate the capacity for educating youth alone. This is true for all youth, but it is especially true for youth whose social and political capital, as well as health and familial structures, might be compromised due to poverty, racism, or lack of economic opportunities. Most teachers and school administrators, whose ranks are overwhelmingly white and middle-class, need to expand their capacity to educate these youth; most parents and civic leaders in these neighborhoods can do more to enhance their own capacities to lead, guide, and support this work.

There is a reciprocal relationship between educational organizing, community capacity building, and school improvement. Sustainable school reform is only built through education organizing that develops leaders, builds power, and engenders the kinds of social and political capital (skills to communicate successfully with key decision makers) necessary to make substantive and lasting change. Leaders, power, and social/political capital all lead to commitments and procedures of accountability to the school improvements being implemented as a result of organizing.[82]

A sense of accountability among educators and school officials to poor and working-class families of a district or school is one of the primary intangible goods that education organizing generates. The agreements and commitments to new resources or programs are one thing, but the sense of accountability to these families, and the families' empowerment to hold school accountable for these new resources, is the important condition for bringing these agreements to fruition. Forms of accountability generated through organizing campaigns are not the stiff and standardized "one-size-fits-all" kind of accountability generated through high-stakes standardized testing laws. It is instead a more local and relational understanding of accountability, based on transparent agreements and new norms generated through the collaborative work of organizing.

Neighborhoods and communities retain the benefits of these capacities after education organizing goals have been reached. Individuals experience the positive results of new leadership skills, increased knowledge about schools and organizations, and new expectations and aspirations derived from their political work. Organizing work teaches citizenship skills, and these skills can enable future projects and problem solving. In a survey of adult leaders (n=241 respondents) who had participated in eight organizing projects across the United States, "more than 70 percent . . . say they are more knowledgeable about how to resolve community problems, and are more active on community issues." Among young people surveyed (n=124 respondents) in this same study,

> 87 percent report that they attended a rally or press event for the first time through the organizing group; 69 percent signed a petition for the first time, and 63 percent contacted or met with a public official for the first time. Compared with their peers in a national sample, young people in our survey sample were seven times more likely to have attended an action, three times more likely to dhave been involved in community problem-solving efforts, and three times more likely to have contacted a public official.[83]

Practices of collaborative creation within education organizing build networks of accountability, new skills of civic and political engagement, and new avenues for enhanced political legitimacy. As schools and districts work in good faith to live up to the agreements negotiated through organizing campaigns, their standing as fair, effective public institutions will also be enhanced.

Conclusion

> A pluralist democracy needs to make room for dissent and for the institutions through which it can be manifested. Its survival depends on collective identities forming around clearly differentiated positions, as well as on the possibility of choosing between real alternatives.[84]

There are clearly patterns of power and influence in school governance and in the outcomes of public schooling. Differentials in academic success, completion rates, and resources are well known. These differentials clearly reflect what sociologists tell us about school governance trends and patterns: poor and working-class people's interests are often overlooked or disregarded in the allocation of resources, curricular planning, and in decision-making processes in schools. "Who are 'not really speaking beings' in the scenes of schooling?"[85] There are historic and distinct patterns of educational inequality and influence that plague public education; clearly, not all beings "speak" powerfully in school governance.

No Child Left Behind has produced no magical solutions to this problem, and in many ways the legislation has deepened the challenges of educating poor children. In fact, recent scholarship documents how the high-stakes standardized testing regimes of NCLB have thwarted some of the successes of CBOs in recent years.[86] Yet education organizing continues to provide a forum for local voices to shape their schools. In an age of unprecedented federal control over schools, organizing is a form of dissent that attempts to create "speaking beings" through practices of communication, leadership development, building power, and collaborative creation. These practices do not simply create power for organizing groups; they build capacity and legitimacy for public schools and the people who work in them. They create knowledge and resources, opportunities, and partnerships for schools and their communities that can last far beyond one organizing campaign.

Organizing for education reform is a human practice, however. It is thus subject to all the foibles and errors of any other type of political work. Since the practices it employs are complex, and since the building of power can involve all sorts of trade-offs and compromises, education organizing is a messy business. The best efforts of organizers and those school officials who genuinely attempt to collaborate with them can derail. Partnerships between faith-based organizing groups and public schools can go awry as religiously motivated work spills over into inappropriate religious activity in school settings. Education organizing is also a limited political intervention; it does not substitute for reformed state and national educational policies, for example. As Dennis Shirley notes in a recent article summing up the state of education organizing and research, it is an important but limited strategy.

> Education is also far too complex and nuanced of a field for any single political perspective or even the most gutsy and determined activists to attain an exclusive purchase on the many problems of reform. When adapted and infused into a broader repertoire of change strategies, however, community organizing has much to offer for the way ahead.[87]

In his more recent work, Shirley calls for community organizing to be a starting point, an avenue toward a model of "'empowered participatory governance' that aspires to maximize the benefits of grassroots reform while acknowledging the need for systems-level accountability systems."[88] The next chapter describes yet another strategy for such empowerment: democratic deliberation.

Schools are composed of many webs of governance and resource-allocation, and many layers of decision makers and actors. As a strategy for building publics *for* schools, education organizing can contribute to school reform efforts by constituting the *demos* in endless formations. Without the people acting on behalf of their political will, the very project of public education is substantially weakened. Organizing is one powerful way to enable a group of citizens to understand and assert their political will for their local schools. Another powerful way, which can often supplement organizing efforts or act as a stand-alone initiative, are the forms of associative democracy fostering the deliberations of citizens.

Chapter 6
Deliberative Democracy and Public Schools

Deliberative democracy, as applied to educational contexts, consists of multiple types of gatherings and forums that bring diverse citizens together (often physically but sometimes virtually) to talk, listen, learn, and better understand their shared educational problems. These forums enable citizens to express their conflicts, build collective understanding, and make or shape decisions and policies for their schools. In localities around the United States, the public is experimenting with these practices on behalf of the future of their public schools. As Matt Leighninger writes in *The Next Form of Democracy,*

> Over the last twenty years, ordinary people have developed new civic attitudes and capacities; they are better educated, more diverse, less apt to defer to government and other forms of authority, more adept at using new technologies, and more willing to take productive (or disruptive) roles in public decision making.[1]

Deliberative democracy theory and practice has been a field of growing interest and innovation in recent decades; public schools and districts around the country have witnessed the fruits of this innovation. In cities like Plainfield, New Jersey; Winston-Salem, North Carolina; and Kansas City, Kansas, leaders have developed imaginative new ways to help citizens deliberate issues and challenges facing their schools, and more broadly, problems that are affecting the well-being of children and youth.

Deliberative democracy represents "any one of a family of views according to which the public deliberation of free and equal citizens is the core of legitimate political decision making and self-governance."[2] James Bohman describes public deliberation as "a dialogical process … for the purpose of resolving problematic situations that cannot be settled without interpersonal coordination and cooperation."[3] Deliberation is ultimately about weighing various options and trying to come to public judgment shaped by the voices and views of all constituents, or as Noëlle McAfee puts it, "a process through which people grapple with the consequences of various public problems and proposals."[4] As discussed in Chapter 2, legitimacy is one of the key challenges for schools today. Deliberative processes can help school leaders earn more political legitimacy by enabling publics to form and achieve maturity. Through forums, citizen's juries, study circles, or a number of other deliberative venues, citizens shape goals, purposes and programs for their local schools.

Legitimacy, as argued earlier, cannot be achieved in school governance simply through the correct aggregation of the individual, preformed opinions of voters. Deliberative democracy supplements school governance when there is no simple aggregation available, when thorny problems of value—"wicked problems"—are at hand.[5] Wicked problems do not have technical solutions; they are characterized by competing underlying values and priorities, whose solutions will usually involve tradeoffs. In the face of these problems, deliberative processes are concerned with the formation of a political will through good processes of deliberation and reflective thinking. "Deliberation is not so much a form of discourse or argumentation as a joint, cooperative activity."[6] Building legitimacy thus requires school governance that can help facilitate processes of decision making among diverse citizens, and requires the kinds of school boards and education authorities able to heed the advice and direction of their citizens. A brief look at just three examples of districts that have engaged in such deliberative work illustrates these possibilities.

Deliberative Democracy and the Schools

Portsmouth, New Hampshire, has been host to a range of deliberative innovation, and the public schools have been part of this activity. In 1999, two hundred sixth-graders and seventy-five adult community members met to engage in study circles on the topics of bullying and related behavior issues. A study circle is a voluntary, small group (5–25) of citizens who meet multiple times to explore a critical social issue. Each meeting lasts a few hours and is directed by a moderator; citizens can elect to read assigned materials between sessions as springboards to learning and further discussion. The study circles led to a greater awareness of bullying in the school, but it also helped connect diverse groups across the community in dialogue around common concerns. One year later, members of these study circles encouraged a Portsmouth school board member to help implement a similar deliberative process for a school redistricting issue they needed to tackle. This is a good example of a "wicked" problem; there are many possible technical and "correct" solutions to enrollment/overcrowding issues, but a good solution will be based on those particular values and priorities among parents, educators, students, and community members in a district. "Prior attempts to resolve the schools' lopsided enrollments and space problems had failed in the wake of bitter public argument over the issue during city council meetings."[7]

Over one hundred residents participated in four-week facilitated small group discussions, each held at a different school location that was feeling the effects of overcrowding. Citizens could thus learn more about the issues firsthand. The group's final report, *Rethinking Instead of Redistricting*, provided input directly to the Board of Education Redistricting Committee. "The resulting plan developed by the school board received broad support for increased funding of school renovations, and resulted in only sixty-five students switching schools."[8]

A different, more ambitious deliberative project was launched in central Texas a few years later. Multiple school districts and nonprofit agencies collaboratively organized and convened a series of dialogues called *Too Many Children Left Behind: Closing the Education Gaps in Central Texas.* Over six hundred people participated in dialogues in six school districts, organized to "provide a mechanism for community change, a platform of understanding across communities for *regional* solutions, and a set of grass roots input from parents, students, teachers, and community members into the strategic planning process for systemic education reform in the region."[9] These dialogues were organized using the National Issues Forum (NIF) model, a structured deliberative format developed from research by the Kettering Foundation. NIF has developed materials for communities to use in discussing the achievement gap in educational outcomes between racial and class groups in US public schools, among other issues.[10] NIF materials, like those of other national deliberative organizations, use research to help "frame" a divisive issue so that it can be productively discussed among diverse stakeholders in a locality; framing is a key part of preparing to deliberate an issue. Central Texas project collaborators used the NIF materials as a guide, customizing the materials for each school district hosting a deliberative forum in its region. The result of these dialogues was a Blueprint for Educational Change, a statement of recommendations and plans that encompass thirty-five school districts, fifteen charter schools, and seven higher education institutions across the region.[11]

In South Carolina, a series of deliberative forums were convened in three diverse districts in the late 1990s. "South Carolina's students had scored near the bottom of national rankings for decades, but in the mid-1990s, the public seemed to have lost patience with the assurances of administrators and school boards that improvement was just around the corner."[12] A partner in this project was Public Agenda, a national nonpartisan organization devoted to improving democratic problem solving. A statewide survey sponsored by Public Agenda yielded data showing widespread dissatisfaction with public schools on a range of issues: lack of accountability for student performance, inequitable distribution of resources, and schools' inability to enforce discipline and ensure safety. The "Reconnecting" project was the response to these findings, initiated by the School Boards Association in collaboration with the State Department of Education as well as Public Agenda.

> Reconnecting represented a self-consciously innovative approach to public engagement. In each community, a series of neighborhood public meetings would be held under the auspices of a steering committee comprising citizens selected by the school district as broadly representative of the community, but who would operate independently of the school district. At the meetings, participants would be asked to discuss their aspirations for the community; what keeps people apart and what brings them together in the community; and what role the schools should play in the community. After completion of the neighborhood meetings, the steering committee would select 50 citizens reflecting the demographics of the school district ... to come together in a 'community conversation' to forge an agreement that would outline hopes and expectations for actions different segments of the community would do to rebuild the connection [between citizens and their schools].[13]

These examples from New Hampshire, Texas, and South Carolina are illustrative of the possibilities of public deliberation. Each describes a different way of enacting deliberation, a type of citizen inquiry process related to issues and problems facing their schools. *Their* schools, the citizens' schools, are at the heart of the inquiry here, for deliberative venues and processes are explicitly structured to show citizens how their public schools belong not just to the state, or to the paid experts or public officials they hire, appoint, or elect to run them. Deliberation processes help give citizens the means and venues for thinking through the "wicked" problems facing their schools, and developing the will, commitment, and means for tackling them.

The Theory of Deliberative Democracy

> The ancient Greeks called deliberation the talk we use to teach ourselves before we act. Deliberation is the kind of reasoning and talking we do when a difficult decision has to be made, a great deal is at stake, and there are competing options or approaches we might take. At the heart of deliberation is weighing possible actions and decisions carefully by examining their costs and consequences in light of what is most valuable to us. Deliberation can take place in any kind of conversation—including dialogue, debate and discussion.[14]

Among political theorists, democratic theory took a decisively deliberative turn in the late twentieth century. While representative bodies regularly deliberate on behalf of citizens in democratic states, deliberative democracy theorists advocate an approach to politics in which citizens themselves deliberate. Deliberative democrats want to improve the quality of democracy through expanding its franchise, scope, and authenticity. They wish to expand the proportion of citizenry actively engaged in politics (franchise), extend the range of issues under control of citizens' power (scope), and expand the degree to which citizen control is substantive rather than symbolic (authenticity).[15]

Expanding the franchise of decision making through deliberative processes is central to this theory. "Deliberative democracy itself began ... as a theory for which democratic legitimacy depends upon the ability of *all* those subject to a decision to participate in authentic deliberation."[16] Much attention has been paid in deliberative theory and practice to the inclusiveness of deliberative forums and processes to ensure, in particular, that citizens who may be often excluded from political proceedings are full, equal participants. Good deliberative forums are diverse in terms of ideological viewpoints as well as identities of participants (along the lines of, for example, social class, race/ethnicity, religion, nationality, sexuality, and gender). "Diversity ensures that the issue under deliberation is considered from multiple angles. It also reduces the likelihood of enclave deliberation among like-minded people, where views are strengthened rather than questioned."[17]

Deliberative democratic theorists also wish to expand the scope of issues that citizens can directly shape through deliberative processes and agreement outcomes. Local governments have begun to experiment with a range of deliberative processes for addressing budgets and public financing, environmental and conservation issues, city planning, and police-community relations.[18] Deliberative forums have also been used to address various school issues, including redistricting, school facilities, funding, integration, racial-ethnic disparities in school achievement, teacher quality, school violence, and affirmative action policies in higher education.[19]

Finally, deliberative democracy seeks to make citizen voice more authentic and substantive. As discussed earlier, citizen's powers to shape their local schools' vision and policies are mostly limited to participating in local school board elections or, more indirectly, one-way communications with their local/state/national legislative representatives. School boards will hear from a few more motivated or vocal citizens at compulsory open forum times at school board meetings, but the random and irregular nature of citizens' comments in such forums means that board members cannot rely (in terms of quantity or quality) on such irregular input for decision making. Yet on a consistent basis, school boards and administrators encounter the wicked problems that are perfectly suited for citizens, in deliberation, to exercise a more substantive voice in school decision making.

In order for citizens to be able to have a more authentic influence in school decision making, much depends upon the quality and tenor of the deliberations among the diverse constituents. How can citizens make sound judgments together about issues that are controversial and that excite passionate views? Amy Gutmann and Dennis Thompson remind us that moral disagreement is inevitable, and certainly this is true when it comes to educational matters.[20] As human beings, we have limited generosity toward others, and given limited and ever shrinking educational resources, our generosity is even more tested. Moreover, given the ways in which Americans often surround ourselves with like-minded friends, neighbors, and news sources, our exposure and openness to different and perhaps opposing views can be very limited. All these realities present challenges for deliberative politics. However, the quality of deliberation is critical; our ability to come to agreement with strangers rests upon the principles, assumptions, and facilitation skills that structure good deliberative processes, so that such challenges are not insurmountable.

Gutmann and Thompson offer three important characteristics of good public deliberation: reciprocity, publicity, and accountability.[21] Reciprocity is "a form of mutuality in the face of disagreement."[22] It is the ability to engage in "reasonable" debates with others wherein participants carefully listen to others and offer up their own stances or beliefs in terms that they believe would be understandable to others. This does not mean that deliberators have to be hyper-rational philosophers. Reciprocity is a fundamental principle of deliberative democracy, but it does not require "reasonable" deliberation to exclude people's beliefs and opinions that may not always be based in "reason" per se. Rather, reciprocity requires that we set up processes of talk and discussion wherein people can find ways to listen and understand through their differing perspectives. "Beliefs, opinions, and so forth do not quash reason. Rather, [reciprocity] suggests that citizens and officials should have open minds, seek moral agreement when they can, maintain mutual respect when they cannot and create laws and policies that will continue to be open to challenge, critique, and ongoing deliberation."[23] Deliberative agreements, then, must be based on mutual justification—the idea that the grounds for agreement are based on justifications to which even those who disagree can consent.

Reciprocity is not, however, an automatic condition of deliberation; it must be constructed. Good deliberative practitioners set up deliberations with the intent to foster and build the potential for mutual justification. This is why Martín Carasson, director of Colorado State University's Center for Public Deliberation, describes the "first order goals" of deliberation to be (1) issue learning, (2) improved democratic attitudes and skills, and (3) improved relationships.[24] Trying to solve wicked problems through deliberation requires first learning about the issue or problem under discussion, as we often bring our own narrow views and experiences to any controversial issue, without all the relevant facts. Many deliberation participants also learn to listen to those who do not share their viewpoint, and how to speak out about their views to those who may not agree with them. Importantly, this requires that majority views, as well as the views of experts, are not allowed to dominate deliberative processes. This is the "the non-tyranny constraint" of sound deliberative decision making, where decisions are made "in light of broadly convincing reasons rather than based on power asymmetries."[25] Similarly, Claus Offe and Ulrich Preuss describe "enlightened" political judgment to be "fact-regarding" (as opposed to ignorant), "other-regarding" (as opposed to narrowly self-interested), and "future-regarding" (as opposed to myopic or short-sighted).[26]

Reciprocity refers not only to the condition of mutual justification that good deliberations foster but also to the underlying principle of equality central to deliberative theory. To further challenge and mitigate the power asymmetries that occur in public life and in deliberative processes, norms and processes that promote equality are central to deliberative practice.

> Regardless of its content, a norm of equality has to be operative in democratic deliberation and decision making. For example, if the decision making process is defined in terms of discussion and debate, then every citizen must have an equal chance to speak and to employ the full range of expressions available to everyone else; everyone must also have equal access to all relevant arenas for debate and discussion, as well as equal standing and opportunities in the decision making process.[27]

The problems and challenges of inequality in deliberative politics has been the focus of much research and writing on deliberative theory, about which I will elaborate later in this chapter.

The principle of publicity is identified by a number of deliberative theorists as central to the practice. Gutmann and Thompson tell us that publicity is about both accountability and accessibility.[28] Deliberative politics makes public officials more accountable to their constituents; deliberative processes often yield public agreements, goals, and choices that citizens wish to see carried out by education officials. This accountability, for schools, is a two-way street. "A conception of accountability that connects schools and communities broadens the base of stakeholders who then feel responsible for improving public education and builds added public pressure for these improvements."[29]

But publicity also refers to the wide accessibility that deliberative politics should provide. Deliberative politics should both happen in public—in venues and settings open and welcoming to all citizens—and be public in their content. As John Dryzek notes, such public forums should be

> ideally hosting free-ranging and wide-ranging communication, with no barriers limiting who can communicate, and few legal restrictions on what they can say.... The locations might involve Internet forums, the physical places where people gather and talk (e.g., cafés, classrooms, bars, and public squares), public hearings, and designed citizen forums of various sorts (which limit participation on the basis of numbers, but do not restrict the kinds of persons who can deliberate).[30]

I have spent much of this discussion of deliberative theory on the qualities of good deliberation, but a clear focus must also be put on the outcomes that deliberative democracy can yield. Carcasson describes three second-order goals in deliberative democracy: (1) transformed conflicts, (2) individual and collective action, and (3) improved institutional decision making.[31] In our sound-bite and partisan political culture, conflict characterizes much of politics; deliberation does not erase differences in view or belief, but enables citizens to find productive avenues for their disagreements. As the codirector of Healthy Democracy Oregon states, deliberative democracy "can play a meaningful role in moving past partisan gridlock, conflicts of interest, etc., if done with integrity and transparency. As cynical as politics is, I think there is keen interest on both sides of the aisle to find innovative ways to move past old debates."[32] Dryzek provides much evidence from studies and experiments around the world of how deliberative forums can improve the quality and legitimacy of decision making in governance.[33]

If conflicts are productively transformed in deliberation, they can yield decisions and direction for action—what many believe to the heart of any good deliberative process. Many citizens are drawn into deliberations with the promise that their participation will help yield a good decision about a problem faced by their community. A key component of deliberative democracy is thus the quality of the agreements produced and the force these agreements have in shifting individual action, collective action, and/or policy directives guiding an institution.

The multiple outcomes of deliberative politics are made clear in a three-year qualitative case study conducted of two districts implementing different forms of democratic governance processes, including deliberation.[34] Julie Marsh's *Democratic Dilemmas* outlines the numerous and mixed outcomes that were witnessed in these districts. In the district called Highland, where the relatively successful deliberations were a key part of a long-term strategic planning process, participants agreed on four key strategies, with detailed plans for achieving each strategy, "including an articulation of specific results, actions, individuals responsible, timelines, and expected costs."[35] Marsh found that "deliberations in Highland yielded decisions that offered new solutions to old problems."[36] And while the ultimate responsibility of achieving these solutions fell to district administrators and teachers, Marsh emphasizes the two-way feel of the accountability ethic that was built during the process, and the affective outcomes in the community: "Strategic planning appeared to cultivate the deliberative skills of participants (e.g., how to weigh evidence and arrive at decisions aimed at the common good) and expand their understanding of the education system and the district. It also may have enhanced citizens' commitment to support the district and reform in the future."[37]

Deliberative democracy advocates see such outcomes and forms of accountability as enhancing the political legitimacy of public institutions. By expanding the franchise and scope of decision making—and by constructing deliberative processes that are based on reciprocity, equality, and publicity—deliberative politics offers a promising way for schools to achieve publics for their schools.

To discuss the promise and drawbacks of deliberative politics in a finer grain as it applies to educational leaders, I now turn to the specific habits and skills that these types of public work require. Citizens, along with civic and school leaders of all types, sponsor and conduct the deliberative experiments described thus far in this chapter. Their work is not achieved through magic or luck but through particular kinds of habits or skills. Parallel to the work of education organizing described in the previous chapter, four broad categories of public-building skills encourage the development and achievement of powerful publics for public schooling: communication, building power, leadership development, and collaborative creation. How do these four skills specifically shape our assumptions, theories, and practices of deliberative politics in school-based governance and decision making?

Habits and Skills of Communication

Deliberative democracy is based on an assumption that communication processes are transactional; that citizens can learn and sometimes evolve their views on political issues through that learning. A parent who walks into a hearing on controversial curriculum might be dead-set against one set of positions but through a good deliberative process may come to at least be able to consent to a policy that she would originally never have considered supporting. Deliberative democracy, as a way to build publics for schools, is a process of will formation, not simply the structured clash of preformed wills and opinions. Deliberative forums are therefore designed to help a diverse array of citizens with a range of opinions on a subject come together to talk with and—far more challenging—to listen to one another. Deliberation assumes diversity and disagreement among participants. Deliberative practitioners rely on faith in human intelligence and communication abilities, as well as carefully planned and executed deliberative strategies, to find sources or points of agreement within that pluralism. As Carcasson and Sprain note,

> Deliberation puts considerable faith in human nature, assuming that despite quirks of human nature that can make collaborative problem-solving difficult, people are capable of deliberating when provided productive spaces and processes to do so. Adversarial political processes too often take advantage of and intensify the flaws of human nature, such as selective listening and the inherent impulse to prefer simple "good vs. evil" framings over engaging tough choices. The deliberative perspective, on the other hand, seeks to overcome those flaws and nurture the more positive democratic potentials of citizens.[38]

While deliberative democrats rely on a degree of confidence in human nature, they are not simple-minded in this faith. Deliberative communicative processes and venues are based on the assumption that society is characterized by both deep pluralism and conflict. Deliberation is a political process used for school or district governance regarding problems or decisions about which there is initially little available consensus. Deliberative processes ask participants to deal with the messiness of their disagreement through a structured process and challenge them to find directions in which they might move as a polity, *within* that disagreement. While most deliberative processes attempt to build working agreements among participants, failure to do so can still yield progress in the process of democratic decision making. Even "when interests or values conflict irreconcilably, deliberation ideally ends not in consensus but in a clarification of conflict and structuring of disagreement, which sets the stage for a decision by non-deliberative methods, such as aggregation or negotiation among cooperative antagonists."[39] The object of democratic deliberation, however, is to try to find agreement, transforming an "I" into a "we" around a particular problem or challenge. As McAfee argues, the object of deliberation is not the unification of diverse views but an integration of views to find ways forward that accommodate the pluralism of the citizenry.

> Participants use their disagreements as productive constraints, helping them identify in which, albeit few, possible directions the polity might move. In the many deliberations . . . I have observed, participants leave saying that even when they did not agree with other participants, they did come to see why the others held the views they did. They came to change their views of others' views. Even

in the face of trenchant disagreement, participants would focus on coming up with a direction that would accommodate the plural concerns in the room.[40]

In the process of finding a direction that can accommodate a broad cross-section of citizens, deliberations ideally allow for a range of communication venues as well as styles. Town meetings, collaborative forums, citizen advisory boards, and public hearings all structure communications differently. More collaborative forums will rely on a range of both large and small-group venues to promote dialogue across difference and promote reflection among participants. Some kinds of deliberative structures lend themselves to more adversarial kinds of talk.[41] Depending on the goal and venue, degrees of contestation and disagreement are to be expected in deliberative communications. Indeed, "deliberative authenticity exists to the extent that communication induces reflection on preferences in non-coercive fashion. Provided that this standard is met, the kinds of communication admissible can be quite wide-ranging, and contestation in particular should be welcomed for its ability to induce reflection."[42] The giving and taking of views and opinions in a deliberation can take an array of forms, including greeting, story-telling, and emotional expressions of preference or viewpoint. Deliberative communication should not be viewed as a starchy, hyper-rational exchange of polite views, but can and should accommodate the diverse styles and modes of communication that are infused with the fullness and charge of powerful human expression. "Deliberation is a process that inherently involves passion as well as reason."[43] It is for this reason that good deliberations involve good facilitators, people who are trained to move discussions forward through the passions and conflicts that will inevitably be raised in trying to resolve wicked problems.

Deliberation facilitators keep in mind several factors that help a group "sustain the recognition, acceptance, and productive nurturing of conflict while searching for outcomes that will attract genuine consensus."[44] One is the assembling of deliberative processes that include groups characterized by what political scientists call "cross-cutting cleavages," which "encourage individuals to ally first with one set of others and then with another set on different issues."[45] For example, in a deliberation about a controversial new high school facility, citizens involved with the local Tea Party group might find alliances in a deliberative hearing with elderly citizens who are fearful of tax increases on their limited incomes; yet these same citizens might also be sympathetic to citizens with differing views who are familiar members of their church congregations. Cross-cutting cleavages help prevent deliberations from becoming entrenched in partisan and predictable group stances and patterns of interest.

Another factor enhancing a deliberative group's ability to communicate and reach agreement across difference is the mix of issues on the agenda. A group process constructed around challenges ranging from relatively consensual to relatively conflictual, in that order, builds mutual respect and communicative exchanges that can pave the way for productive discussions about problems in which interests clash more directly. On a similar note, certain deliberative structures and strategies can help build potential for better communication. In a study of sixteen organizations that conduct and promote deliberative forums, David Ryfe discusses some of the explicit relationship-building activities that deliberative organizations use to get difficult conversations started.[46] Finally, the abilities of deliberators are obviously a key factor in the productive nurturing of conflict in the search for acceptable outcomes and agreements. Deliberative practitioners and facilitators (see Appendix) are developing a range of methods to build the abilities of deliberators within the confines of actual deliberative processes, but a longer-term development of the larger citizenry's capacities in this regard requires reformed civics curriculum and pedagogy, among other efforts.

While most communications in formal deliberation have been face-to-face, again, the Internet and social media are expanding possibilities. The frontier of digital deliberative practices is brand new, and this is certainly true for education-oriented deliberation as well. "The notion of government-as-a-platform, where we—citizens and public officials alike—use the web to make the boundary between the public and the government more porous and our interactions more collaborative and participatory, simply hasn't gotten very far. Yet."[47]

But some online experiments and new applications are promising. In Colorado, Wisconsin, New Mexico, and Minnesota cities, online conversations about local issues, called e-forums, are inclusive, free spaces where participants can discuss local or national issues. Sponsored by e-democracy.org, these local online discussion boards are "a place where citizens, local officials, or journalists post their questions and get an idea of how residents feel about these issues."[48] Other uses of online communication technologies combine face-to-face deliberations with online networks that expand and extend the work done in the real-time forums. An example of this kind of innovation is found in Kansas City.

Starting in 2008, Public Agenda helped the Kansas City Regional METS Leadership Coalition (regional leaders dedicated to supporting Math, Engineering and Science achievement) to implement a multi-year public engagement initiative to improve opportunities for young people and support economic growth through METS. Community Conversations were held in multiple communities around the region to discuss issues and ideas locally. Each of the participating communities joined an overarching, region-wide online social network as a platform to continue the conversation amongst the participants of their own events, but also to learn from each other and connect people interested in improving METS education across the region.[49]

These examples illustrate the expanding possibilities for deliberative politics unfolding in online venues and show how, rather than replacing face-to-face civic forums, these tools will enable new ways of expanding and deepening citizen participation.

Habits and Skills of Building Power through Deliberative Democracy

Deliberative democracy makes public policies and decisions more reflective of the concerns and interests of a broader array of citizens, expanding the franchise of democratic participation and decision making. This is why some advocates call the deliberative ideal "power neutralizing" in its aims:

> In the ideal case, collective decision making through deliberation also neutralizes the political role of arbitrary preferences and power by putting collective decisions on a footing of common reasons. In ideal deliberation, the only power that prevails is, as Habermas puts it, the "force of the better argument"—and that is a force equally available to all.[50]

Of course, there are no "ideal" deliberations. While many deliberative practitioners have worked toward this ideal, deliberative practice is still challenged by the relatively privileged and white identities of most of its experts and facilitators.[51] The field still has work to do in diversifying its own ranks and practices. Yet the very legitimacy of deliberative decision making rests upon the degree to which deliberations truly incorporate the views of the diverse range of citizens affected by the problems under deliberation. The challenges of creating fully inclusive processes in democratic politics generally and in deliberative politics more specifically are essential to understand and face. "Calls for inclusion arise from experiences of exclusion—from basic political rights, from opportunities to participate, [and] from the hegemonic terms of debate."[52]

Deliberation processes must be designed to combat the multiple ways in which different types of citizens—and especially less powerful citizens—are left out of decision making in our society. Private negotiations and back-door agreements with more powerful citizens, who have access to the primary decision makers in a representative democracy, are too prevalent in political life, including school politics. Some kinds of public decision-making processes in school districts are formally "open" but in practice, not authentically open to the input of citizens, and subject to too many decisions made during confidential, private, or closed-door sessions.[53] Even those forums that are open to any citizen, when run without facilitators or a good process, are all too often simply stages for the loudest and most organized to air their views. To counter these trends, those who use deliberative strategies must understand how such forums help build power and influence among all voices, in the face of much inequality within the society at large.

Both external and internal exclusions hamper democratic decision making. External exclusion "names the many ways that individuals and groups that ought to be included are purposely or inadvertently left out of fora for discussion and decision making." How are deliberative processes in school districts planned so that all factions, stakeholders, and perspectives in the school or district are both attending *and* actively participating? Internal exclusion "concern[s] ways that people lack effective opportunity to influence the thinking of others even when they have access to fora and procedures of decision-making."[54] How does the deliberative process actively enable all kinds of perspectives, even some of the more "unpopular" views, to be expressed and heard?

Vigorous recruitment and planning strategies can go a long way toward remedying problems of external exclusion. In Ryfe's study of deliberative organizations, he found that most of these organizations actively worked to recruit diverse participants from all corners of the community or region. These efforts are challenging, as "inclusiveness entails an incredible amount of work. After all, who wants to engage in a discussion of a difficult, often uncomfortable issue with people dramatically different than oneself if not compelled to do so?"[55] A group of parents who feel excluded and silenced in their school district may resist repeated invitations to the deliberation process. Yet some organizations come up with labor-intensive but creative ways of approaching this problem.

Simply to get individuals to participate in a broadened community discussion with people unlike themselves, these organizations conduct a great deal of pre-meeting exercises with participants.... This work is intended to probe individual values and expectations [e.g., through one-on-one meetings], to confront participants with opposing views before the group meets, and to allow the organizations to develop a game plan for actual discussions.[56]

Getting citizens identified with marginalized populations or positions in a school or a district to a deliberation forum is only part of the inclusion battle; "internal exclusions" are also powerful ways that less popular or dominant voices, once in the room, can be diminished in deliberation. These internal exclusions might show up in two different ways. One is through the creation of a "logocracy," in which the power in a deliberative setting goes to the "rhetorically or laryngically gifted" in the group—that is, to the most verbally talented or even most talkative deliberators; in which the "rule of the reasoners (and not of reason) is likely to compound existing social inequalities" along race, gender, social class, sexuality, and ability lines in a school or district.[57]

The other kind of internal exclusion happens when rhetoric of "the common good" or shared interests discourages people from voicing their legitimate, particular interests and perspectives on a problem. This exclusion takes shape in arguments appealing to the alleged "common interests" of all participants but that fail to shift the status quo of current power arrangements and fall along existing lines of influence. "The advantaged will find some way to defend self-serving proposals with appeals to ideas of the common advantage, but press a conception of the common advantage that assigns great weight to the *status quo*." Common advantage will be understood relative to the "existing framework of inequality, with that framework itself left off the deliberative table."[58]

An example of such an internal exclusion is documented in research on a series of public meetings on desegregation issues facing a New Jersey school district in the 1990s.[59] At the time, the town of Englewood (population 24,850) was 45 percent white, 36 percent African American, and 14 percent Hispanic; its high school was 92 percent African American and Hispanic. Surrounding towns of Englewood Cliffs, Leonia, and Tenafly had large white majorities and a small but growing middle-class Asian population and school enrollment. Plans to regionalize the school district as a way of remedying segregation in Bergen County were discussed at a series of public hearings. Tali Mendelberg and John

Oleske witnessed and analyzed these hearings in terms of rhetoric and speech. The researchers focused on the first and last hearings in their analysis, which were also the two most well-attended public hearings: one of these, overwhelmingly populated by white citizens, was nearly completely homogenous in the views expressed against the desegregation plans; and the other, more racially integrated meeting, saw a more heterogeneous mix of interests expressed from diverse speakers about the proposed desegregation remedy. In analyzing the speech content of both meetings, Mendelberg and Oleske reached several conclusions:

> We find that (a) deliberation at the segregated meeting maintained consensus among segregated Whites; (b) these citizens used coded rhetoric that appeared universal, well-reasoned, and focused on the common good, but in fact advanced their group interest; (c) deliberation at the integrated meeting maintained the conflict between segregated Whites and others; and (d) there, rhetoric that seemed universal to segregated Whites was decoded by the integrated audience as racist and group interested.[60]

Particularly when the issue of race is involved, deliberative speakers in the United States wield a tricky, murky rhetoric. Those opposing the regionalization plan for a racially integrated school district were much more likely to use appeals to "neighborhood schools" and to predict that any regionalization plan to integrate would fail to work because of the problem of "white flight." "Speakers repeatedly attempted to 'deracialize' their arguments by disclaiming racism, thus appearing to meet the deliberative criterion of tolerance. (In fact, the word segregation was never mentioned by anyone speaking against integration.)"[61]

Those speakers opposing integration are not being demonized here; the point of these observations is to show how challenging and slippery the internal exclusions of deliberative processes can be. Our communications and use of language can often be wielded in ways that, intentionally or intentionally, wield power and influence benefiting our own positions.

Yet Mendelberg and Oleske's research also points to several other important factors to be considered when contemplating the use of deliberation processes for school-based decision making. One crucial factor shaping the inclusive quality of deliberative politics is the type and quality of the venue or forum used to deliberate. In a public-meeting style deliberation, there is exceedingly little "deliberation" at all, if that word implies at least some degree of exchange of views through genuine dialogue among diverse participants. This type of venue has been an unfortunately popular one for soliciting public opinion during school controversies (recall the R-rated movie conflict discussed in Chapters 3 and 4). The public hearing is supposed to be an open forum for all viewpoints, but it is usually a space where "two kinds of 'voices' tend to predominate: the angriest and the most organized. The *general* public, and certainly those who have been traditionally marginalized, are rarely represented in any meaningful fashion."[62] Good deliberations are highly interactive, building on the assumptions about communication discussed earlier in this chapter.

Mendelberg and Oleske's analysis also points to a set of questions and considerations that should preempt the decision to engage a school or district in a deliberative process, including: what are the primary goals and purposes of this deliberative process? What is the nature of the current relationship between relevant stakeholders? What is the state of understanding, generally, in the community? In what ways can the issue or goals be productively framed to allow for multiple perspectives but also to enable citizens to choose among distinct, reasonable, realizable options?[63] There are a range of deliberative structures, some much more appropriate for deeply divisive and sensitive problems than others. In addition, the entire question of whether a particular issue can productively be deliberated at all is essential to consider. Mark Warren discusses race as an example of a deliberative topic that, in the United States, is difficult to deliberate in ways that are productive and not harmful to participants, especially to those racial minorities whose views may not always be received well.

> Race is one of a variety of topics to which I shall refer as "sensitive" in ways that make deliberation difficult. *Sensitive issues,* as I shall use the term here, are those that *necessarily and involuntarily reference inherited status inequalities of speakers as part of the content of speech in ways that destabilize deliberation.* That is, the *who* of the speakers undermines the *what* of statements, such that the speech loses its forcefulness as a means of resolving conflicts.[64]

Warren challenges those planning deliberative dialogues to ask themselves, what are the moral and cultural resources that participants may draw upon to ensure that this deliberation about sensitive issues is both honest and respectful? What are ways that well-designed deliberations can help people tackle such issues?[65] As this discussion of power dynamics within deliberative democracy shows, the decision to deliberate an issue is only the first decision among many that school leaders and their deliberative partners need to answer before proceeding to facilitate such processes.

Habits and Skills of Leadership Development

Of particular focus in this chapter are the habits and skills necessary for achieving publics through deliberative political processes. School administrators and school board members interested in publics for their schools can develop leadership resources for schools outside school building walls by working with collaborative partners and institutions. Developing and encouraging leadership for school improvement in communities around their district is a key habit for those who are paid, elected, or appointed by the public to run public schools.

When it comes to using deliberative politics as a venue for achieving public schools, building and relying upon the leadership outside the school building is essential. Good deliberative processes are *not* usually run by school district employees, as these people usually lack the training, time, and the trust among all constituents required to achieve their deliberative goals. School district administrators and school board members are best used as partners and collaborators with external organizations who bring some of the necessary background, resources, and "neutral" reputation among constituents to help the process succeed.

While successful deliberative processes require that school administrators and other types of experts take a very carefully prescribed role, diverse types of leadership are an essential dimension to deliberative politics. Jonathan Kuyper argues that "good leadership (or a good leadership structure) is one that enables and facilitates meaningful deliberation and is geared toward mitigating a coercive environment."[66] Leaders initiate deliberative work; solicit the material, physical, political, and financial support required to stage and run deliberative sessions; and provide important "uptake" roles, ensuring that decisions reached in deliberative processes are properly channeled to policy-making venues in the proper governance bodies.[67]

Let us examine some examples of the types of leadership required for deliberative efforts for educational problems. In a community engagement process run in the Plain Local School district in northeast Ohio, the district partnered with the Harwood Institute for Public Innovation.[68] They called their collaborative process the Reconnecting Communities and Schools (RCS) initiative, and they began by identifying a steering committee for the effort. This committee included a broad representation of community stakeholders and was the group responsible for planning the activities of the RCS. The Harwood Institute provided training for committee members on citizen participation and the philosophies behind it, and simulated deliberative conversations for the group to help them learn about the process. The committee also benefited from a facilitator/coach, a former school administrator in a nearby district who had helped to implement a similar process there. This facilitator/coach attended planning sessions, offered advice, and checked in with committee members regarding their progress.

Growing the necessary local leadership for deliberation has been assisted by the creation of networks and nonprofit institutions that are building regional and national resources for deliberative democracy. Mentioned earlier in this chapter, the National Issues Forum and Public Agenda (as well as others listed in the Appendix) are two prominent organizations. The Public Education Network, as another example, has helped to launch Local Education Funds operating in thirty-two states in the United States.[69] Local Education Funds, or LEFs, are not affiliated with school districts but are nonprofit organizations designed to be critical friends to districts engaged in sustained school improvement. By working collaboratively with schools as independent nonprofits, LEFs are able to build local leadership and initiatives, serving as a catalyst for greater involvement in the reform of their public schools. LEF network members "actively promote involvement in public education by all segments of their communities. They work for accountability and achievement of high standards by all students, and improvement in the quality of public schools. They also generate resources for public education by facilitating and managing investments from government, businesses, and philanthropic organizations."[70] Such intermediary organizations can provide excellent resources for building civic leadership on behalf of deliberative processes, including personnel to help plan, organize, and find funding such projects. In places as diverse as Boston, New Orleans, Pittsburgh, and Berea, Kentucky, LEFs have successfully addressed school issues while adapting to local culture and policy contexts.[71]

When local organizations such as LEFs are not present, many districts rely on national groups for assistance in deliberative work. The National Issues Forum and Everyday Democracy are two organizations that help provide resources, training, and support for groups interested in deliberation. In addition, university-based public deliberation centers, local YWCAs, and League of Women Voters chapters have all served as intermediary institutions for school-based deliberations. All these different kinds of organizations help to create what are sometimes called "deliberative entrepreneurs" in the deliberative democracy literature, people who help build the interest and skills within regions, cities, or towns for deliberative work.[72]

Developing local leaders outside school walls helps activate, engage, and sustain the local citizenry's interest and work on behalf of public schools. Such development is best approached as a long-term commitment. Deliberative work is ideally developed when local school and community leaders are committed not to simply holding one deliberation around a wicked school issue, but to creating a culture of deliberation in a district and community. In a recent report that helps to sum up the field of practice in deliberative democracy and lay a foundation for its future, Elena Fagotto and Archon Fung describe the goal of "embeddedness" in deliberative democracy.[73] "Embeddedness" is a way of describing deliberation as a habit, when the practice is "embedded in a community's political institutions and social practice" and people in a community or region regularly help shape public decisions and take collective actions "through processes that involve discussion, reasoning, and citizen participation rather than through the exercise of authority, expertise, status, political weight, or other such forms of power."[74] This does not mean every decision is made through deliberative processes, but that avenues and processes for helping citizens discuss and weigh in on solutions to the problems in their communities are part of the political culture of a city, town, or region. It also means that leadership for planning and facilitating such deliberative processes is part of the ongoing organizational and civic life in that place.

Habits and Skills of Collaborative Creation

Habits of collaborative creation generate enhanced capacity for educating youth on the part of citizens, parents, educators, elected officials, and civil society associations. This skill focuses on efforts to collaborate and create initiatives, structures, policies, or agreements that enhance educative ends. The goal of building publics for public schools is ultimately to help educators and others who work directly with youth to achieve greater success with larger numbers of children and youth. Skills of collaborative creation help build such initiatives, structures, and agreements through deliberative processes and work.

Gary Anderson, in his research on participatory decision-making processes in schools, notes the significance of such habits. He argues that "many well-intended participatory restructuring and reform efforts in education fail because they undermine institutional spaces within which a relatively clear set of rules, norms, and identities regulate social interactions, creating what Warren calls *arenas of social groundlessness,* without a plan for the collaborative reconstruction of a new social ground."[75]

Deliberations in schools result in decisions, agreements, or new understandings about complex, "wicked" problems. Yet these decisions and agreements are always constructed in the midst of new norms, roles, and rules around democratic decision making and participation in school governance. When school district leaders decide to build a culture of deliberation to help supplement their representative structures of governance, they are giving up some forms of control and sharing their authority to make decisions. What's being created, as new forms of control and shared authority are put into place, are new ideas and norms around school improvement, decision making, and shared accountability.

This is a reconstructed social ground, reconstructed from an expert-only approach to a more collaborative mindset. As Chris Gates of Philanthropy for Active Civic Engagement states, the hurdles of adopting deliberative strategies such as online engagement tools or other deliberative innovations are often philosophical as much as technological.

> Embedded in the DNA of these tools are two principles: transparency and democracy. The problem is that everyone wants to use the tools, but they're not comfortable with the DNA that comes along with them. As soon as you start using these tools, your organization has to become more transparent and small "d" democratic. If you want to use these tools, you have to be comfortable with volunteers, taxpayers, etc., helping to set the priorities of the institution.[76]

While Gates is speaking of online engagement tools, the same can be said of any deliberation strategy. Embedded in the very structure of these strategies and tools are very different forms of shared authority, accountability, and transparency than seem comfortable for most school leaders. We discuss these forms of public leadership in the next chapter. Suffice it to say, schools do not educate alone; as public institutions partly responsible for the well-being of children and youth, they are partners and collaborators with multiple constituencies. Habits of collaboration are thus key to building publics for schools.

Collaborative creation begins with the shared planning of deliberative processes. We can see an excellent example in the decade-long effort in Connecticut designed to "help communities find common ground for public action and ways to work together to address educational issues."[77] Citizens working with the League of Women Voters in the state could apply for grants from the league to fund local deliberative processes, but the criteria for getting grant money built collaborative creation habits into the planning processes themselves. To get a grant, applicants had to find five cosponsors for the effort to begin the coalition-building process. They had to secure moderators in their community, compile all conversation notes into a document, and circulate it. Follow-up criteria were also stipulated: "the League strongly recommends that conveners organize follow-up meetings—often announced at the beginning or at the end of a conversation—to build on the recommendations emerged during the deliberation," sending the critical message that "deliberation is not held in a vacuum, but is rather the first step of a process to promote change."[78] The outcomes of these Connecticut deliberations on education were numerous.

> First, conversations improve communication between the school system and families, by bringing to surface needs that schools are unaware of, or available resources that families ignore. Second, they provide a valuable source of community input to improve the design and delivery of public services. Third, since they are organized by broad coalitions of public and non-profit service providers, advocacy groups, funders, and the school system, they improve coordination and collaboration among different actors. By and large, conversations seem to be more successful at providing community input to the school system or other local organizations than at mobilizing citizens in a sustained way. Hiring of staff to reach out to minority parents, changing the school start time to address the problem of sleep deprivation among students, expanding options for early childcare, and making school facilities more accessible for the community are just some of the changes that were prompted by Community Conversations.[79]

Skills of collaborative creation help school administrators and school board leaders work inventively and interactively with multiple stakeholders and organizations in their community.

These skills also help shape the goals and intended outcomes of a deliberation. Where do deliberations lead? What outcomes do they generate? These questions rightly challenge many deliberative practitioners. Such practitioners regularly face the challenge of failure, where despite a productive dialogue, "their groups' action efforts often fell flat." This practitioner concluded that rather than simply training citizens in deliberative processes alone, "dialogue participants *and* organizers needed to be trained and educated in social change methods like policy advocacy and community organizing."[80] Thus, collaborative creation often doesn't end with deliberative processes or agreements they produce. Deliberation, like community organizing, is only one type of political strategy in a democracy. Successful deliberations may very well be part of a diverse range of political work related to school improvement, including not only community organizing, as discussed in the previous chapter, but also lobbying, campaigning, or voting as well. Deliberative agreements are important points along what can be a much longer road of community problem solving and school improvement, one where a variety of political strategies may be needed.

Deliberative Politics in School Governance

Some school administrators and board members may find it hard to reconcile their current views on school governance with those presented in this chapter. Deliberative processes may sound like a direct challenge to the authority of the school board and superintendent. Deliberative processes may be considered simply unnecessary for districts with good boards and good public relations. Moreover, deliberative processes might be avoided because administrators fear such processes will unleash adversarial politics and intractable public conflicts that will be bad for the school's public relations. I will try to answer these objections.

Deliberative processes are designed to complement current forms of school governance, necessary because of the eroding of political legitimacy that US public schooling has experienced over the past several decades. Typically, school governance happens within school board meetings and superintendents' and principals' offices; it emanates from the halls of state-houses and the federal House and Senate. It is a process that comes from, and follows the predictable channels of, expert power and representative authority of "government" as we understand it in our society.

There is a significant shift in moving from the assumption that something called the "government" runs our schools, to thinking about processes of "governance" that can shape and direct administrators and teachers in their work. "Governance intimates a paradigm shift in the meaning of democracy and civic agency," writes Harry Boyte, challenging us to shift the way we think of expertise and decision making in education. "The shift involves a move from citizens as simply voters, volunteers, and consumers to citizens as problem solvers and co-creators of public goods; from public leaders, such as public affairs professionals and politicians, as providers of services and solutions to partners, educators, and organizers of citizen action; and from democracy as elections to democratic society."[81] Luvern Cunningham captures this shift when he states that "*governing* education" consists of "the aggregate of formal and informal influences and decisions that create and sustain the conditions for learning and the consistent focus on learning."[82] It is a shift from "customers" of education or "voters" in elections to "constituents" and "citizens," with whom school representatives should actively be engaged, and to whom they are responsive. As Abe Feuerstein argues, "periodically held school board elections do little to engender [this] kind of accountability."[83] The same can be said for district websites, no matter how frequently they are updated. One-way communication does not suffice.

Some may protest that the centralization of school decision making over the past century, discussed in earlier chapters, takes away much authority from local officials to engage in the kinds of governance suggested here. Indeed, tightening state and federal pressures on local school officials makes the process of local governance more challenging. But as Larry Cuban notes, local practitioners and administrators still ultimately determine what happens in their own schools. "Local school boards, superintendents, principals, and teachers act as policy brokers who revise state and federal policies. Centralizing state and federal policymaking has not left local officials impotent."[84]

As stated several times over, bringing in more deliberative processes and even embedding deliberation into the culture of decision making in a school or district does not mean we fire all the experts and give up the representative forms of governance that run schools. Schools need experts in pedagogy, mathematics, reading, civics, the law, counseling, and a host of other fields; representative governance structures like school boards, though much weakened today, help keep our schools periodically responsive to voters. The right places to bring in deliberative processes to help achieve publics for our schools are when wicked educational problems of value and priority are present, where experts alone cannot decide for themselves the ways a diverse district may want to proceed, and where representatives cannot possibly understand all the views and opinions held by constituents in their district. Yet schools cannot do this work alone. It is too time-consuming and usually ineffective when schools are not able to partner with intermediary organizations that bring expertise and resources.

Even with the help of capable intermediary groups, deliberations will bring to light the conflicts and multiple perspectives on a school issue or problem within a district. Because deliberative democracy is a process resting on the principle of publicity and open governance, its processes entail risks for district officials.

But for that matter, so does the status quo of school governance. School officials are not widely trusted, school boards are under increasing fire as an outdated mode of running schools, and the public's estimation of school quality is far from positive. Far greater than the possible controversies that deliberations may air in a district are the risks of doing nothing new or different when it comes to governance.

CHAPTER 7
PUBLIC LEADERSHIP FOR PUBLIC SCHOOLS

Steven R. Thompson and Kathleen Knight Abowitz

Unhappy the land that is in need of heroes.
—Bertolt Brecht

While *leadership* denotes a broad field of study today, much of its literature is overrepresented by scholars, consultants, and writers in business and corporate work, followed closely by those in electoral politics and the military. As Carole Elliot and Valerie Stead note, large business organizations have "tended to provide the majority of research sites, with the great corporate leader becoming a dominant archetype. Political and military contexts have also traditionally been a rich source for leadership studies, and ... they continue to be a source of fascination in the media and in popular culture more broadly."[1] While we in education certainly can learn from business and military sectors about leadership, this bias in the leadership literature means that too many educational leaders are formally trained with a literature largely lacking theoretical resources for understanding and navigating the *public* contexts of educational leadership. Leadership for public schools and public life constitutes a particular kind of leadership. Public leadership, we contend in this chapter, is unique, particularly as it applies to public schools.

Traditionally, public leadership has referred to a thread of leadership studies focusing on the work of elected officials and those at the top of organizational hierarchies in political or military life. There are signs that the field is growing in richness and diversity.[2] The field remains hampered, however, by a relative lack of empirical and theoretical research, as well as by rapid changes in the real world of institutions.[3] Educational leadership research comes closer to addressing this deficit, as the work of much school leadership is in at least nominally public contexts, though explicit theorization of educational leadership's *public* contexts and parameters is rare even in this literature. While public leadership for schools resists reduction into techniques, stand-alone models, or singular skills, we sketch its distinguishing features in this concluding chapter.

Leadership Challenges of Our Complex Global Age

Many observers of our current condition report how our societies and lives have grown in complexity.[4] The roles each individual must fill are ever-expanding in number, and the demands of these roles seem to be rapidly evolving. As in the past, contemporary parents must attend to the safety and education of their children, but such responsibility now requires knowledge of the Internet and our electronic world, which their children already have more of than their parents. A child's educational options now include charter schools, online programs, new media sources, and home schooling. Physically, children mature earlier than in the past. Our new communications technology brings information to families and children more quickly than even twenty years ago. And the challenges of growing-up now include pressures to become global consumers and citizens in a new global political-economy. Being an effective citizen now requires knowledge of science, legal principles, economics, global cultures, and a new media literacy that parents and grandparents of the twentieth century rarely needed.

Whether in fashion, diet, housing, or other kinds of goods or services, the available choices require a consumer to be a student of the marketplace who never quite finishes the course of study, for the subject matter is always evolving. New products emerge at an astonishing rate. Over 250,000 books are published in English each year. There are at least 575 models of automobiles available in the United States, not counting the varieties that could be created by selecting options. Soon will come the day in many middle-class homes when refrigerators, coffee makers, and dishwashers are all connected to the Internet, with touchscreens to manage their functions. Workers entering the job market today are advised to prepare for careers that will include multiple jobs over a lifetime, many in categories that do not even exist yet.[5] The new and emerging forms of family life—increasing numbers of single-parent families, common-law marriages, intentional extended families, and increasing acceptance of same-sex partnerships—expand the varieties and the complexities of family life.

Simply understanding what is happening may exceed the capabilities of most of us. The European Enlightenment established modern notions of science, politics, and society. These modernist views include a belief that all of nature can be understood through science. This view, in turn, lead to the belief that much of nature could be manipulated or controlled by applying this understanding. Society came to be seen not as shaped by God or natural law but by men through human decisions and the social contract. Individuals who in medieval times were believed to be living lives ordained by God in a social order established by heavenly powers were regarded in the Enlightenment as individuals with rights, responsibilities, and the freedom to manage their own lives in the pursuit of satisfaction and happiness. But while many among us have not yet mastered the basic understandings of the Enlightenment, much of the knowledge and wisdom of that era have been displaced by new postmodern worldviews. These worldviews—characterized by pluralism, discontinuity, hybridity, and difference—while liberating for many, are undeniably more complex than their Enlightenment precedents.[6]

Moreover, this complexity brings disenchantment. Postmodern critiques are rooted in disillusionment with the promises of modernism. Earlier confidence in the power of science to guide our actions has fallen to the view of our environment as polluted and damaged by the engines of modern technology and the hidden complexities of unintended consequences. Society is seen as manipulated by special interests motivated by greed or power. Neither government nor business earns trust; and academia, the legal system, and religious organizations are viewed as serving the affluent and powerful in unfair ways. The promise of democratic societies in which diverse publics collaborate around shared interests is doubted as incivility, bigotry, and violence persist. Individuals are seen as acting in ways shaped by their individual experiences of culture, family, education, and work. Unconscious motives and perceptions cause us to behave in ways that are often self-centered if not self-serving. Increasingly, individuals retreat from social interaction in an era of "cocooning" and experience much more of life than previous generations through electronic media.

A similar experience of complexity and intensification has beset schools, as society has required more of schools through the varied and accumulating educational policies of the twentieth and early twenty-first centuries. A list of responsibilities that have been added to the national agenda for schools in the past fifty years would have to include equal athletic opportunities for women, integration of disabled learners into mainstream social activity, health and medical services to the young, nutritional support for the poor, the provision of equal access to learning for speakers of literally dozens of languages, closing the achievement gap (regardless of causes rooted in broader societal issues), and enforcement of a host of laws relating to child abuse, immigration status, weapons, drugs, disease control, and homeland security.

The anthropologist Joseph Tainter has written that such increasing complexity is a common condition in societies throughout history.[7] He has argued that societies exist to solve problems and that to solve them requires increasing social complexity. For example, if a community needs to defend itself from hostile neighbors, some military function must be provided. If military solutions fail to provide the desired security, a combination of military and diplomatic functions might develop. To strengthen diplomacy, perhaps improved communications will be required. All of these expansions of function in response to emerging problems require role specialization, new technologies, and ultimately, a more complex society. Seen this way, such growing complexity is not an affliction but a normal social tendency as we become more sophisticated, knowledgeable, and effective.

But Tainter goes on to suggest that societies have limited capacity to understand and cope with this increasing complexity; it can outpace our ability to support and sustain it. In *The Collapse of Complex Societies*, Tainter proposes that societies such as the Roman Empire and Mayan civilization fell as a result of a collective inability to contend with and continue to support the ever-increasing complexity of social systems. Whether the challenge is economic or technical, he suggests that there is a limit to our capacity for complexity. And in the face of these limits, we search for heroes to restore our sense of stability and security. John Dewey wrote in 1929 that great social change and complexity draw humans toward people and ideas that promise "perfect certainty." "The quest for certainty is a quest for a peace which is assured, an object which is unqualified by risk and the shadow of fear which action casts."[8] Our heroes habit is an outgrowth of our yearning to control and manage complex changes in our social, scientific, and school lives.

Our Addiction to Heroes

Ronald Heifetz and others have pointed out that our natural tendency when faced with uncertainty or instability is to turn to leaders to provide us answers and restore our missing security—to seek heroic leaders.[9] According to anthropologists such as Joseph Campbell, traditional myths and the heroes they featured were developed to help us learn the values of the community and to understand how to contribute to society in appropriate ways.[10] They helped new generations understand that our ancestors had shared our experience and had lessons to offer. These mythic lessons were intended to be guidelines for living our lives and for becoming the best human beings we could be as described by whatever culture to which we belonged. Usually, the lessons required some hard work, enduring a trial or a rite of passage, remaining true to a cherished value, achieving an informed perspective, or facing a human weakness. Our rites of passage marked the lessons learned. But whatever the details, traditional heroes were those who showed the way through our own personal difficulties to achieve responsible adulthood. Heroes were to be emulated. They were models to help us meet the challenges of life.

But somewhere along the way, we came to seek heroes not to teach us, but to deliver us from our most difficult work and to make our lives easy. Popular culture is overflowing with examples of heroic saviors. Look for show times at your local multiplex cinema and you will find some—probably from comic books—vanquishing evil in many forms. Look on the athletic field and you find some scoring touchdowns or hitting home runs. Look at your television and you will find them locking up criminals, saving lives, and putting idiots in their proper place. Log on to your video game and you will find an avatar that will allow you to do all this and imagine yourself the hero or heroine. In short, we are taught by all our entertainments that heroes are real and that they are clear-eyed, steadfast, and relatively free of flaws (though maybe not free of scars).

Relying on heroic leaders presents problems. It is simplistic to point out that popular notions of heroism are illusory and that no single human is so wise and skilled as to be able to know how we can solve contemporary problems. Yet we continue to seek such iconic leaders and to place faith, or at least hope, in their abilities to provide solutions. Part of this fruitless search no doubt lies with the androcentric or male-centered orientation of much leadership theory, and the continued association between "leadership" and occupancy of appointed or elected position.[11] This androcentrism and the preoccupation with positional leadership are among the many faulty assumptions guiding our search for heroic leaders.

One other aspect of our preoccupation with heroes deserves mention. Our most heroic leaders are often martyrs. In M. Mitchell Waldrop's book on the emerging science of complexity, he notes, "[In Ireland,] the highest peak of heroism is to lead an absolutely hopeless revolution."[12] In fact, many of our cultural heroes suffer tragic ends. From Socrates to Martin Luther King Jr., there is a smell of death surrounding the heroic. No wonder it is hard to hire, appoint, recruit, or retain good school and community leaders at so many levels. We expect not only heroes but perhaps their tragic ends as well.

A democratic society requires that all citizens share the responsibilities of running its institutions and solving its problems. Contemporary leaders must avoid acting as solitary heroes and find ways to urge all stakeholders to contribute to the success of the community.

Our Faulty Assumptions about Organizations and Communities

The first of these faulty assumptions is that systems can be controlled. Management schools across our nation name "control" as one of the primary functions of management, and many executives hold the title of "Controller." But Robert Heller, an American businessman and consultant, is famously quoted as saying "the first myth of management is that it exists." New scholarship in systems and organizational behavior argues that while systems have order, human behavior within those systems cannot be controlled or even reliably predicted.[13]

Perhaps this belief that our organizations and communities can be controlled grows out of a second faulty assumption: that people do what they are told. Some will argue that the right combination of incentives—rewards and punishments— can compel certain behavior, but psychologists have long studied motivation and behavior, and no sober student of human behavior will support the idea that people will behave as they are told to behave simply because someone in authority tells them to—at least, not for long. Yet our popular culture celebrates the authoritative hero who "takes names and kicks butt," the hired gun, the tough coach, the drill sergeant.

And finally, these first two beliefs join to produce the faulty assumption that leaders can and should know all the answers. For if our social systems can be controlled and if people will do as they are told, then all that is needed is for a knowledgeable, expert leader to provide the road map and implement the rules—a courageous, strong, usually masculine person with a simple, easily understood solution for what ails us and our communities.

So at all levels of community governance, we search for leaders who are rarely found. When we do find leaders, approval rates for their work are embarrassingly low and the eagerness to "throw the bums out" is often palpable. An Internet search for "failure of leadership" produces over 121 million sites. It appears that all publics, whether rooted in some cultural interest, political goal, or geographic convenience, find cause to be disappointed in their leaders. And so we live out a paradox: we hunger for leadership, yet we mistrust those in leadership roles.

But even if citizens get what they ask of a leader, it is rarely what they want. For what most of us want is security and reduced stress—a sense that our communities are safe and prosperous and stable. We seek what will allow us to be comfortable and capable individuals, to reduce the threat to our security and competence. Nature has prepared us well to survive such threats—when they take the form of predators and physical adversaries. When the threat is a predicament of our own creation—such as the complex challenges we face in many strained public school organizations—we are less well prepared for the conflict.

Pitfalls on the Road toward Social Intelligence

In societies as complex as those we find in the world today, it is understandable that we should want to control social forces through leadership conceived as individual intelligence and capacity for decisive, authoritative decision making. Such faulty assumptions of what leadership is, and what we expect school leaders to do, are partly based on our cultural notions of intelligence. Rather than simply one individual's power to come to know and judge, "intelligence" is also something possessed by social groups and organizations, shared among people. Social intelligence is "the power of observing and comprehending social situations—and social power—trained capacities of control—at work in the service of social interest and aims."[14] Groups become more intelligent through asking questions, posing problems, and inquiring together to come to plausible answers. Certain forms of leadership enable social groups to engage in the constant formation and testing of social intelligence. Tom Atlee calls this "collective intelligence" and describes ways that groups, organizations, communities, states, and even nations can create and exhibit such capacities in the face of complex problems.[15] Leadership for public institutions and public life explicitly fosters these capacities. Yet these forms of leadership are often upstaged by far more seductive ways of thinking about leadership in US society. We tend to think of leadership in "how to" terms, as a technique to be implemented, as a forum for individual authority and ego, and as a means to organizational control. These three beliefs about leadership all contribute to the difficulty many school leaders face in attempting to achieve publics for public schools.

Leadership as Technique

One of these mistaken beliefs is the view that leadership is a technical task that is synonymous with management. It leads to the view that successful leaders know what to do and can do it by following the right rules or techniques. Philosopher Alisdair MacIntyre famously criticized contemporary management practice as drone-like, with regard only to measureable outcomes: "The manager treats ends as given, as outside his scope; his concern is with technique, with effectiveness."[16] This simplistic faith in technique has given rise to a whole industry of leadership publications with titles like *The Ten Steps to Leadership,* or *The Twelve Secrets of Successful Leaders,* or *Six Keys to Unlocking Your Leadership Potential.* (Try searching the Internet for "steps to leadership.") Certainly, the push for ever-higher test scores in public education since the passage of NCLB has fed this tendency in modern management.

The knowledge that leadership is something different from simply implementing management rules or techniques is well established. For literally decades, leadership researchers have distinguished leadership from technical skills in various ways. Warren Bennis wrote of the distinction by suggesting that leaders master the context and managers surrender to it.[17] Heifetz describes the need for leadership in adaptive situations, those that require learning and problem-solving, while he argues management will suffice for technical change.[18] Chris Argyris wrote of this distinction by discussing two types of learning required of organizations that face difficult challenges. The first is single-loop learning, which is straightforward and simply involves adjusting strategies and actions. Double-loop learning, because its roots are in values and mental models, requires substantial learning.[19]

There is certainly a need in organizations for leaders who know how to "keep the doors open," efficiently continue routine operations, and sustain valued behavior. There are, in other words, aspects of our school organizations and communities that depend on competent administrative technique, but while technical management skill is generally effective for accomplishing familiar tasks and solving problems that are well-understood, it is inadequate to solve problems that are unfamiliar and persistent. In fact, persistence of a problem usually indicates that it is poorly understood or has been addressed using inadequate management techniques rather than with skills characteristic of a broader leadership approach. Maintaining or repairing an automobile requires technical skill. There are manuals and training programs that can teach us what to do. But planning and developing an efficient and effective transportation system for city is more than a technical challenge. It requires an understanding of the values of a population surrounding environmental issues, life style, and use of public resources. It requires the ability to develop commitment to a long-term financial plan and economic structures. It requires some anticipation of technologies and social developments not yet evident. And it requires developing political will.

Writers have, for decades, proposed models that distinguish between problems that respond to the more mechanical behaviors associated with administering organizational activity, and the more complex and persistent problems for which there is no proven or generally accepted approach. This difference between the domain of technique and that of approach are so profound that many writers have written of it in fields other than leadership. Educator Parker Palmer writes of this distinction as it applies to teaching, noting that successful teaching is a personal act that emerges from the identity of the teacher and that simply applying technique to the practice of teaching reduces instruction to wooden, mechanical exercises that are uninspiring and ineffective.

> Good teaching cannot be reduced to technique; good teaching comes from the identity and integrity of the teacher ... in every class I teach, my ability to connect with my students and connect them with the subject, depends less on the methods I use than on the degree to which I know and trust my selfhood and am willing to make it available and vulnerable in the service of learning.[20]

In his books, *Stewardship: Choosing Service Over Self Interest* and *The Answer to How Is Yes: Acting on What Matters*, Peter Block goes so far as to suggest that the search for technique is an obstacle to action. "Our search for manuals, recipes, the practical is endless. The nonfiction best-seller list is filled with recipe books that have nothing to do with cooking." He continues with this telling story:

> I was in a group that wanted to know how to promote empowerment and participation. Who doesn't? I asked how many had read the books *Thriving on Chaos, Seven Habits of Highly Effective People, The Empowered Manager, The Fifth Discipline.* Most of the group raised their hand. In those four books are more than 925, count them, specific suggestions on how to move the workplace in high performing and customer-centered directions. So if we have seen those books and others, and there are more practical suggestions than we can use in a lifetime, why are we still asking the question "How?"[21]

So the search for some set of steps or techniques to use as a leader is not only likely to lead to uninspiring management of the status quo. Such preoccupation with technique will lead us to fail in solving our most important public educational challenges, the ones that are poorly understood, complex, and urgent.

Leadership as Individual Platform

Our current view of leaders-as-heroes has another important effect. As we celebrate strong, individualistic leaders we encourage them to behave with steadfast conviction, for to acknowledge uncertainty would be to recognize the limits of our knowledge and is distinctly unheroic. The qualities we often seek in leaders include being strong-willed, having unwavering convictions, and having an unwillingness to change positions. One needs only to consider political attack ads to see that changing one's position is not viewed as a result of learning or growth, but as a sign that a leader is untrustworthy, a "flip-flopper." So those who seek positions of authority often take pride in being unyielding and stubborn.

Leaders are certainly individuals, but they are individuals-in-society, working from within social groups and as actors in public life. Advocating the achievement of publics, espousing leadership habits that invite participation, communication, and even conflict, we have consistently argued in this book that leadership is not seen in the individual performance of decisive lone-rangers. Yet certainly we acknowledge the multiple cases where individual leaders do have to act or make decisions alone, without consultation, without deliberation with others. Leaders working in public realms, however, will see leadership as a role rather than a platform, as a particular set of habits that encourage the development of social intelligence and collaborative forms of action, rather than the development of individual ego, prestige, or professional status. While human beings may certainly be creatures of ego, the best leaders are not solely or wholly governed by this motive. In writing about political leaders, Debbie Walsh, director of the Center for American Women and Politics at Rutgers University, has described this as the difference between running for office to do something and running for office to be somebody.[22]

Effective leaders must be open to the influence of others and focus on the goals of the community, not on the image or prestige of the leader. Indeed, the leader may be called on to practice humility in leadership often as he or she shares responsibility, considers other points of view, or confronts problems that are only poorly understood.

Leadership as Control

William Foster's writing on educational administration analyzes how "an administrative mentality pervades modern society" and is exerted through "technologies of thought" that enable leaders to control or govern organizations or groups of people.[23] Administrators in educational organizations exert control over key technologies that govern schooling: technologies of numeracy (statistics, data, and budgets), of information systems, and of language—the important ways we linguistically frame and organize organizational work with others and to the publics we serve. Foster writes that "leadership is language and language is how leadership is exerted."[24] Often, leadership language conveys decisiveness, bold decision making, and authoritative direction. Our language of leadership is often a language conveying control, corresponding to desires for decisive heroes who bring certainty to a complex world.

This language of control is, in fact, an artifact of the positivistic and modernist views that persist in the leadership literature in spite of the continuing and growing sense that they are no longer sufficient to face our current challenges. Yet, as argued earlier, these views rest on the assumption, among others, that organizations can be understood as operating on knowable laws and therefore can be controlled. Systems theory has provided additional insight into the trouble with placing faith in our ability to control organizations. Margaret Wheatley writes in her book *Leadership and the New Science*:

If organizations are machines, control makes sense. If organizations are process structures, then seeking to impose control through permanent structure is suicide. If we believe that acting responsibly means exerting control by having our hands into everything, then we cannot hope for anything except what we already have—a treadmill of effort and life-destroying stress.[25]

But if instead of machines we were to think of school organizations as a set of relationships, and as a story in which each person plays a part, then perhaps what good public leaders do is more akin to narration than control. "Narrative, reflecting the 'local knowledge' of organization participants, provides a language and structure of discourse to guide administration. To participate in the narrative of the school is to share in the self-conscious construction of social text."[26] A school's story, or its cumulative tale of failure, success, history, and future, is a narrative that leadership helps to construct. Those in leadership cannot and should not seek to individually author or exclusively control a public organization's story. Such exclusive control is as fictional as it is unethical, for it violates the moral and political spirit of public institutions—institutions whose existence and direction should be animated by and integrally connected with the political will of publics and diverse citizens.

Public Creation: Leadership Habits and Skills

Communication: Seeking a Sense of Community

When we use the term *communication,* especially when writing about leadership, we usually mean the intellectual activity of presenting and receiving information, making arguments, and sharing points of view. While this primarily intellectual activity is indeed key to developing social intelligence, there is another role played by communication that is usually overlooked—building community and shared identity, forging an inclusive sense of "we" around a school mission. For at the root of leadership in public life is openness, or "the willingness to entertain a variety of alternative perspectives, be receptive to contributions from everyone regardless of previous attainment or current status, and create dialogic open spaces [in which] multiple opportunities for diverse voices and opinions [can] be heard."[27] This entails building participatory forms of leadership and school governance in public schools that help build the relational networks needed for diverse perspectives and dialogues.

As explained in Chapter 5, community organizers have long used a variety of group activities and events to bring people together to talk and learn from one another, and to develop shared purpose and identity. This sense of belonging to the same social group is key to community action and is a vital part of the "narration" of a public institution or organization by its citizens and publics. The power of this bonding or bridging communication, however, is not solely in the strength of the content of a message (though particularly weak or inappropriate content can discourage the goal of building community). Rather, the power of the communication to promote public bonding comes from shared experience, a form of social capital. By simply being together, talking, and listening together, groups can develop a history of shared experience that becomes a foundation for a sense of shared identity. Robert Putnam has explored this phenomenon extensively. In his book *Better Together,* he describes examples of communities that have done this successfully and writes that "they all involve making connections among people, establishing bonds of trust and understanding, building community. In other words, they all involve creating social capital: developing networks of relationships that weave individuals into groups and communities."[28]

Building bonds of trust and understanding across social class, race, and ethnic divides requires authentic participation in the life of the school and its governance. This authenticity is difficult to cultivate for many educational administrators in schools today, as both standards of "good practice" and common-sense notions of heroic leadership fail to promote authentic participation models that build communal, relational networks. As Anderson notes, participatory reforms in schools can be authentic or they can be strategic, designed more as a "sophisticated technology of control" than a genuine site of inclusive participation for all classes and races of citizens, students, and teachers.[29]

Leadership Development: Trusting Others

The reasons to share leadership in public organizations like schools are many. Democratic principles such as fair participation and respect for diversity may be sufficient reasons to share leadership responsibility, but a more practical argument is simply that the functions of leadership have never been limited to those granted formal authority. Informal leaders have always existed, and a public leader cannot effectively control who becomes a leader. Philip Woods explains:

> The practice of distributed and democratic leadership is not limited to those in formal positions of leadership at the apex of a school hierarchy—headteachers and principals, and other senior school managers. It extends to all who contribute to leadership as an organisational force emergent from collective and interactive effort. This means everyone in the school community who exercises initiative which influences other people, stimulates action, change and a sense of direction, ... in other words, all who share in the circulation of initiative.[30]

But how does a contemporary formal school leader nurture leadership skills and develop a larger reservoir of leadership talent that can be relied upon to move thought and practice in the school community in positive directions? The development of new models such as "distributed leadership" and "sustainable leadership" signals new paradigms organized around this important question.[31]

Beginning with John Locke, there is much in political literature about trusting our leaders and striking a balance between holding them accountable and allowing them the necessary discretion to make decisions on our behalf, or granting those with authority the discretion to make decisions that will affect the community. There is less written about how leaders can share or develop leadership in others.

> In the modern administrative state, the story of trust is the decision when and under what conditions we grant discretion to others. With only slight exaggeration, we might even claim that *the* dilemma of modern administrative leadership as it confronts the demands of democracy is establishing equilibrium between accountability and discretion, between setting limits on leaders' activities while allowing them the flexibility to act.[32]

One of the lessons from community organizing for education is that intentional processes of leadership development are a key component of building constituencies that can advocate for and help implement plans for school improvement. While community organizers exert an important leadership in this work through their expertise about politics and political decision making, the success of their work is largely defined by how well they can build grassroots leadership to define and sustain campaigns. Similarly, paid school leaders (principals, superintendents) cannot succeed in their work without authentic plans for building grassroots leadership within schools and in the civic contexts surrounding them.

Building Power: Empowering Others

Formally appointed and elected leaders in public institutions such as schools are responsible to the electorate, the constitutional principles of the state and nation, and the children who attend their schools. Those leaders who are hired by elected school boards wield professional, contractual, and bureaucratic authority for decision making in schooling. Professional authority comes from the specialized knowledge of education, contractual or legal authority is derived from the terms of the contract of employment, and bureaucratic authority comes from educational system's organizational governance traditions.[33] These forms of authority, as well as other types, "authorize" people like superintendents and principals to make decisions on behalf of many other people within the educational system.

Building publics for public schools entails a challenge to these traditional types of authority. Organic publics arise when citizens, parents, or students pose a problem in a school community and seek some authority to help define and solve the problem. What does "shared governance" of public schooling in a democratic society actually mean in practice? Many leadership theories often stand in tension with democratic principles, as leadership often "means persuading people to do something they originally may not have wanted to do or perhaps even fashioning policies that may require them to do something they will never want to do."[34] Leadership practices often threaten individual liberty and the power of individuals to have a say in their own life experiences and circumstances. Thus, one of the key problems that public leaders face is how to share authority with others who as citizens/parents possess rights and intelligence to participate in the governance of their public institutions, and who as employees/teachers/staff will benefit from the opportunity to share in the making of their own workplace organization.

A well-meaning but often detrimental leadership habit that disempowers citizens from meaningfully participating in their public schools is that of "bringing in the experts." One of the patterns we see in both deliberation and community organizing as public-building strategies is that "expertise" is never seen as a replacement for "experience," that is, the experience of students, parents, community members, teachers, or other leaders in a school–community organization. Public deliberation advocates tap into the experiences of various constituents, help them to connect their experiences with those of others' in their school or community, and use their experiences and relationships to inquire more deeply into the problem at hand. Only when expertise is required is expertise consulted, and in ways that *inform,* not *conclude,* the deliberations about possible outcomes or solutions. Similarly, community organizing begins with tapping into the experiences of parents, students, and community members who are living with deep dissatisfactions or problems with their school. Organizers use these experiences to help citizens hone a particular agenda as they build their own expertise around their local educational system. In this way, the power of citizens' lived experiences is at the center of the public-building work, driving its energies and motivating individuals to step into leadership roles within organizations.

A. Belden Fields and Walter Feinberg call "dialogical authority" the kind that "assumes an open-ended system in which rules, the division of labor, and systems of accountability are objects to be determined by deliberation among the relevant parties."[35] While we are not calling to eliminate other forms of authority that school leaders possess in a public school (this is neither legally possible nor politically prudent), we are urging leaders to help the citizens of their district cultivate the power and skills of dialogical authority, and to be open to its influence in their decision making.

Collaborative Creation: Transcending Individualism

Much of what passes for deliberation in our communities today is simply structured argument. Deborah Tannen in *The Argument Culture* explains how our popular culture and media are consumed with relentless contention.[36] Whether because we have learned and continue to practice competition as the preferred way to approach our fellow citizens or because we are thrilled by the drama of emotional confrontation, we seem unable to work together to understand and rationally consider differing points of view. At its worst, such argument degenerates into ad hominem attacks as we resort to vilifying those we see as unyielding to our will. In such a climate the goal becomes to win at an opponent's expense, to prevail in a contest of wills, all the while remaining unable to think of neighbors and colleagues as our allies with a shared interest.

Peter Senge and his colleagues, adapting an idea originally offered by leadership theorist Chris Argyis, offer a response to this kind of climate of argument. They name behaviors that promote a single view, idea, or conclusion "advocacy," including those behaviors like selling, explaining, and directing actions intended to enlist support and accomplish a task. But Senge and his colleagues argue that too much advocacy can obstruct learning; that learning requires that we become tentative in our conclusions, more reserved about our certainty, and open to deepening our understanding by considering the views of others. This effort to understand opposing or other views they call "inquiry."[37] In inquiry, equal effort is devoted to understanding the views and beliefs of others, and to the work of presenting one's own views and beliefs, or advocacy. Advocacy and inquiry together contribute to a better outcome. Moreover, by balancing these two activities, group members collaborate in discovering insights that no one yet has. That is, they engage in group inquiry and learning.

At the root of this approach is a trust in the power of dialogue to produce wise choices and sound decisions. James Surowiecki in *The Wisdom of Crowds* provides evidence of why such trust is well placed. Whether in formal groups such as committees and teams or in informal or accidental groups like markets and consumer groups, group decisions are perceptive, wise, and reliable most of the time. Surowiecki writes, "collective intelligence can be brought to bear on a wide variety of problems, and complexity is no bar."[38] He goes on to argue that such trust is a good idea for other reasons: "A healthy democracy inculcates the virtues of compromise—which is, after all, the foundation of the social contract—and change. The decisions that democracies make may not demonstrate the wisdom of the crowd. The decision to make them democratically does."[39] Robert Greenleaf in *Servant Leadership,* and more recently, Peter Block in *Stewardship: Choosing Service over Self-Interest,* propose an approach to leadership that values humility as well as confidence.[40] Greenleaf writes that power, often disproportionately invested in leaders, is a corrupting influence, and that those who assume to know what is good or virtuous for the community also assume great moral risk. Similarly, Block warns that much of contemporary organizational dysfunction can be traced to paternalistic, even sovereign views of leadership. Too many leaders, like kings of old, believe privilege and power are the prerogative of the leader and necessary for the control they would exercise. The alternative is to recognize not only our potential as communities but also our limits as individuals and as individual institutions. This second recognition requires what Senge and his colleagues name "personal mastery."[41] It includes, among other things, the willingness of the leader to become a learner him- or herself. It includes the commitment to awareness, cognition of the diversity of values and views that inhabit a public, and recognition that as humans, leaders have room to improve.

Being a humble learner, however, does not mean a leader aims to be powerless and to never take a position. Anderson's advocacy leadership model provides very important frames for public achievement.[42] An explicitly political model that sees the job of school leader as being a tireless advocate for the most marginalized groups and families in the school community, advocacy leadership prevents shared participation and collaboration from simply reproducing the privilege of middle-class students and families. Advocacy leadership views current centralized educational "reforms" with a critical distance, attempting to use local participatory and empowerment strategies to build school capacity through collaborative networks.

Whether based on a heroic or an entitled view of leadership, one person cannot expect to understand and respond wisely to the complexity of our contemporary predicaments. Nor can one model of leadership hope to capture the endlessly shifting dynamics of educational leadership today. Successful leaders will be those who build the sense of belonging and shared interest that characterize healthy community, who trust others to share leadership responsibility, who promote learning and empowerment throughout the community, and who are willing to subordinate their own self-interest and pride to the broad interests of diverse school communities.

Conclusion

In June of 2010, twenty-five school superintendents met in northeast Ohio to discuss the challenges they face as leaders. A report summarizing the event described their conversation this way:

> Superintendents expressed their frustrations over increasingly inadequate funding, staff and communities that continue to expect business as usual, and a lack of clarity for the future of education.... These superintendents want to take on this new challenge, but they're not quite sure where to begin. They recognize that in many respects, they're fighting the wrong battles—battles from past wars that will no longer move them forward. Even with this recognition, they're not sure how to shift the tide since staffs and communities are so invested in the past. Complicating things more, they are not really clear themselves about the future of education.[43]

Clearly, this moment in public education is one where citizens may seem to yearn for heroic leadership from these superintendents, but formal public school leaders must resist this temptation. The most important challenges we face are shared challenges, what deliberative practitioners call "wicked problems." These are problems of direction, value, and ultimate purposes of educational institutions. The answers do not lie in the constraining, narrow ideas of education built into federal policies like NCLB, or in the traditional, seductive notions of heroic leaders who make authoritative, expert decisions. For leaders, finding the answers to these challenges is to help educators and citizens, who share the challenges, to build responses together. As Keith Grint argues, "the leader's role with a Wicked Problem is to ask the right *questions* rather than provide the right *answers* because the answers may not be self-evident and will require a collaborative process to make any kind of progress."[44] There are many reasons to be discouraged in this work, as the political impediments as well as our own "bad habits" of leadership can seem overwhelming. But there are reasons to be hopeful, as well.

Recognition of the potential contributions developed within public forms of deliberation and organizing has grown in the last generation. Knowledge of how to organize and conduct effective dialogue and group decision making is significant. Many organizations have emerged offering expertise and support to those who are serious about conducting the business of our publics in more effective ways. We list some of those organizations in the Appendix.

The proliferation of these civic organizations points to another key source of hope in developing publics for public schools: the forgotten role of the local in public institutions and decision making. As William Foster points out, "the decline of the local in the conduct of the affairs of institutions such as schools is a decline in the promise of a truly democratic regime."[45] As we "celebrate" a decade of NCLB, political movements from both the left and the right are coming to see the limits of federal and state control in educational governance. Though each plays important roles, they have combined over the past several generations to eclipse the role that local and regional civic groups and organizations might play in reviving and redefining public schools. There is growing recognition of this fact, the product of a convergence of social movements oriented toward renewed visions of democracy, justice, opportunity, and education. There is growing acknowledgment that "our public school system—one of the great achievements of American democracy—is not just a service for the public to consume. It is a lifelong compact among Americans to continually renew our nation's future, to be actively supported by all citizens, whether or not they have children of school age."[46] This new recognition of the import of local governance and civic participation in public schooling could lead to changes in the culture of educational leadership as well as in the policy-making milieu of US public schooling. Such change will not happen without much grassroots leadership and political work, however. The forces for standardization and privatization remain powerful in our society, and undoing these trends remains challenging work for us all.

AFTERWORD

A popular refrain today in the social sciences is that humans are strongly predisposed to in-group thinking at the expense of understanding and cooperation across difference. Jonathan Haidt, a psychology professor at the University of Virginia, has received a lot of press for his new book, *The Righteous Mind: Why Good People Are Divided by Politics* (2012). Haidt argues that our political disagreements are constructed within the very life narratives that construct our understandings of who we are, and what constitutes right and wrong behavior or action. "Morality binds us into ideological teams that fight each other as though the fate of the world depended on our side winning each battle. It blinds us to the fact that each team is composed of good people."[1] This thesis has gotten much media play, in part because it fits so well with popular refrains that contemporary political discourse is hopelessly divisive and lacking in true substantive dialogue across party lines. Pew polls show hardening partisanship in the American populace, at levels higher than at any other point measured in the past twenty-five years.[2] If the public is hopelessly gridlocked, originating even at a psychological level, then why should we bother with trying to engage the public in public education? If politics is somehow predestined to be unproductive, why should local educational and community leaders attempt to involve local groups and marginalized voices into the governance of schooling?

We should be skeptical in the face of over-simplified claims and excuse-making questions. It is simplistic to say that we might be easily dropped into boxes of "right" and "left" or "conservative" or "liberal." On any range of issues, many citizens may fall along several places along the right-left spectrum. This is particularly true in education, where many issues in a local school district defy easy partisan categories. In the face of declining enrollments in this elementary school, should we close the school? If we see trends in higher dropout rates for poorer students in our community, how should the district be responding? There is no Republican or Democratic playbook that answers these questions. Many things in educational politics have this particular and local flavor, and it is in these local contexts that we can envision politics beyond partisan gridlock.

"We need to radically refocus on the local," writes Eric Liu.[3] The power of local, participatory political engagement is crucial to this book's central idea, that publics for public schooling are not given but achieved. The local is where our problems sting us most sharply and where problems of governance affect us most acutely; it is literally where we live and where we send our kids to school. The local is where our publics often come to fruition in light of real problems, whether that be the need for a stoplight or addressing a high dropout rate in the local high school. It is not theoretical or abstract, but concrete and more understandable in scope for everyday citizens. This is not your grandmother's "local," however. It is not the localism of nineteenth-century America but of twenty-first-century networked global society, where a school district in Maine or California can work toward resolution of a complex problem with assistance from national or international organizations or individuals, using innovative social media tools developed by these organizations, but with the autonomy and local participation to make their resolution fit with their distinct context. It is not an isolated local, devoid of national priorities; it is a local bound by constitutional principles of equity, liberty, and pluralism. It is not a romantic, idealized local; it is filled with tight budgets, radical wealth disparities, and antigovernment sentiments. Yet it is an essential space to reclaim for democratic governance writ large and public educational governance in particular.

The timing of this book's thesis will seem unrealistic to some. Never have US schools been under so much centralized control. After a decade of No Child Left Behind, many school leaders have given up hope of such creative possibility in their local governance. This book respectfully but directly challenges that cynicism and failure of imagination. As activists, politicians, and parents on all sides of the aisle experience dissatisfaction with the centralized, top-down control of public education today, new possibilities for local public work are emerging. This book takes the (small-d) democratic bet that this new possibilities can bring new forms of school governance in the next decades of American educational politics (if, however, any semblance of "public schooling" remains in attempts by some to eradicate the institution and make all education a so-called free market). While this era will be filled with its own stresses, imperfections, and hard work, it will represent a positive turn from our present moment.

Appendix

A list of resources for educational or community leaders interested in engaging in public-building work related to public education.

Resources for Community Organizing

Annenberg Institute of School Reform at Brown University— Center for Education Organizing

http://annenberginstitute.org/project/center-education-organizing

The Center for Education Organizing (CEO) supports and amplifies local and national demands for educational justice in underserved communities. The CEO integrates the expertise of a university-based research center, years of on-the-ground experience supporting education organizing, and a long-standing reputation as a seasoned convener of diverse education stakeholders.

DART: Direct Action Research Training Center

www.thedartcenter.org

The Direct Action and Research Training Center, or DART, is a national network of nineteen affiliated grassroots, nonprofit, congregation-based community organizations. DART organizations bring people together across racial, religious, and socioeconomic lines to pursue justice in their communities.

Gamaliel Foundation
www.gamaliel.org
Gamaliel is a grassroots network of nonpartisan, faith-based organizations in eighteen US states, South Africa, and the United Kingdom that organizes to empower ordinary people to effectively participate in the political, environmental, social, and economic decisions affecting their lives.

Industrial Areas Foundation
www.industrialareasfoundation.org
The leaders and organizers of the Industrial Areas Foundation build organizations whose primary purpose is power—the ability to act—and whose chief product is social change.

People's Institute for Community Organizing
www.piconetwork.org
People's Institute for Community Organizing, or PICO, is a national network of faith-based community organizations working to create innovative solutions to problems facing urban, suburban, and rural communities.

Resources for Deliberation and Engagement

Center for Public Deliberation at Colorado State University
www.cpd.colostate.edu
The center is dedicated to enhancing local democracy through improved public communication and community problem solving.

**Center for Public Deliberation (CPD) at
University of Houston–Downtown**
www.uhd.edu/academic/colleges/humanities/uhd_cpd/index.html
The Center for Public Deliberation (CPD) is a collaborative, nonpartisan group that encourages citizens to actively participate in the deliberative democracy process through public discussions about issues that affect their lives.

Everyday Democracy

www.everyday-democracy.org

A national leader in the field of civic participation and community change, Everyday Democracy helps people of different backgrounds and views talk and work together to solve problems and create communities that work for everyone.

National Coalition for Dialogue and Deliberation (NCDD)

http://ncdd.org

The National Coalition for Dialogue and Deliberation (NCDD) promotes the use of dialogue, deliberation, and other innovative group processes to help people come together across differences to tackle our most challenging problems.

National Issues Forums

http://nifi.org

National Issues Forums (NIFs) bring people together to talk about important issues. Each forum focuses on a specific issue, such as illegal drugs, Social Security, or juvenile crime. The forums help people of diverse views find common ground for action on issues that concern them deeply. NIFs are structured deliberative discussions, led by trained moderators. Using nonpartisan issue books, participants weigh possible ways to address a problem. They analyze each approach and the arguments for and against.

The Harwood Institute

www.theharwoodinstitute.org

The Harwood Institute is a leading change organization, recognized nationally for a unique approach to breaking down barriers and empowering people to make progress in improving their communities.

Kettering Foundation

www.kettering.org

The Kettering Foundation is an independent, nonpartisan research organization rooted in the American tradition of cooperative research. Everything Kettering researches relates to one central question: What does it take for democracy to work as it should? Or, put another way: What does it take for citizens to shape their collective future?

Public Agenda

www.publicagenda.org

Public Agenda, an innovative public opinion research and public engagement organization, works to strengthen our democracy's capacity to tackle tough public policy issues.

Public Education Network (PEN)

www.publiceducation.org

Public Education Network is a national association of local education funds (LEFs) and individuals working together to advance public school reform in low-income communities across the United States. PEN believes an active, vocal constituency is the key to ensuring that every child, in every community, benefits from a quality public education.

Penn State Center for Democratic Deliberation (CDD)

http://cdd.la.psu.edu

The Center for Democratic Deliberation (CDD) was founded in 2006 as a non-partisan, interdisciplinary center for research, teaching, and outreach on issues of civic engagement and democratic deliberation.

West Virginia Center for Civic Life

www.wvciviclife.org

The West Virginia Center for Civic Life is a nonpartisan, nonprofit organization that helps engage citizens in community discussions of important public issues that affect West Virginia and the nation.

Resources for Education for Democracy

Forum for Education and Democracy

www.forumforeducation.org

The Forum for Education and Democracy is a national education "action tank" committed to the public, democratic role of public education—the preparation of engaged and thoughtful democratic citizens.

John Dewey Society

http://doe.concordia.ca/jds/

Founded in 1935, the John Dewey Society exists to keep alive Dewey's commitment to the use of critical and reflective intelligence in the search for solutions to crucial problems in education and culture. JDS promotes open-minded, critical reconsiderations of Dewey's influential ideas about democracy, education, and philosophy.

New DEEL

www.temple.edu/education/newdeel/index.html

A partnership of educators around the world dedicated to democratic, ethical educational leadership.

Notes

Chapter 1

1. David Mathews, president of the Kettering Foundation in Dayton, Ohio, authored *Is There a Public for Public Schools?* (Dayton: Kettering Foundation, 1997), now required reading for educators interested in public engagement work. The title of this chapter and the book itself salutes Mathews's work and honors the continuing importance of Mathews's question.

2. This view was articulated and popularized by John E. Chubb and Terry M. Moe in *Politics, Markets, and America's Schools* (Washington, DC: Brookings Institution, 1990), who argued that consumers and markets, rather than government and publics, should govern schools.

3. Joe Smydo, "Pittsburgh Schools Drop 'Public' from Name to Boost Image," *Pittsburgh Post-Gazette,* Wednesday, July 11, 2007. Available at www.post-gazette.com.

4. Ibid.

5. Laura Ries, quoted in Nora Carr, "Must Public Education Restore Its Image as Great Equalizer?" *Education Digest* 72, no. 4 (December 2006): 29.

6. Katherine Mangu-Ward, "Public Is Now a Four-Letter Word," *Reason Hit and Run,* July 12, 2007. Accessed January 19, 2010. Available at http://reason.com/blog.

7. Gerald W. Bracey, "Schools-Are-Awful Bloc Still Busy in 2008," *Phi Delta Kappan* 90, no. 2, 103.

8. "Public Change of Heart: Superintendent Wise to Respond to Naming Concern," editorial, *Pittsburgh Post-Gazette,* July 23, 2007. Accessed October 19, 2009. Available at www.post-gazette.com.

9. Ibid.

10. Mark E. Warren, "Democracy and the State," in *The Oxford Handbook of Political Theory,* ed. John S. Dryzek, Bonnie Honig, and Anne Phillips (New York: Oxford University Press, 2006), 382. See also Mark E. Warren, "What Can Democratic Participation Mean Today?" *Political Theory* 30, no. 5 (October 2002): 678.

11. Joel Spring, *The American School: 1642–1993,* 3rd ed. (New York: McGraw-Hill, 1994), 70.

12. William Reese, *America's Public Schools: From the Common School to "No Child Left Behind"* (Baltimore: Johns Hopkins University Press, 2005), 37.

13. From Du Bois's *Black Reconstruction in America,* 641–649; quoted in James D. Anderson,

The Education of Blacks in the South, 1860–1935 (Chapel Hill: University of North Carolina Press, 1988), 6.

14. Stephen Macedo, *Diversity and Distrust* (Cambridge, MA: Harvard University Press, 2000), 112.

15. William Reese, *History, Education, and the Schools* (New York: Palgrave-MacMillan, 2007), 97.

16. Ibid., 101.

17. Progressive-era school reformer Ellwood Cubberley, quoted in Kathryn A. McDermott, *Controlling Public Education: Localism versus Equity* (Lawrence: University of Kansas Press, 1999), 15.

18. David F. Labaree, "Public Goods, Private Goods: The American Struggle over Educational Goals," *American Educational Research Journal* 34, no. 1 (Spring 1997): 46.

19. See William Reese, "Public Schools and the Elusive Search for the Common Good," in *Reconstructing the Common Good in Education: Coping with Intractable American Dilemmas,* Larry Cuban and Dorothy Shipps, eds. (Palo Alto, CA: Stanford University Press, 2000), 13–31.

20. As told to Robert and Helen Lynd (1929, 194), in Labaree, "Public Goods, Private Goods," 46.

21. Ibid., 46–47.

22. See David F. Labaree, "Consuming the Public School," *Educational Theory* 61, no. 4, 390.

23. Mike Rose, *Why School? Reclaiming Education for All of Us* (New York: New Press, 2009), ix–x.

24. James M. Giarelli, "Educating for Public Life," in *Critical Conversations in Philosophy of Education,* ed. Wendy Kohli (New York: Routledge, 1994), 201.

25. Kenneth A. Strike, "Liberty, Democracy, and Community: Legitimacy in Public Education," in *American Educational Governance on Trial: Change and Challenges,* 102nd Yearbook of the National Society for the Study of Education, part 1, William Lowe Boyd and Debra Miretzky, eds. (Chicago: University of Chicago Press, 2003), 37–56.

26. John Dewey, *Public and Its Problems* (New York: Henry Holt, 1927), chapter 4.

27. Michael K. Briand, *Practical Politics: Five Principles for a Community That Works* (Urbana: University of Illinois Press, 1999), 205.

28. Ibid.

Chapter 2

1. Michael Smith, "New Principals: You Can't Say I Didn't Warn You," The Principal's Page, published August 6, 2009. Available at www.principalspage.com/theblog/archives/2009/08.

2. Mark Niquette, "Ohio's Voter Turnout Rebounds," *Dispatch Politics, Columbus Dispatch,* November 5, 2009. Available at www.dispatch.com.

3. Jonah Goldberg, "Do Away with Public Schools," *Los Angeles Times,* June 12, 2007. Available at www.latimes.com.

4. William Lowe Boyd, "Public Education's Crisis of Performance and Legitimacy: Rationale and Overview of the Yearbook," in *American Educational Governance on Trial: Change and Challenges,* 102nd Yearbook of the National Society for the Study of Education, part 1, ed. William Lowe Boyd and Debra Miretzky (Chicago: University of Chicago Press, 2003), 1–19.

5. John W. Meyer and W. Richard Scott, *Organizational Environments: Ritual and Rationality* (Beverly Hills, CA: Sage, 1983), 201.

6. Psychologists call the tendency to heed information that supports our prior positions and discard or discount contrary information a manifestation of "my-side bias" or "confirmation bias." Daniel B. Klein, "I Was Wrong, and So Are You," *The Atlantic,* December 2011, 68.

7. The actual quality and quantity of substantive journalistic news reporting on school issues,

however, is often poor today. In 2009 the Brookings Institute released *Invisible: 1.4 Percent Coverage for Education Is Not Enough,* documenting that only 1.4 percent of national news coverage from TV, newspapers, news websites, and radio dealt with education. Available at www.brookings.edu/reports/2009/1202_education_news_west.aspx.

8. Walter C. Parker, "Constructing Public Schooling Today: Derision, Multiculturalism, Nationalism," *Educational Theory* 61, no. 4 (2011): 417.

9. Parker explains the term and documents the influence of this discourse on public schooling today. Ibid., 416–421.

10. Cynthia Stark, "Hypothetical Consent and Political Legitimacy," *Paideia,* paragraph 2. Available at www.bu.edu/wcp/Papers/Poli/PoliStar.htm

11. Kenneth A. Strike, "Liberty, Democracy, and Community: Legitimacy in Public Education," in *American Educational Governance on Trial: Change and Challenges,* 37.

12. Ibid., 38.

13. Ibid., 40–41.

14. Iris Marion Young, *Inclusion and Democracy* (New York: Oxford University Press, 2000), 19.

15. Michael W. Kirst, "The Evolving Role of School Boards: Retrospect and Prospect," in *The Future of School Board Governance: Relevancy and Revelation,* ed. Thomas L. Alsbury (Lanham, MD: Rowman and Littlefield Education, 2008), 45.

16. Ibid., 48.

17. Clyde Brown, Annie Miller, Kathleen Knight Abowitz, and Stephanie Raill Jayanandhan, *Ohio's Civic Health Index 2009: Civic Engagement in Hard Economic Times* (Washington, DC: National Conference on Citizenship, 2009), 19–20. Available at www.ham.muohio.edu/cce. See also Ron Fournier and Sophie Quinton, "In Nothing We Trust," *National Review,* April 19, 2012. Available at www.nationaljournal.com.

18. Kenneth Strike, *Ethical Leadership in Schools: Creating Community in an Environment of Accountability* (Thousand Oaks, CA: Corwin, 2007), 98.

19. Piotr Perczynski, "Active Citizenship and Associative Democracy," in *Democratic Innovation: Deliberation, Representation, and Association,* ed. Michael Saward (New York: Routledge, 2000), 163.

20. For more detail on this case, see Richard Fossey, "'I Support My Gay Friends': Free Speech Is Alive and Well in the Schools of the Florida Panhandle," *Teachers College Record,* August 18, 2008. Available at www.tcrecord.org.

21. Ibid., para 16.

22. James Davison Hunter, *Culture Wars: The Struggle to Define America* (New York: Basic Books, 1991).

23. Boyd, "Public Education's Crisis of Performance and Legitimacy," 3.

24. David L. Kirp, "Making Schools Work," Sunday Review, *New York Times,* May 20, 2012, 1.

25. Bonnie C. Fusarelli and William Lowe Boyd, "Introduction: One Nation Indivisible? An Overview of the Yearbook," *Educational Policy* 18, no. 1 (January and March 2004): 7.

26. Larry Cuban, "A Solution that Lost Its Problem: Centralized Policymaking and Classroom Gains," in *Who's in Charge Here? The Tangled Web of School Governance and Policy,* ed. Noel Epstein (Denver: Education Commission of the States, 2004), 120.

27. Joel Kline, Michelle Rhee, Peter Gorman, Ron Huberman, Carole R. Johnson, Andrés Alonso, Tom Boasberg, Arlene Ackerman, William R. Hite Jr., Jean-Claude Brizard, José M. Torres, Terry B. Grier, Paul Vallas, Eugene White, and LaVonne Sheffield, "How to Fix Our Schools: An Education Reform Manifesto," *New York Times,* October 10, 2010. Available at www.washingtonpost.com/wp-dyn/content/article/2010/10/07/AR2010100705078.html.

28. Executive Summary, *A Rotting Apple: Education Redlining in New York City,* Schott Foundation for Public Education, April 2012, 7. Available at http://schottfoundation.org/publications-reports/education-redlining.

29. Jonathan Rothwell, "Housing Costs, Zoning, and Access to High-Scoring Schools," Brookings Institute, April 19, 2012. Available at www.brookings.edu/research/papers/2012/04/19-school-inequality-rothwell.

30. Kenneth Strike discusses the pervasive and damaging effects of this mythology in his book review of *Class and Schools: Using Social, Economic, and Educational Reform to Close the Black-White Achievement Gap* by Richard Rothstein, in *American Journal of Education* 111, no. 3 (May 2005): 414–420.

31. "Child Poverty and Family Income," ChildStates.gov Forum on Child and Family Statistics. Available at www.childstats.gov/americaschildren/ecol.asp.

32. UNICEF, *Child Poverty in Rich Countries 2005*, Innocenti Research Centre Report Card No. 6 (Florence, Italy: UNICEF Innocenti Research Centre, 2005), 2. Available at www.unicef-irc.org/publications/pdf/repcard6e.pdf.

33. While Strike terms this principle "political socialization," I prefer the label "political education." Socialization is the process by which people learn to adopt the cultural patterns of their environment, whereas education refers to the broader process of liberation from ignorance through the pursuit and learning of knowledge, and is not limited to schooling. Socialization can be and often is a subconscious process, whereas education is more intentional and conscious and thus more likely to be the subject of critical scrutiny and assessment. Such scrutiny is required for political education in a pluralist democratic republic, where parents of diverse political views will need to be able to assess and discuss such educational aims and their outcomes.

34. Walter Feinberg, *Common Schools/Uncommon Identities: National Unity and Cultural Difference* (New Haven, CT: Yale University Press, 1998), 9.

35. Mordechai Gordon (ed.), *Reclaiming Dissent* (Rotterdam: Sense Publishers, 2009); and Sarah M. Stitzlein, *Teaching for Dissent: Citizenship Education and Political Activism* (Boulder, CO: Paradigm, 2012).

36. *The Civic Mission of Schools* (New York: Carnegie Corporation of New York and the Center for Information and Research on Civic Learning and Engagement, 2003), 12–13.

37. Ibid., 14.

38. See the 2012 report from the Educational Testing Service with distressing evidence for a serious civic education gap: Richard Coley and Andrew M. Sum, *Fault Lines in Our Democracy: Civic Knowledge, Voting Behavior, and Civic Engagement in the United States* (Princeton, NJ: Educational Testing Service, 2012). Available at www.ets.org/s/research/19386/. See also Meira Levinson, *No Citizen Left Behind* (Cambridge, MA: Harvard University Press, 2012).

39. Katherine Kristen, "Our Schools Can Do a Far Better Job of Teaching Patriotism," *Center of the American Experiment*, September 11, 2002. Available at www.americanexperiment.org.

40. David F. Labaree, *Education, Markets, and the Public Good: The Selected Works of David F. Labaree* (New York: Routledge, 2007), 43; The Holmes Group, *Tomorrow's Teachers: A Report of the Holmes Group* (Michigan: Holmes Group, 1986); Carnegie Forum on Education and Economy, *A Nation Prepared: Teachers for the 21st Century: The Report of the Task Force on Teaching as a Profession* (St. Paul, MN: Forum, 1986).

41. "Better Teaching, Better Learning, Better Schools," National Board for Professional Teaching Standards. Available at www.nbpts.org.

42. David F. Labaree, "Public Goods, Private Goods: The American Struggle over Educational Goals," *American Educational Research Journal* 34, no. 1 (Spring 1997): 43.

43. Strike, *Ethical Leadership in Schools,* 99.

44. See Michael Fullan and Andy Hargreaves, "Reviving Teaching with 'Professional Capital,'" *Education Week,* June 5, 2012. Accessed June 8, 2012. Available at www.edweek.org.

45. Harry Boyte, "Constructive Politics as Public Work," in *Democraticizing Deliberation: A Political Theory Anthology,* ed. Derek W. M. Barker, Noëlle McAfee, and David W. McIvor (Dayton, OH: Kettering Foundation Press, 2012), 173.

46. Strike, *Ethical Leadership in Schools,* 107. For a relevant take on the power of the local and the "local knowledge" of teachers as it relates to student assessment, see Sarah Stitzlein, Walter

Feinberg, Jennifer Greene, and Luis Miron, "Illinois Project for Democratic Accountability," *Educational Studies,* 42, no. 2 (2007): 139–155.

47. Mark E. Warren, "Democracy and the State," in *The Oxford Handbook of Political Theory,* ed. John S. Dryzek, Bonnie Honig, and Anne Phillips (New York: Oxford University Press, 2006), 384. Italics mine.

48. John W. Meyer and W. Richard Scott, "Centralization and the Legitimacy Problems of Local Government," in *Organizational Environments: Ritual and Rationality,* 202.

49. Harry Brighouse, *On Education* (New York: Routledge, 2005), 126.

Chapter 3

1. Michael Warner, *Publics and Counterpublics* (New York: Zone, 2002), 7.

2. Jon Cohen, "Budget Talks in a Word: 'Ridiculous,' 'Disgusting' and 'Stupid' Top Poll," *Washington Post Politics,* August 1, 2011. Available at www.washingtonpost.com/blogs.

3. *American Beauty* (Universal City, CA: Dreamworks, 1999). Directed by Sam Mendes and written by Alan Ball. The website Common Sense Media rates this film as "iffy" for ages 17–18. "Parents need to know that this movie's rating comes from graphic, bloody violence (including child abuse), extremely raw language, nudity, sex (including teen sex), and drug use that is very positively portrayed." ("What Parents Need to Know," Common Sense Media, www.commonsensemedia .org/movie-reviews/American-Beauty.html.)

4. Bernard Crick, *In Defense of Politics,* cited in Harry Boyte, *Everyday Politics: Reconnecting Citizens and Public Life* (Philadelphia: University of Pennsylvania Press, 2004), 37.

5. Robert Talisse, "Liberty, Community, and Democracy: Sidney Hook's Pragmatic Deliberativism," *Journal of Speculative Philosophy* 15, no. 4 (2001): 288.

6. Chantal Mouffe, *The Democratic Paradox* (New York: Verso, 2000).

7. The term *public work* is borrowed from Harry Boyte's writings and work on citizen movements. See Harry Boyte and Nan Skelton, *Reinventing Citizenship: The Power of Public Work* (St. Paul: University of Minnesota, 1995). Available at www.extension.umn.edu/distribution/ citizenship/dh6586.html.

8. John J. Stuhr, *Pragmatism, Postmodernism, and the Future of Philosophy* (New York: Routledge, 2003), 20.

9. Michael Briand, *Practical Politics: Five Principles for a Community That Works* (Urbana: University of Illinois Press, 1999), 16.

10. Albert O. Hirschman, *Exit, Voice, and Loyalty* (Cambridge, MA: Harvard University Press, 1970).

11. Michael B. Berkman and Eric Plutzer, *Ten Thousand Democracies: Politics and Public Opinion in America's School Districts* (Washington, DC: Georgetown University Press, 2005), 85.

12. Rich Somerville, "Future Generations: 'Citizens' or 'Consumers'?" in *Co-Creating a Public Philosophy for Future Generations,* ed. Tai-Chang Kim and James A. Dator (Westport, CT: Praeger, 1999), 167.

13. Walter C. Parker, *Teaching Democracy: Unity and Diversity in Public Life* (New York: Teachers College Press, 2003), 29.

14. Iris Young, *Inclusion and Democracy* (New York: Oxford University Press, 2000), 19.

15. This discussion draws from Mark E. Warren's *Democracy and Association* (Princeton, NJ: Princeton University Press, 2000).

16. I use the idea of "shared fate" here as an adapted version of that developed by Melissa S. Williams, "Citizenship as Identity, Citizenship as Shared Fate, and the Functions of Multicultural Education," in *Citizenship and Education in Liberal-Democratic Societies,* ed. Kevin McDonough and Walter Feinberg (New York: Oxford University Press, 2003), 208–247.

17. As I argue elsewhere, "the summoning of the ideal of community signals an identitarian politics of sameness, unifying and fixing individual selves in order to construct stability and order

in a disorderly world. Schools are frequently sites of such constructions." See "Reclaiming Community," *Educational Theory* 49, no. 2 (1999): 143.

18. Eva Gold, Jeffrey Henig, and Elaine Simon, "Calling the Shots in Public Education: Parents, Politicians, and Educators," *Dissent,* Fall 2011, 36. (Emphasis in original.)

19. Ibid.

20. For a discussion of youth activism for schools and the Urban Youth Collaborative's work, see Kavitha Mediratta, "A Rising Movement," *National Civic Review* 95, no. 1 (Spring 2006): 15–22.

21. Aaron Schutz and Marie Sandy, *Collective Action for Social Change: An Introduction to Community Organizing* (New York: Palgrave MacMillan, 2011), 188.

22. Alastair Hannay, *On the Public* (New York: Routledge, 2005), 78.

23. John B. Thompson, "Shifting Boundaries of Public and Private Life," *Theory, Culture & Society* 28, no. 4 (2011): 64.

24. Chris Higgins and Kathleen Knight Abowitz, "What Makes a Public School Public? A Framework for Evaluating the Civic Substance of Schooling," *Educational Theory* 61, no. 4 (2011): 367.

25. Gary Miron and Christopher Nelson, *What's Public about Charter Schools? Lessons Learned about Choice and Accountability* (Thousand Oaks, CA: Corwin Press, 2002), 195.

26. Frank Lutz and Laurence Iannaccone suggest, "Local school district elections usually fall below 40 percent, even as low as 15 percent or less." In "The Dissatisfaction Theory of American Democracy," *The Future of School Board Governance: Relevancy and Revelation,* ed. Thomas L. Alsbury (Lanham, MD: Rowman and Littlefield, 2008), 4.

27. See Maia Bloomfield Cucchia, Eva Gold, and Elaine Simon, "Contracts, Choice, and Customer Service: Marketization and Public Engagement in Education," *Teachers College Record* 113, no. 11 (2011): 2460–2502.

28. James Giarelli, "Educating for Public Life," in *Critical Conversations in Philosophy of Education,* ed. Wendy Kohli (New York: Routledge, 1994), 202.

29. Paul Shaker and Elizabeth E. Heilman, "The New Common Sense of Education: Advocacy Research Versus Academic Authority," *Teachers College Record* 106, no. 7 (July 2004): 1444.

30. Ibid., 1445.

31. Julie Underwood and Julie F. Meade, "A Smart ALEC Threatens Public Education," *Phi Delta Kappan* 93, no. 6 (March 2012): 50–55.

32. Linda M. McNeil, "Private Asset or Public Good: Education and Democracy at the Crossroads," *American Educational Research Journal* 39, no. 2 (Summer 2002): 243. See also Patricia Burch, *Hidden Markets: The New Education Privatization* (New York: Routledge, 2009).

33. Stephan J. Ball, "Privatising Education, Privatising Education Policy, Privatising Educational Research: Network Governance and the 'Competition State,'" *Journal of Education Policy* 24, no. 1 (2009): 83–99. For excellent resources on the scope of public school privatization, visit "Privatization," The Education Commission of the States. Available at www.ecs.org/html/IssueSection.asp?issueid=92&s=Selected+Research+%26+Readings.

34. David Tyack, "School Governance in the United States: Historical Puzzles and Anomalies," in *Decentralization and School Improvement: Can We Fulfill the Promise?* ed. Jane Hannaway and Martin Carnoy (San Francisco: Jossey-Bass, 1993), 24.

35. McNeil, "Private Asset or Public Good," 244.

36. Robert J. Franciosi, *The Rise and Fall of American Public Schools: The Political Economy of Public Education in the Twentieth Century* (Westport, CT: Praeger, 2004), 133.

37. Dennis Shirley, *Community Organizing for Urban School Reform* (Austin: University of Texas Press, 1997), 73. See also Aaron Schutz, "Home Is a Prison in the Global City: The Tragic Failure of School-Based Community Engagement Strategies," *Review of Educational Research* 76, no. 4 (2006): 691–743.

38. Leonard J. Waks, "Dewey's Theory of the Democratic Public and the Public Character of Charter Schools," *Educational Theory* 60, no. 6 (2010): 16.

Chapter 4

1. Margaret Canovan, "The People," *The Oxford Handbook of Political Theory,* ed. John S. Dryzek, Bonnie Honig, and Anne Phillips (New York: Oxford University Press, 2006), 356–357.

2. John Dewey, *The Public and Its Problems* (New York: Henry Holt, 1927), 15–16.

3. Ibid., 67.

4. Noortje Marres, "Issues Spark a Public into Being," *Making Things Public: Atmospheres of Democracy,* ed. Bruno Latour and Peter Weibel (Cambridge: MIT Press, 2005), 209.

5. Iris Young, *Inclusion and Democracy* (New York: Oxford University Press, 2000), 112.

6. Elizabeth Meadows and Katherine Blatchford, "Achieving Widespread Democratic Education in the United States: Dewey's Ideas Reconsidered," *Education and Culture* 25, no. 1 (2009): 40.

7. Ibid., 109.

8. Young, *Inclusion and Democracy,* 112.

9. Aaron Schutz, "Power and Trust in the Public Realm: John Dewey, Saul Alinsky, and the Limits of Progressive Democratic Education," *Educational Theory* 61, no. 4 (2011): 497.

10. U.S. Department of Education, National Center for Education Statistics, *The Condition of Education 2012* (NCES 2012-045), Table A-33-1. Available at http://nces.ed.gov/fastfacts/display.asp?id=16.

11. Nancy Fraser, *Justice Interruptus: Critical Reflections on the "Postsocialist" Condition* (New York: Routledge, 1997), 87.

12. Young, *Inclusion and Democracy,* 110.

13. Chantal Mouffe, *The Democratic Paradox* (New York: Verso, 2000), 2.

14. Ibid., 34.

15. Claudia W. Ruitenberg, "Educating Political Adversaries: Chantal Mouffe and Radical Democratic Citizenship Education," *Studies in Philosophy and Education* 28 (2009): 272.

16. Seyla Benhabib, "Toward a Deliberative Model of Democratic Legitimacy," in *Democracy and Difference: Contesting the Boundaries of the Political,* ed. Seyla Benhabib (Princeton, NJ: Princeton University Press, 1996), 69.

17. Jürgen Habermas, *The Structural Transformation of the Public Sphere: An Inquiry into a Category of Bourgeois Society,* trans. Thomas Burger with the assistance of Frederick Lawrence (Oxford: Polity Press, 1962/1989).

18. Thomas McCarthy, "Practical Discourse: On the Relation of Morality to Politics," in *Habermas and the Public Sphere,* ed. Craig Calhoun (Cambridge, MA: MIT Press, 1992), 54.

19. See Nicole M. Rishel, "Digitizing Deliberation: Normative Concerns for the Use of Social Media in Deliberative Democracy," *Administrative Theory and Praxis* 33, no. 3 (September 2011): 415. For an informative recent history of deliberative democracy theory, see Derek W. M. Barker, Noëlle McAfee, and David W. McIvor, "Introduction: Democratizing Deliberation," in *Democratizing Deliberation: A Political Theory Anthology* (Dayton, OH: Kettering Foundation, 2012), 1–20.

20. See Matt Leighninger, *Using On-Line Tools to Engage—and Be Engaged by—the Public* (Washington, DC: IBM Center for the Business of Government, 2011); and such websites as the Civic Commons: Sharing Technology for the Public Good, a collection of apps and sites that help citizens around the world engage with government. Available at http://civiccommons.org/engagement-commons.

21. Rishel, "Digitizing Deliberation," 420.

22. See, for example, Suzanne Ashby, Cris Garza, and Maggie Rivas, "Public Deliberation: A Tool for Connecting School Reform and Diversity," Southwest Educational Development Laboratory (Austin, TX: Southwest Educational Development Laboratory, 1999). Accessed October 28, 2009; available at www.sedl.org/pubs/lc06. See also examples found on websites of deliberative organizations listed in the Appendix.

23. In a review of popular public relations textbooks for school administrators conducted within a larger study of school-community literature, Schutz notes that "these texts provide a broad range of tools that administrators can use to lead their schools' 'publics' in the directions that the administrators themselves desire ... [and] emphasize the dangers inherent in allowing independent power bases to develop." See Aaron Schutz, "Home Is a Prison in the Global City: The Tragic Failure of School-Based Community Engagement Strategies," *Review of Educational Research* 76, no. 4 (2006): 707.

24. David Mathews, "The Lack of a Public for Public Schools," *Phi Delta Kappan* 78, no. 10 (June 1997): 742.

25. Mouffe, *The Democratic Paradox*, 102.

26. Ibid.

27. Unlike some other accounts of Mouffe's agonistic democratic model, I read it as compatible with certain forms of deliberative democracy, following interpretations such as that of Andrew Knops in "Debate: Agonism as Deliberation—Mouffe's Theory of Democracy," *Journal of Political Philosophy* 15, no. 1 (2007): 115–126.

28. For more on participatory democracy, see Carole Pateman, *Participation and Democratic Theory* (Cambridge: Cambridge University Press, 1970); David Held, *Models of Democracy*, 3rd ed. (Palo Alto, CA: Stanford University Press, 2006), 209–216; and Jeffrey D. Hilmer, "The State of Participatory Democratic Theory," *New Political Science* 32, no. 1 (March 2010): 43–63.

29. Robert Fisher and Eric Shragge, "Contextualizing Community Organizing: Lessons from the Past, Tensions in the Present, Opportunities for the Future," in *Transforming the City: Community Organizing and the Challenge of Political Change,* ed. Marion Orr (Lawrence: University of Kansas Press, 2007), 195.

30. Saul D. Alinsky, *Rules for Radicals: A Pragmatic Primer for Realistic Radical* (New York: Vintage Books, 1971).

31. Mark R. Warren, "Communities and Schools: A New View of Urban Education Reform," *Harvard Educational Review* 75, no. 2 (Summer 2005): 15. Warren also analyzes the educational organizing work of the Texas IAF in *Dry Bones Rattling* (Princeton, NJ: Princeton University Press, 2001); another excellent source here is Dennis Shirley's *Community Organizing for Urban School Reform.*

32. Kavitah Mediratta, Seema Shah, Sara McAlister, Norm Fruchter, Christina Mokhtar, and Dana Lockwood, *Organized Communities, Stronger Schools: A Preview of Research Findings* (Providence, RI: Annenberg Institute for School Reform at Brown University, 2008), 1. Available at www.annenberginstitute.org/Products/Mott.php.

33. See Aaron Schutz, "Social Class and Social Action: The Middle-Class Bias of Democratic Theory in Education," *Teachers College Record* 110, no. 2 (February 2008): 405–442. My response to this opposition of social action and deliberative strategies can be found in Kathleen Knight Abowitz, "What's Pragmatic about Community Organizing?" *Philosophical Studies in Education* 41 (2010). Available at http://ovpes.org/2010Final.htm.

34. Chantal Mouffe, "Deliberative Democracy or Agonistic Pluralism," in *Political Science Series* 72, ed. Christine Neuhold (Vienna: Institute for Advanced Studies, 2000), 11. Available at www.ihs.ac.at/publications/pol/pw_72.pdf.

35. John S. Dryzek, *Deliberative Democracy and Beyond: Liberals, Critics, Contestations* (New York: Oxford University Press, 2000), 86.

36. For rationale of combining these two democratic theories, see Jane Mansbridge with James Bohman, Simone Chambers, David Estlund, Andreas Føllesdal, Archon Fung, Cristina Lafont, Bernard Manin, and José Luis Marti, "The Place of Self-Interest and the Role of Power in Deliberative Democracy," *Journal of Political Philosophy* 18, no. 1 (2010): 64–100; and Denise Vitale, "Between Deliberative and Participatory Democracy: A Contribution on Habermas," *Philosophy and Social Criticism* 32, no. 6 (September 2006): 739–766.

37. By "facilitating organizations" I mean regional or national networks of foundations, and nonprofit organizations that enable citizens to become organized and/or to formally deliberate

their shared problems and concerns. These organizations can provide the know-how, experience, and personnel to help citizens do public work. See Appendix for a suggestive list.

38. Benhabib, "Toward a Deliberative Model of Democratic Legitimacy," 84.

39. Nancy Salvato, "Salvato: Notes on Democracy: And to the Republic for Which It Stands," *GOPUSA,* May 24, 2011. Available at www.gopusa.com/commentary.

40. Ibid.

41. Held, *Models of Democracy,* 1.

42. Ibid., 2.

43. Robert B. Westbrook, *John Dewey and American Democracy* (Ithaca, NY: Cornell University Press, 1991), 282. For a good discussion of this problem and the rich history of this debate, see Tony DeCesare, "The Lippmann-Dewey 'Debate' Revisited: The Problem of Knowledge and the Role of Experts in Modern Democratic Theory," *Philosophical Studies in Education* 42 (2011). Available at www.ovpes.org/journal.htm.

44. Larry Cuban, "A Solution that Lost Its Problem: Centralized Policymaking and Classroom Gains," in *Who's in Charge Here? The Tangled Web of School Governance and Policy,* ed. Noel Epstein (Denver: Education Commission of the States, 2004), 109.

45. Robert Franciosi, *The Rise and Fall of American Public Schools: The Political Economy of Public Education in the Twentieth Century* (Westport, CT: Praeger, 2004), 143.

46. For a valuable sketch of the proper federal role in public education, see Frederick M. Hess and Linda Darling-Hammond, "How to Rescue School Reform," *Education Week,* December 5, 2011. Available at www.nytimes.com/2011/12/06/opinion/how-to-rescue-education-reform .html?_r=2.

47. Cuban, "A Solution That Lost Its Problem," 116.

48. Eric Liu, "Democracy Is for Amateurs: Why We Need More Citizen Citizens," *Atlantic,* May 11, 2012. Available at www.theatlantic.com.

49. William R. Caspary, *Dewey on Democracy* (Ithaca, NY: Cornell University Press, 2000), 37.

50. Kenneth Strike, *Ethical Leadership in Schools: Creating Community in an Environment of Accountability* (Thousand Oaks, CA: Corwin, 2007), 95.

51. Mark E. Warren, *Democracy and Association* (Princeton, NJ: Princeton University Press, 2000), 16.

Chapter 5

1. Dennis Shirley, "Community Organizing for Educational Change: Past Illusions, Future Prospects," in *The Future of Educational Change: International Perspectives,* ed. Ciaran Sugrue (New York: Routledge, 2008), 89.

2. Celina Su, *Streetwise for Book Smarts: Grassroots Organizing and Education Reform in the Bronx* (Ithaca, NY: Cornell University Press, 2009), 23.

3. This synopsis compiled from Eva Gold and Elaine Simon, with Chris Brown, "A New Conception of Parental Engagement: Community Organizing for School Reform," in *The Sage Handbook of Educational Leadership,* ed. F. W. English (Thousand Oaks, CA: Sage, 2005), 237–268.

4. Kavitha Mediratta, Seema Shah, and Sara McAlister, *Building Partnerships to Reinvent School Culture: Austin Interfaith* (Providence, RI: Annenberg Institute for School Reform at Brown University, 2009), 1.

5. Eva Gold and Elaine Simon, *Successful Community Organizing for School Reform* (Chicago: Cross City Campaign for Urban School Reform, 2002), 23–24. Available at www.lsna.net/Issues -and-programs/Schools-and-Youth/Strong-Neighborhoods-Strong-Schools-Case-Study-LSNA .html.

6. See Matthew Corritore, "Why Conservatives Should Love Community Organizing," *Brown Daily Herald,* October 17, 2008. Available at www.cbsnews.com/stories/2008/10/18/politics/

uwire/main4530674.shtml. See also Robert Fisher and Sally Tamarkin, "What ACORN and the New Right Can Teach Us about Current Trends in Community Organizing," *Social Policy,* Spring 2009, 48–50. For an excellent overview of organizing trends in the United States, see Aaron Schutz and Marie Sandy, *Collective Action for Social Change: An Introduction to Community Organizing* (New York: Palgrave MacMillan, 2011), chapter 3.

7. Mediratta, Shah, and McAlister, *Building Partnerships,* 3.

8. Dennis Shirley, "Promoting Participatory Democracy through Community Organizing," in *Partnering to Prepare Urban Teachers: A Call to Activism,* ed. Francine P. Paterman (New York: Peter Lang, 2008), 59.

9. Gary L. Anderson, "The Politics of Participatory Reforms in Education," *Theory into Practice* 38, no. 4 (Autumn 1999): 191–195; Betty Malen, "The Promises and Perils of Participation on Site-Based Councils," ibid., 209–216.

10. See, for example, E. M. Horvat, E. B. Weininger, and Annette Lareau, "From Social Ties to Social Capital: Class Differences in the Relations between Schools and Parent Networks," *American Educational Research Journal* 40 (2003): 319–351. See also Dennis Shirley, "Teacher Education and Community Organizing," in *Teacher Education with an Attitude: Preparing Teachers to Educate Working-Class Students in Their Collective Self-Interest,* ed. Patrick J. Finn and Mary E. Finn (Albany: State University of New York, 2007), especially 81–84.

11. Mediratta, Shah, and McAlister, *Building Partnerships,* 3.

12. Gold and Simon, "A New Conception of Parent Engagement," 239.

13. Quote from Ed Chambers in Frances Polletta, *Freedom Is an Endless Meeting: Democracy in American Social Movements* (Chicago: University of Chicago Press, 2002), 181.

14. Dennis Shirley, "Community Organizing and Educational Change: A Reconnaissance," *Journal of Educational Change* 10 (April 2009): 230. For more on this, see Sara McAlister, "Community Organizing as an Education Reform Strategy," Annenberg Institute for School Reform, Brown University, February 3, 2011. Available at http://annenberginstitute.org/commentary.

15. Kavitha Mediratta, Seema Shah, and Sara McAlister, *Community Organizing for Stronger Schools: Strategies and Successes* (Cambridge, MA: Harvard Education Press, 2009), 40.

16. Ibid., 52.

17. John Dewey, *Democracy and Education* (New York: Free Press, 1916), 46.

18. Alison Kadlec, *Dewey's Critical Pragmatism* (Lanham, MD: Rowman and Littlefield, 2007), 72. The embedded Dewey quote is from *Democracy and Education,* 52–53.

19. Dewey, *Democracy and Education,* 5.

20. For an illustration of this process as it applies to students and teachers in schools, see Kathleen Knight Abowitz, "A Pragmatist Revisioning of Resistance Theory," *American Educational Research Journal* 37, no. 4 (2000): 877–907.

21. Shirley, "Community Organizing for Educational Change," 91.

22. Ibid.

23. Kavitha Mediratta and Norm Fruchter, *Mapping the Field of Organizing for School Improvement: A Report on Education Organizing in Baltimore, Chicago, Los Angeles, the Mississippi Delta, New York City, Philadelphia, San Francisco, and Washington, D.C.* (New York: Institute for Education and Social Policy, New York University, 2001), 32 [ERIC Document ED 471 052].

24. Ibid., 26.

25. Polletta, *Freedom Is an Endless Meeting,* 186.

26. Ibid.

27. Shirley, *Community Organizing for Urban School Reform,* 61.

28. Mediratta, Shah, and McAlister, *Community Organizing for Stronger Schools,* 60.

29. Polletta, *Freedom Is an Endless Meeting,* 222.

30. See also Paul S. Adler and Seok-Woo Kwon, "Social Capital: The Good, the Bad, and the Ugly," in *Knowledge and Social Capital: Foundations and Applications,* ed. E. L. Lesser (Boston: Butterworth/Heinemann), 106–108.

31. Gold and Simon, *Successful Community Organizing for School Reform,* 17.

32. Mediratta and Fruchter, *Mapping the Field of Organizing for School Improvement,* 33.

33. Described in Jeannie Oakes, John Rogers, and Martin Lipton, *Learning Power* (New York: Teachers College Press, 2006).

34. Mark R. Warren, *Dry Bones Rattling* (Princeton, NJ: Princeton University Press, 2001), 27.

35. M. Elena Lopez, *Transforming Schools through Community Organizing: A Research Review* (Cambridge, MA: Family Involvement Network of Educators [FINE], Harvard Family Research Project, 2003), 4.

36. Gold and Simon, *Successful Community Organizing for School Reform, 7;* Mark R. Warren, Soo Hong, Carolyn Heang Rubin, and Phitsamay Sychitkkhong Uv, "Beyond the Bake Sale: A Community-Based Relational Approach to Parent Engagement in Schools," *Teachers College Record* 111, no. 9 (September 2009): 2231. For an in-depth account of the Logan Square Neighborhood Association's work, see Soo Hong, *A Cord of Three Strands: A New Approach to Parent Engagement in Schools* (Cambridge, MA: Harvard University Press, 2011).

37. Bonnie Young Laing, "The Universal Negro Improvement Association, Southern Christian Leadership Conference, and Black Panther Party: Lessons for Understanding African American Culture-Based Organizing," *Journal of Black Studies* 39, no. 4 (March 2009): 635–656.

38. John Dewey, "Policies for a Third Party," *New Republic,* April 8, 1931, 203. Quoted in Cara A. Finnegan, "Elastic, Agonistic Publics: John Dewey's Call for a Third Party," *Argumentation and Advocacy* 39, no. 3 (Winter 2003): 168.

39. Ben Brandzel, "What Malcolm Gladwell Missed about Online Organizing and Creating Big Change," *Nation,* November 15, 2010. Available at www.thenation.com. For a similar story about students using social media to organize protests, see Elbert Chu and Chris Palmer, "For Legacy High School Students, a Lesson in Activism Hits Home," *New York Times,* February 7, 2012.

40. Brandzel, "What Malcolm Gladwell Missed about Online Organizing."

41. Ronald Heifetz, *Leadership without Easy Answers* (Cambridge, MA: Belknap of Harvard University Press, 1994), 20.

42. Schutz and Sandy, *Collective Action for Social Change,* 60.

43. Warren, *Dry Bones Rattling,* 24.

44. Richard Couto, "Defining a Citizen Leader," in *Public Leadership Education: The Role of Citizen Leadership* (Dayton, OH: Kettering Foundation, 1992), 9–10.

45. Warren, *Dry Bones Rattling,* 212.

46. An excellent example of this kind of learning is found in Oakes, Rogers, and Lipton, *Learning Power,* as well as in Michael Fabricant, *Organizing for Educational Justice: The Campaign for Public School Reform in the South Bronx* (Minneapolis: University of Minnesota Press). University researchers or centers can be key collaborators, providing important resources for this stage of inquiry and leadership development. Some CBOs have partnerships with local universities, using the social capital and research capabilities and resources of universities to help with organizing work.

47. Shirley, *Community Organizing for Urban School Reform,* 64.

48. John M. Beam and Sharmeen Irani, "Acorn Education Reform Organizing: Evolution of a Model," National Center for Schools and Communities, Fordham University, April 8, 2003, 18. Available at http://stage.web.fordham.edu.

49. Gender is one difference that likely shapes how "leadership" in organizing is envisioned and developed. For a discussion of how gender identities shape organizing work, see Susan Stall and Randy Stoecker, "Community Organizing or Organizing Community? Gender and the Crafts of Empowerment," *Gender and Society* 12, no. 6 (December 1998): 729–756.

50. Warren et al., "Beyond the Bake Sale," 2233, italics in original.

51. Lopez, *Transforming Schools through Community Organizing: A Research Review,* 3.

52. Warren, *Dry Bones Rattling,* 212.

53. Gold and Simon, *Successful Community Organizing for School Reform,* 13.

54. Warren, *Dry Bones Rattling,* 210–211.

55. Ibid., 35. See also Aaron Schutz's discussion of leadership trends in organizing as they relate to social class in "Social Class and Social Action: The Middle-Class Bias of Democratic Theory in Education," *Teachers College Record* 110, no. 2 (February 2008): 405–442.

56. Warren, *Dry Bones Rattling,* 213.

57. Ibid., 214.

58. Participation in school decision-making processes is *authentic* if it "includes relevant stakeholders and creates relatively safe, structured spaces for multiple voices to be heard. Authentic participation in school governance should result in the "constitution of a democratic citizenry and redistributive justice for disenfranchised groups or, in educational terms, more equal levels of student achievement and improved social and academic outcomes for *all* students." See Gary L. Anderson, "Toward Authentic Participation: Deconstructing the Discourses of Participatory Reforms in Education," *American Educational Research Journal* 35, no. 4 (Winter 1998): 575.

59. Fabricant, *Organizing for Educational Justice,* 23.

60. Ibid., 206. For an account of resistance, see Beatrice S. Fennimore, "Brown and the Failure of Civic Responsibility," *Teachers College Record* 107, no. 9 (September 2005): 1905–1932.

61. Anderson, "Toward Authentic Participation," 580. For more analysis of inauthentic participation and community engagement practices in urban schools, see Schutz, "Home Is a Prison in the Global City," 691–743.

62. Mediratta, Shah, and McAlister, *Building Partnerships,* 3.

63. Celina Su, in her study of the organizational cultures of CBOs in the Bronx, found two distinct patterns. Organizations tended to use the "Alinskyite tool kit," which tended to be more confrontational in tone, or the "Freirean tool kit," which made use of more relational, collaborative kinds of strategies. See *Streetwise for Book Smarts,* 17–19.

64. Schutz, "Home Is a Prison in the Global City," 717.

65. Shirley, *Community Organizing for Urban School Reform,* 69.

66. National Center for Schools and Communities, *From Schoolhouse to Statehouse: Community Organizing for Public School Reform* (New York: Fordham University, 2002), 19.

67. Aaron Schutz, "Rethinking Domination and Resistance: Challenging Postmodernism," *Educational Researcher* 33, no. 1 (January/February 2004): 20.

68. Chantal Mouffe, "Deliberative Democracy or Agonistic Pluralism," in *Political Science Series* 72, ed. Christine Neuhold (Vienna: Institute for Advanced Studies, 2000), 15. Available at www.ihs.ac.at/publications/pol/pw_72.pdf.

69. Schutz, "Rethinking Domination and Resistance," 718. The research done on educational organizing as reported in *From Schoolhouse to Statehouse* also echoes this finding, as discussed on page 19.

70. Shirley, *Community Organizing for Urban School Reform,* 85.

71. Warren, "Communities and Schools," 5.

72. Warren et al., "Beyond the Bake Sale," 2213.

73. Industrial Areas Foundation, "IAF in Action." Accessed September 11, 2009; available at www.industrialareasfoundation.org/iafaction/iafactionschools.htm.

74. Warren, "Communities and Schools," 20.

75. Ibid., 21. Shirley also offers an instructive portrait of San Antonio's IAF organizing efforts in *Community Organizing for Urban School Reform,* chapter 7.

76. Fischer and Tomarkin, in "What ACORN and the New Right Can Teach Us About Current Trends in Community Organizing," warn of "the perils of romanticizing local-only efforts" and remind of the importance of national organizing and policy groups in much of this work (49).

77. Fabricant, *Organizing for Educational Justice,* 206–210.

78. Mediratta, Shah, and McAlister, *Community Organizing for Stronger Schools,* 155.

79. Eva Gold, Elaine Simon, Leah Mundell, and Chris Brown, "Bringing Community Organizing into the School Reform Picture," *Nonprofit and Voluntary Sector Quarterly* 33 (Supplement), no. 3 (September 2004): 65S–66S.

80. Ibid., 66S.

81. R. Chaskin, P. Brown, S. Venkatesh, and A. Vidal, *Building Community Capacity* (New York: Aldine De Gruyter, 2000), 7; as quoted in Gold et al., "Bringing Community Organizing into the School Reform Picture," 58S.

82. Ibid., 68S.

83. Mediratta, Shah, and McAlister, *Community Organizing for Stronger Schools*, 155, 157.

84. Chantal Mouffe, "Democracy as Agonistic Pluralism," in *Rewriting Democracy: Cultural Politics in Postmodernity*, ed. Elizabeth Deeds Ermarth (Burlington, VT: Ashgate, 2007), 43.

85. Claudia Ruitenberg quoting Jacques Rancière ["Introducing Disagreement," *Angelaki: Journal of Theoretical Humanities* 9, no. 3 (2004): 5] in "What If Democracy Really Matters," *Journal of Educational Controversy* 3, no. 1 (Winter 2008). Available at www.wce.wwu.edu/Resources/CEP/eJournal/v003n001/a005.shtml.

86. See Dennis Shirley and Michael Evans, "Community Organizing and No Child Left Behind," in *Transforming the City: Community Organizing and the Challenge of Political Change*, ed. Marian Orr (Lawrence: University Press of Kansas, 2007), 109–132.

87. Shirley, "Community Organizing and Educational Change: A Reconnaissance," 235–236.

88. Shirley, "Promoting Participatory Democracy through Community Organizing," 61.

Chapter 6

1. Matt Leighninger, *The Next Form of Democracy: How Expert Rule Is Giving Way to Shared Governance ... and Why Politics Will Never Be the Same* (Nashville: Vanderbilt University Press, 2006).

2. James Bohman, "The Coming of Age of Deliberative Democracy," *Journal of Political Philosophy* 6, no. 4 (1998): 401.

3. James Bohman, *Public Deliberation: Pluralism, Complexity, and Democracy*, Studies in Contemporary German Social Thought (Cambridge, MA: MIT Press, 1997), 27.

4. Noëlle McAfee, "Three Models of Democratic Deliberation," in *Democratizing Deliberation: A Political Theory Anthology*, ed. David Barker, Noëlle McAfee, and David McIvor (Dayton, OH: Kettering Foundation, 2012), 31.

5. Martín Carcasson, "'Toward a More Perfect Union': An Introduction to the Deliberative Democracy Movement," Citizens' Toolbox conference, March 16, 2011, Miami University, Oxford, OH. The source of the "wicked problem" label is Horst W. J. Rittel and Melvin M. Webber, "Dilemmas in a General Theory of Planning," *Policy Sciences* 4 (1973): 155–169.

6. Bohman, *Public Deliberation*, 27.

7. Gloria Mengual, "Portsmouth, N.H.: Where Public Dialogue Is a Hallmark of Community Life," Everyday Democracy, June 1, 2003. Available at www.everyday-democracy.org/en/Article.141.aspx.

8. National Coalition for Dialogue and Deliberation, *Resource Guide on Public Engagement*, October 2010, 15. Available at www.ncdd.org.

9. E3 Alliance, *Achievement Gaps Deliberative Dialogues Final Report*, December 18, 2007, 1. Available at www.e3alliance.org/dialogues.html.

10. National Issues Forums information, available at www.nifi.org/forums/index.aspx. For a good list of deliberative resources such as this one, please see the Appendix.

11. National Coalition for Dialogue and Deliberation, *Resource Guide on Public Engagement*, 16.

12. M. Stephen Weatherford and Lorraine M. McDonnell, "Deliberation with a Purpose: Reconnecting Communities and Schools," in *Deliberation, Participation, and Democracy: Can the People Govern?* ed. Shawn W. Rosenberg (New York: Palgrave-MacMillan, 2007), 189.

13. Ibid., 190.

14. Sandy Heierbacher, *NCDD Project Report for the Kettering Foundation* (Boiling Springs, PA: National Coalition for Dialogue and Deliberation, 2009), 3.

15. John S. Dryzek, *Deliberative Democracy and Beyond: Liberals, Critics, Contestations* (New York: Oxford University Press, 2000), 86.

16. Ibid., 85–86.

17. Carolyn M. Hendriks, John S. Dryzek, and Christian Hunold, "Turning Up the Heat: Partisanship in Deliberative Innovation," *Political Studies* 55 (2007): 366.

18. For a discussion of public financing and budget deliberations, see Leighninger, *The Next Form of Democracy,* chapter 8. For an example of deliberative strategies used in habitat conservation, see Craig W. Thomas, "Habitat Conservation Planning," in *Deepening Democracy: Institutional Innovations in Empowered Participatory Governance,* ed. Archon Fung and Eric Olin Wright (New York: Verso, 2003), 144–172. Deliberation used to address the US health care crisis is described in John Doble, Jared Bosk, and Samantha DuPont, *Coping with the Cost of Health Care: How Do We Pay for What We Need? Outcomes of the 2008 National Issues Forums* (Dayton, OH: Kettering Foundation, June 2009). Available at www.publicagenda.org/citizen/researchstudies/health-care-medical-research.

19. For example, Leighninger, *The Next Form of Democracy,* chapter 7; Steven R. Thompson, *Engaging Citizens through Conversation: Reconnecting Communities and Schools in the Plain Local School District* (Cincinnati: KnowledgeWorks Foundation and the Harwood Institute for Public Innovation, 2004); Julie A. Marsh, *Democratic Dilemmas: Joint Work, Education Politics, and Community* (Albany: State University of New York Press); Tali Mendelberg and John Oleske, "Race and Public Deliberation," *Political Communication* 17 (2000): 169–191.

20. Amy Gutmann and Dennis Thompson, *Democracy and Disagreement* (Cambridge, MA: Harvard University Press, 1996), 22.

21. Ibid., 12.

22. Ibid.

23. Nancy Thomas, "Educating for Deliberative Democracy: The Role of Public Reason and Reasoning," *Journal of College and Character* 9, no. 2 (November 2007): 6.

24. Martín Carcasson, *Beginning with the End in Mind: A Call for Goal-Driven Deliberative Practice,* cited in Heierbacher, *NCDD Project Report for the Kettering Foundation,* 14.

25. James Fishkin quoted in Bohman, *Public Deliberation: Pluralism, Complexity, and Democracy,* 35.

26. Claus Offe and Ulrich Preuss, "Democratic Institutions and Moral Resources," in *Political Theory Today,* David Held, ed. (Cambridge: Polity, 1991), 156–157; cited in Held, *Models of Democracy,* 3rd ed. (Palo Alto, CA: Stanford University Press, 2006), 232.

27. Bohman, *Public Deliberation: Pluralism, Complexity, and Democracy,* 36.

28. Amy Gutmann and Dennis Thompson, *Why Deliberative Democracy?* (Princeton, NJ: Princeton University Press, 2004), 4.

29. Marsh, *Democratic Dilemmas,* 161.

30. John Dryzek with Simon Niemeyer, *Foundations and Frontiers of Deliberative Governance* (New York: Oxford University Press, 2011), 11.

31. Carcasson, cited in Heierbacher, *NCDD Project Report for the Kettering Foundation,* 14.

32. Ibid., 17.

33. Dryzek, *Foundations and Frontiers of Deliberative Governance,* chapter 8.

34. Marsh, *Democratic Dilemmas.*

35. Ibid., 53.

36. Ibid., 163.

37. Ibid., 162.

38. Martín Carcasson and Leah Sprain, "Key Aspects of the Deliberative Democracy Movement," *Public Sector Digest* (July 2010). Available at www.publicsectordigest.com.

39. Jane Mansbridge et al., "The Place of Self-Interest and the Role of Power in Deliberative Democracy," *Journal of Political Philosophy* 18, no. 1 (2010): 68.

40. McAffe, "Three Models of Democratic Deliberation," *Democratizing Deliberation,* 32–33.

41. See Abigail Williamson and Archon Fung, *Mapping Public Deliberation: A Report for the*

William and Flora Hewlett Foundation (Cambridge, MA: Taubman Center for State and Local Government, John F. Kennedy School of Government, 2005). Available at www.hewlett.org/library/mapping-public-deliberation.

42. Dryzek, *Deliberative Democracy and Beyond,* 76. See also the work of Iris Marion Young in *Inclusion and Democracy* (New York: Oxford University Press, 2000), chapter 2; and Jane Mansbridge, "Practice—Thought—Practice," in *Deepening Democracy: Institutional Innovations in Empowered Participatory Governance,* ed. Archon Fung, Erik Olin Wright, and Rebecca Abers (New York, NY: Verso, 2003), 188–189.

43. Cheryl Hall, "Recognizing the Passion in Deliberation: Toward a More Democratic Theory of Deliberative Democracy," *Hypatia* 22, no. 4 (Fall 2007): 82.

44. Mansbridge, "Practice—Thought—Practice," 189.

45. Ibid., 190.

46. David Michael Ryfe, "The Practice of Deliberative Democracy: A Study of 16 Deliberative Organizations," *Political Communication* 19 (2002): 367.

47. Micah Sifry, from the Pew Report *Government Online,* quoted in Matt Leighninger, "How Should Citizens and Public Managers Use Online Tools to Improve Democracy?" *National Civic Review,* Summer 2011, 24. A collection of online engagement and deliberative tools can also be found at www.civiccommons.org, described as a "community-driven civic app store."

48. Scott Bittle, Chris Haller, and Alison Kadlec, *Promising Practices in Online Engagement,* Center for Advances in Public Engagement, Public Agenda, Occasional Paper #3 (2009), 14.

49. Ibid., 11.

50. Joshua Cohen and Joel Rogers, "Power and Reason," in *Deepening Democracy: Institutional Innovations in Empowered Participatory Governance,* ed. Archon Fung and Eric Olin Wright (New York: Verso, 2003), 242.

51. Caroline W. Lee, "Five Assumptions Academics Make about Public Deliberation, and Why They Deserve Rethinking," *Journal of Public Deliberation* 7, no. 1 (2011). Lee provides an excellent assessment of where the field stands with regard to these matters.

52. Young, *Inclusion and Democracy,* 6.

53. See, for example, Mark Walsh, "School Boards Struggle with Sunshine Laws," *Education Week* 22, no. 4, September 25, 2002, 1–15.

54. Young, *Inclusion and Democracy,* 53–55.

55. Ryfe, "The Practice of Deliberative Democracy: A Study of 16 Deliberative Organizations," 365.

56. Ibid.

57. Cohen and Rogers, "Power and Reason," 244–245.

58. Ibid., 248.

59. Mendelberg and Oleske, "Race and Public Deliberation."

60. Ibid., 169.

61. Ibid., 181–182.

62. Center for Advances in Public Engagement, *Essentials* (New York: Public Agenda, 2008). Available at www.publicagenda.org/reports/public-engagement-primer-public-agenda. (Emphasis in original.)

63. See Martín Carcasson, "Choosing, Combining, and Adapting Methods," Project Process Brainstorming Worksheet. Fort Collins: Colorado State University Center for Public Deliberation, n.d.

64. Mark E. Warren, "What Should and Should Not Be Said: Deliberating Sensitive Issues," *Journal of Social Philosophy* 37, no. 2 (Summer 2006): 163. (Emphasis in original.)

65. See Alison Kadlec and Will Friedman, "Deliberative Democracy and the Problem of Power," *Journal of Public Deliberation* 3, no. 1 (2007). Available at http://services.bepress.com/jpd/vol3/iss1/art8.

66. Jonathan W. Kuyper, "Deliberative Democracy and the Neglected Dimension of Leadership," *Journal of Public Deliberation* 8, no. 1 (2012): 8.

67. Ibid.

68. The process described here is taken from Thompson, *Engaging Citizens through Conversation.*

69. "Supporting Local Education Funds," Public Education Network, accessed June 21, 2011. Available at www.publiceducation.org/lefs.asp

70. Ibid.

71. For more on LEF work, see Diane Brown, Jolley Bruce Christman, Tracey Hartmann, and Elaine Simon, *Locating Local Education Funds: A Conceptual Framework for Describing LEFs' Contribution to Public Education* (Washington, DC: Research for Action and Public Education Network, 2004). Available at www.publiceducation.org/LEFresearch.asp.

72. Elena Fagotto and Archon Fung, *Embedded Deliberation: Entrepreneurs, Organizations, and Public Action* (Cambridge, MA: Taubman Center for State and Local Government, Kennedy School of Government, Harvard University, 2006). Available at www.prevnet.org/ru21/common/pdf/hewlett-masterfile-april06.pdf.

73. Elena Fagotto and Archon Fung, *Sustaining Public Engagement: Embedded Deliberation in Local Communities* (East Hartford, CT: Everyday Democracy and the Kettering Foundation, 2009). Available at www.everyday-democracy.org//en/Research.aspx.

74. Ibid., 1.

75. Gary L. Anderson, "Toward Authentic Participation: Deconstructing the Discourses of Participatory Reforms in Education," *American Educational Research Journal* 35, no. 4 (Winter 1998): 592.

76. Chris Gates quoted in Leighninger, "How Should Citizens and Public Managers Use Online Tools to Improve Democracy?," 25.

77. The Connecticut case is one of four profiled in Fagotto and Fung, *Embedded Deliberation,* 16.

78. Ibid.

79. Ibid., 17.

80. Heierbacher, *NCDD Project Report for the Kettering Foundation,* 26. See also Michael Walzer, "Deliberation, and What Else?" in *Deliberative Politics: Essays on Democracy and Disagreement,* ed. Stephen Macedo (New York: Oxford University Press, 1999), 58–69; and Kadlec and Freidman, "Deliberative Democracy and the Problem of Power," 15–23.

81. Harry C. Boyte, "Reframing Democracy: Governance, Civic Agency, and Politics," *Public Administration Review* 65, no. 5 (September/October 2005): 536.

82. Luvern Cunningham, "Rethinking the Role of the Community," in *American Educational Governance on Trial: Change and Challenges,* ed. William L. Boyd and Debra Miretzky (New York: National Society of the Study of Education, 2003), 162.

83. Abe Feuerstein, "Elections, Voting, and Democracy in Local School District Governance," *Educational Policy* 16, no. 1 (January and March 2002): 31.

84. Larry Cuban, "A Solution that Lost its Problem: Centralized Policymaking and Classroom Gains," in *Who's in Charge Here? The Tangled Web of School Governance and Policy,* ed. Noel Epstein (Denver: Education Commission of the States, 2004), 116.

Chapter 7

1. Carole Elliott and Valerie Snead, "Learning from Leading Women's Experience: Towards a Sociological Understanding," *Leadership* 4, no. 2 (2008): 159–160. See also Keith Grint, "Problems, Problems, Problems: The Social Construction of 'Leadership,'" *Human Relations* 58, no. 11 (November 2005): 1467–1494.

2. Barbara Kellerman and Scott Webster, "The Recent Literature on Public Leadership: Reviewed and Reconsidered," *Leadership Quarterly* 12 (2001): 485–514.

3. Ibid., 487.

4. Robert Kegan, *In Over Our Heads* (Cambridge, MA: Harvard University, 1994); Joseph A. Tainter, *The Collapse of Complex Societies* (Cambridge, UK: Cambridge University, 1988); Jeremy Rifkin, *The Empathic Civilization* (New York: Penguin/Tarcher, 2009).

5. Daniel H. Pink, *A Whole New Mind* (New York: Penguin/Riverhead, 2005).

6. Robert J. Starrat, *The Drama of Leadership* (New York: Routledge, 1993).

7. Tainter, *The Collapse of Complex Societies.*

8. John Dewey, "The Quest for Certainty," in *The Collected Works of John Dewey, 1882–1953* (Electronic edition); Dewey, "The Quest for Certainty," in *The Later Works of John Dewey, 1925–1953,* vol. 4 (Carbondale: Southern Illinois University, 2008), 17, 7.

9. Ronald Heifetz, *Leadership without Easy Answers* (Cambridge, MA: Belknap of Harvard University Press, 1994).

10. Joseph Campbell, *Hero with a Thousand Faces,* 3rd ed. (Novato, CA: New World Library, 2008).

11. See, for example, *Reconsidering Feminist Research in Educational Leadership,* ed. Michelle D. Young and Linda Skrla (Albany: State University of New York, 2003).

12. M. Mitchell Waldrop, *Complexity: The Emerging Science at the Edge of Order and Chaos* (New York: Simon and Schuster, 1992), 20.

13. See, for example, Margaret J. Wheatley, *Leadership and the New Science: Discovering Order in a Chaotic World,* 3rd ed. (San Francisco: Berrett-Koehler, 2006).

14. John Dewey, "Ethical Principles Underlying Education" (1897), *Early Works of John Dewey* vol. 5, 75.

15. Tom Atlee, *The Tao of Democracy: Using Co-Intelligence to Create a World That Works for All* (Cranston, RI: Writers' Collective, 2003), chapter 6.

16. Alisdair MacIntyre, *After Virtue: A Study in Moral Theory* (Notre Dame, IN: Notre Dame University Press), 30.

17. Warren Bennis, *On Becoming a Leader* (New York: Addison-Wesley, 1989), 44.

18. Heifetz, *Leadership without Easy Answers.*

19. Chris Argyris, *Reasoning, Learning, and Action: Individual and Organizational* (San Francisco: Jossey-Bass, 1982), 104–106.

20. Parker Palmer, *The Courage to Teach* (San Francisco: Jossey-Bass, 1998), 10.

21. Peter Block, *Stewardship: Choosing Service over Self-Interest* (San Francisco: Berret-Koehler, 1993), 234.

22. Walsh states that "women run for office to do something, and men run for office to be somebody.... Women run because there is some public issue that they care about, some change they want to make, some issue that is a priority for them, and men tend to run for office because they see this as a career path." See Sheryl Gay Stolberg, "When It Comes to Scandal, Girls Won't Be Boys," *New York Times,* June 11, 2011. Available at www.nytimes.com/2011/06/12/weekinreview/12women.html?pagewanted=all.

23. William P. Foster, "The Decline of the Local: A Challenge to Educational Leadership," *Educational Administration Quarterly* 40, no. 2 (April 2004): 177.

24. Ibid., 178.

25. Wheatley, *Leadership and the New Science,* 23.

26. Bill J. Johnston, "Educational Administration in the Postmodern Age," in *Postmodern School Leadership: Meeting the Crisis in Educational Administration,* ed. Spencer J. Maxcy (Westport, CT: Praeger, 1994), 129.

27. Stephen Preskill and Stephen D. Brookfield, *Learning as a Way of Leading: Lessons from the Struggle for Social Justice* (San Francisco: Jossey-Bass, 2009), 21.

28. Robert Putnam, *Better Together: Restoring the American Community* (New York: Simon and Schuster, 1999), 1.

29. Gary L. Anderson, *Advocacy Leadership: Toward a Post-Reform Agenda in Education* (New York: Routledge, 2009), 115.

30. Philip A. Woods, *Democratic Leadership in Education* (Thousand Oaks, CA: Paul Chapman, 2005), 107.

31. Andy Hargreaves and Dean Fink, *Sustainable Leadership* (San Francisco: Jossey-Bass, 2005); James P. Spillane, *Distributed Leadership* (San Francisco: Jossey-Bass, 2006).

32. Kenneth P. Ruscio, *The Leadership Dilemma in Modern Democracy*, New Horizons in Leadership Studies, series ed. Joanne B. Ciulla (Northampton, MA: Edward Elgar, 2004), 32.

33. A. Belden Fields and Walter Feinberg, *Education and Democratic Theory: Finding a Place for Community Participation in Public School Reform* (Albany: State University of New York, 2001), 93–94.

34. Ruscio, *The Leadership Dilemma in Modern Democracy*, 3.

35. A. Belden Fields and Walter Feinberg, *Education and Democratic Theory: Finding a Place for Community Participation in Public School Reform* (Albany: State University of New York, 2001), 95.

36. Deborah Tannen, *The Argument Culture: Moving from Debate to Dialogue* (New York: Random House, 1998).

37. Peter Senge, *The Fifth Discipline: The Art and Practice of the Learning Organization*, rev. ed. (New York: Currency Doubleday, 2006), 183.

38. James Surowiecki, *The Wisdom of Crowds* (New York: Doubleday, 2004), xvii.

39. Ibid., 271.

40. Robert Greenleaf, *Servant Leadership* (New York: Paulist Press, 1977), 169, 171; Block, *Stewardship*, 23.

41. Senge, *The Fifth Discipline*, 129.

42. Anderson, *Advocacy Leadership*.

43. Charlie Irish, *We Need to Speed Up Evolution to Stave Off Revolution* (Unpublished report, Santa Rita Collaborative, 2010).

44. Keith Grint, "Problems, Problems, Problems: The Social Construction of 'Leadership,'" *Human Relations* 58, no. 11 (November 2005): 1473.

45. Foster, "The Decline of the Local," 190.

46. Wendy D. Puriefoy, "Public Engagement and Education Excellence," *Baltimore Sun*, February 8, 2012. Available at www.baltimoresun.com.

Afterword

1. Jonathan Haidt, "Born This Way? Nature, Nurture, Narratives, and the Making of Our Political Personalities," *Reason*, May 2012, 29.

2. Pew Research Center, "Partisan Polarization Surges in Bush, Obama Years: Trends in American Values: 1987–2012," June 4, 2012. Available at http://pewresearch.org.

3. Eric Liu, "Democracy Is for Amateurs: Why We Need More Citizen Citizens," *The Atlantic*, May 11, 2012. Available at www.theatlantic.com.

BIBLIOGRAPHY

Adler, Paul S., and Seok-Woo Kwon. "Social Capital: The Good, the Bad, and the Ugly." In *Knowledge and Social Capital: Foundations and Applications,* edited by E. L. Lesser, 89–113. Boston, MA: Butterworth/Heinemann, 2000.

Alinsky, Saul D. *Rules for Radicals: A Pragmatic Primer for Realistic Radicals.* New York: Vintage Books, 1971.

Anderson, Gary L. *Advocacy Leadership: Toward a Post-Reform Agenda in Education.* New York: Routledge, 2009.

———. "The Politics of Participatory Reforms in Education." *Theory into Practice* 38, no. 4 (Autumn 1999): 191–195.

———. "Toward Authentic Participation: Deconstructing the Discourses of Participatory Reforms in Education." *American Educational Research Journal* 35, no. 4 (Winter 1998): 571–603.

Anderson, James D. *The Education of Blacks in the South, 1860–1935.* Chapel Hill: University of North Carolina Press, 1988.

Argyris, Chris. *Reasoning, Learning, and Action: Individual and Organizational.* San Francisco: Jossey-Bass, 1982.

Ashby, Suzanne, Cris Garza, and Maggie Rivas. "Public Deliberation: A Tool for Connecting School Reform and Diversity." Southwest Educational Development Laboratory. 1999. Accessed October 28, 2009. Available: www.sedl.org/pubs/lc06.

Atlee, Tom. *The Tao of Democracy: Using Co-Intelligence to Create a World That Works for All.* Cranston, RI: Writers' Collective, 2003.

Ball, Stephan J. "Privatising Education, Privatising Education Policy, Privatising Educational Research: Network Governance and the 'Competition State.'" *Journal of Education Policy* 24, no. 1 (2009): 83–99.

Barker, Derek W. M., Noëlle McAfee, and David W. McIvor. "Introduction: Democratizing Deliberation." In *Democratizing Deliberation: A Political Theory Anthology,* edited by David Barker, Noëlle McAfee, and David McIvor, 1–20. Dayton: Kettering Foundation, 2012.

Beam, John M., and Sharmeen Irani. "Acorn Education Reform Organizing: Evolution of a Model." National Center for Schools and Communities, Fordham University, April 8, 2003. Accessed September 28, 2009. Available: http://stage.web.fordham.edu.

Benhabib, Seyla. "Toward a Deliberative Model of Democratic Legitimacy." In *Democracy and Difference: Contesting the Boundaries of the Political,* edited by Seyla Benhabib, 67–94. Princeton, NJ: Princeton University Press, 1996.

Bennis, Warren. *On Becoming a Leader.* New York: Addison-Wesley, 1989.

Berkman, Michael B., and Eric Plutzer. *Ten Thousand Democracies: Politics and Public Opinion in America's School Districts.* Washington, DC: Georgetown University Press, 2005.

"Better Teaching, Better Learning, Better Schools." National Board for Professional Teaching Standards, accessed June 10, 2010. Available: www.nbpts.org.

Bittle, Scott, Chris Haller, and Alison Kadlec. *Promising Practices in Online Engagement.* Center for Advances in Public Engagement, Public Agenda, Occasional Paper #3 (2009). Accessed May 12, 2011. Available: www.publicagenda.org.

Block, Peter. *Stewardship: Choosing Service over Self-Interest.* San Francisco: Berret-Koehler, 1993.

Bohman, James. "The Coming of Age of Deliberative Democracy." *Journal of Political Philosophy* 6, no. 4 (1998): 400–425.

———. *Public Deliberation: Pluralism, Complexity, and Democracy,* Studies in Contemporary German Social Thought. Cambridge, MA: MIT Press, 1997.

Boyd, William Lowe. "Public Education's Crisis of Performance and Legitimacy: Rationale and Overview of the Yearbook." In *American Educational Governance on Trial: Change and Challenges,* 102nd Yearbook of the National Society for the Study of Education, part 1, edited by William Lowe Boyd and Debra Miretzky, 1–19. Chicago: University of Chicago Press, 2003.

Boyte, Harry C. "Constructive Politics as Public Work." In *Democraticizing Deliberation: A Political Theory Anthology,* edited by Derek W. M. Barker, Noëlle McAfee, and David W. McIvor, 153–182. Dayton, OH: Kettering Foundation Press, 2012.

———. *Everyday Politics: Reconnecting Citizens and Public Life.* Philadelphia: University of Pennsylvania Press, 2004.

———. "Reframing Democracy: Governance, Civic Agency, and Politics." *Public Administration Review* 65, no. 5 (September/October 2005): 536–546.

Boyte, Harry C., and Nan Skelton, *Reinventing Citizenship: The Power of Public Work.* St. Paul: University of Minnesota, 1995. Accessed September 24, 2009. Available: www.extension.umn.edu/distribution/citizenship/dh6586.html.

Bracey, Gerald W. "Schools-Are-Awful Bloc Still Busy in 2008." *Phi Delta Kappan* 90, no. 2 (2008): 103–114.

Brandzel, Ben. "What Malcolm Gladwell Missed about Online Organizing and Creating Big Change." *Nation,* November 15, 2010. Accessed May 12, 2012. Available: www.thenation.com.

Briand, Michael K. *Practical Politics: Five Principles for a Community that Works.* Urbana: University of Illinois Press, 1999.

Brighouse, Harry. *On Education.* New York: Routledge, 2005.

Brookings Institute. *Invisible: 1.4 Percent Coverage for Education Is Not Enough.* Accessed February 12, 2010. Available: www.brookings.edu/reports/2009/1202_education_news_west.aspx.

Brown, Clyde, Annie Miller, Kathleen Knight Abowitz, and Stephanie Raill Jayanandhan. *Ohio's Civic Health Index 2009: Civic Engagement in Hard Economic Times.* Washington, DC: National Conference on Citizenship, 2009. Accessed May 12, 2010. Available: www.ham.muohio.edu/cce.

Brown, Diane, Jolley Bruce Christman, Tracey Hartmann, and Elaine Simon. *Locating Local Education Funds: A Conceptual Framework for Describing LEFs' Contribution to Public Education.* Washington, DC: Research for Action and Public Education Network, 2004. Accessed May 12, 2011. Available: www.publiceducation.org/LEFresearch.asp.

Burch, Patricia. *Hidden Markets: The New Education Privatization.* New York: Routledge, 2009.

Campbell, Joseph. *Hero with a Thousand Faces,* 3rd ed. Novato, CA: New World Library, 2008.

Canovan, Margaret. "The People." In *The Oxford Handbook of Political Theory,* edited by John S. Dryzek, Bonnie Honig, and Anne Phillips, 349–362. New York: Oxford University Press, 2006.

Carcasson, Martín. *Beginning with the End in Mind: A Call for Goal-Driven Deliberative Practice.* Public Agenda's Center for Advances in Public Engagement, Occasional Paper, no. 2, 2009. Accessed May 14, 2011. Available: www.publicagenda.org/cape.

———. "Choosing, Combining, and Adapting Methods." Project Process Brainstorming Worksheet (unpublished). Fort Collins: Colorado State University Center for Public Deliberation.

———. "'Toward a More Perfect Union': An Introduction to the Deliberative Democracy Movement." Presentation at Citizens' Toolbox Conference, Miami University, Oxford, Ohio, March 16, 2011.

Carcasson, Martín, and Leah Sprain. "Key Aspects of the Deliberative Democracy Movement." *Public Sector Digest* (July 2010). Accessed May 15, 2011. Available: www.publicsectordigest.com.

Carnegie Corporation of New York, and the Center for Information and Research on Civic Learning and Engagement. *The Civic Mission of Schools.* New York: Carnegie Corporation of New York, and the Center for Information and Research on Civic Learning and Engagement, 2003.

Carnegie Forum on Education and Economy. *A Nation Prepared: Teachers for the 21st Century: The Report of the Task Force on Teaching as a Profession.* St. Paul, MN: Forum, 1986.

Carr, Nora. "Must Public Education Restore Its Image as Great Equalizer?" *Education Digest* 72, no. 4 (December 2006): 29–32.

Caspary, William R. *Dewey on Democracy.* Ithaca, NY: Cornell University Press, 2000.

Center for Advances in Public Engagement. "Essentials." New York: Public Agenda, 2008. Accessed September 12, 2010. Available: www.publicagenda.org/reports.

Chaskin, R., P. Brown, S. Venkatesh, and A. Vidal. *Building Community Capacity.* New York: Aldine De Gruyter, 2000.

"Child Poverty and Family Income," ChildStates.gov: Forum on Child and Family Statistics. Available: www.childstats.gov/americaschildren/eco1.asp.

Chu, Elbert, and Chris Palmer, "For Legacy High School Students, A Lesson in Activism Hits Home." *New York Times,* February 7, 2012. Accessed May 15, 2012. Available: www.nytimes.com.

Chubb, John E., and Terry M. Moe. *Politics, Markets, and America's Schools.* Washington, DC: Brookings Institution, 1990.

Civic Commons: Sharing Technology for the Public Good. Accessed June 1, 2012. Available: http://civiccommons.org/engagement-commons.

Cohen, Jon. "Budget Talks in a Word: 'Ridiculous,' 'Disgusting' and 'Stupid' Top Poll." *Washington Post Politics,* August 1, 2011. Accessed May 20, 2012. Available: www.washingtonpost.com/blogs.

Cohen, Joshua, and Joel Rogers, "Power and Reason." In *Deepening Democracy: Institutional Innovations in Empowered Participatory Governance,* edited by Archon Fung and Eric Olin Wright, 247–264. New York: Verso, 2003.

Coley, Richard, and Andrew M. Sum. *Fault Lines in Our Democracy: Civic Knowledge, Voting Behavior, and Civic Engagement in the United States.* Princeton, NJ: Educational Testing Service, 2012. Accessed May 29, 2012. Available: www.ets.org/s/research/19386/.

Corritore, Matthew. "Why Conservatives Should Love Community Organizing." CBSNews, October 17, 2008. Accessed Mary 12, 2010. Available: www.cbsnews.com/stories.

Couto, Richard. "Defining a Citizen Leader." In *Public Leadership Education: The Role of Citizen Leadership,* 3–9. Dayton, OH: Kettering Foundation, 1992.

Crick, Bernard. *In Defense of Politics.* Chicago: University of Chicago Press, 1993.

Cuban, Larry. "A Solution That Lost Its Problem: Centralized Policymaking and Classroom Gains." In *Who's in Charge Here? The Tangled Web of School Governance and Policy,* edited by Noel Epstein, 104–130. Denver: Education Commission of the States, 2004.

Cucchia, Maia Bloomfield, Eva Gold, and Elaine Simon. "Contracts, Choice, and Customer Service: Marketization and Public Engagement in Education." *Teachers College Record* 113, no. 11 (2011): 2460–2502.

Cunningham, Luvern. "Rethinking the Role of the Community." In *American Educational Governance on Trial: Change and Challenges,* edited by William L. Boyd and Debra Miretzky, 155–176. New York: National Society of the Study of Education, 2003.

DeCesare, Tony. "The Lippmann-Dewey 'Debate' Revisited: The Problem of Knowledge and the Role of Experts in Modern Democratic Theory." *Philosophical Studies in Education* 42 (2011). Accessed September 30, 2012. Available: www.ovpes.org/journal.htm.

Dewey, John. *Democracy and Education.* New York: Free Press, 1916.

_____. "Ethical Principles Underlying Education" (1897), *Early Works of John Dewey,* vol. 5, 54–83. Carbondale: Southern Illinois University Press, 1972.

———. "Policies for a Third Party," *New Republic,* April 8, 1931, 202–205.

———. *The Public and Its Problems.* New York: Henry Holt, 1927.

———. "The Quest for Certainty." In *The Later Works of John Dewey, 1925–1953,* vol. 4. Carbondale: Southern Illinois University, 2008.

Doble, John, Jared Bosk, and Samantha DuPont. *Coping with the Cost of Health Care: How Do We Pay for What We Need? Outcomes of the 2008 National Issues Forums.* Dayton, OH: Kettering Foundation, June 2009. Accessed November 2010. Available: www.publicagenda.org/citizen/researchstudies/health-care-medical-research.

Dryzek, John S. *Deliberative Democracy and Beyond: Liberals, Critics, Contestations.* New York: Oxford University Press, 2000.

Du Bois, W. E. B. *Black Reconstruction in America, 1860–1880.* New York: Free Press, 1999.

E3 Alliance. *Achievement Gaps Deliberative Dialogues Final Report,* December 18, 2007. Accessed October 25, 2009. Available: www.e3alliance.org/dialogues.html.

Elliott, Carole, and Valerie Snead. "Learning from Leading Women's Experience: Towards a Sociological Understanding." *Leadership* 4, no. 2 (2008): 159–180.

Fabricant, Michael B. *Organizing for Educational Justice: The Campaign for School Reform in the South Bronx.* Minneapolis: University of Minnesota Press, 2010.

Fagotto, Elena, and Archon Fung. *Embedded Deliberation: Entrepreneurs, Organizations, and Public Action.* Cambridge, MA: Taubman Center for State and Local Government, Kennedy School of Government, Harvard University, 2006. Accessed February 12, 2009. Available: www.prevnet.org/ru21/common/pdf/hewlett-masterfile-april06.pdf.

———. *Sustaining Public Engagement: Embedded Deliberation in Local Communities.* East Hartford, CT: Everyday Democracy and the Kettering Foundation, 2009. Accessed May 15, 2010. Available: www.everyday-democracy.org//en/Research.aspx.

Feinberg, Walter. *Common Schools/Uncommon Identities: National Unity and Cultural Difference.* New Haven, CT: Yale University Press, 1998.

Fennimore, Beatrice S. "Brown and the Failure of Civic Responsibility." *Teachers College Record* 107, no. 9 (September 2005): 1905–1932.

Feuerstein, Abe. "Elections, Voting, and Democracy in Local School District Governance." *Educational Policy* 16, no. 1 (January and March 2002): 15–36.

Fields, A. Belden, and Walter Feinberg. *Education and Democratic Theory: Finding a Place for Community Participation in Public School Reform.* Albany: State University of New York, 2001.

Finnegan, Cara A. "Elastic, Agonistic Publics: John Dewey's Call for a Third Party." *Argumentation and Advocacy* 39, no. 3 (Winter 2003): 161–173.

Fisher, Robert, and Eric Shragge. "Contextualizing Community Organizing: Lessons from the Past, Tensions in the Present, Opportunities for the Future." In *Transforming the City: Community Organizing and the Challenge of Political Change,* edited by Marion Orr, 193–217. Lawrence: University of Kansas Press, 2007.

Fisher, Robert, and Sally Tamarkin. "What ACORN and the New Right Can Teach Us about Current Trends in Community Organizing." *Social Policy,* Spring 2009, 48–50.

Fossey, Richard. "'I Support My Gay Friends': Free Speech Is Alive and Well in the Schools of the Florida Panhandle." *Teachers College Record,* August 18, 2008. Accessed May 21, 2010. Available: www.tcrecord.org.

Foster, William P. "The Decline of the Local: A Challenge to Educational Leadership." *Educational Administration Quarterly* 40, no. 2 (April 2004): 176–191.

Fournier, Ron, and Sophie Quinton. "In Nothing We Trust." *National Review,* April 19, 2012. Accessed May 1, 2012. Available: www.nationaljournal.com.

Franciosi, Robert J. *The Rise and Fall of American Public Schools: The Political Economy of Public Education in the Twentieth Century.* Westport, CT: Praeger, 2004.

Fraser, Nancy. *Justice Interruptus: Critical Reflections on the 'Postsocialist' Condition.* New York: Routledge, 1997.

Fullan, Michael, and Andy Hargreaves. "Reviving Teaching with 'Professional Capital.'" *Education Week,* June 5, 2012. Accessed June 5, 2012. Available: www.edweek.org.

Fusarelli, Bonnie C., and William Lowe Boyd. "Introduction: One Nation Indivisible? An Overview of the Yearbook." *Educational Policy* 18, no. 1 (January and March 2004): 5–11.

Giarelli, James M. "Educating for Public Life." In *Critical Conversations in Philosophy of Education*, edited by Wendy Kohli, 201–216. New York: Routledge, 1994.

Gold, Eva, Jeffrey Henig, and Elaine Simon. "Calling the Shots in Public Education: Parents, Politicians, and Educators." *Dissent*, Fall 2011, 34–40.

Gold, Eva, and Elaine Simon. *Successful Community Organizing for School Reform*. Chicago: Cross City Campaign for Urban School Reform, March 2002. Accessed August 28, 2009. Available: www.lsna.net/Issues-and-programs/Schools-and-Youth/Strong -Neighborhoods-Strong-Schools-Case-Study-LSNA.html.

Gold, Eva, and Elaine Simon, with Chris Brown. "A New Conception of Parental Engagement: Community Organizing for School Reform." In *The Sage Handbook of Educational Leadership*, edited by F. W. English, 237–268. Thousand Oaks, CA: Sage, 2005.

Gold, Eva, Elaine Simon, Leah Mundell, and Chris Brown. "Bringing Community Organizing into the School Reform Picture." *Nonprofit and Voluntary Sector Quarterly* 33 (Supplement), no. 3 (September 2004): 54S–76S.

Goldberg, Jonah. "Do Away with Public Schools." *Los Angeles Times*, June 12, 2007. Accessed February 9, 2010. Available: www.latimes.com.

Gordon, Mordechai, ed. *Reclaiming Dissent*. Rotterdam: Sense, 2009.

Greenleaf, Robert. *Servant Leadership*. New York: Paulist Press, 1977.

Grint, Keith. "Problems, Problems, Problems: The Social Construction of 'Leadership.'" *Human Relations* 58, no. 11 (November 2005): 1467–1494.

Gutmann, Amy, and Dennis Thompson. *Democracy and Disagreement*. Cambridge, MA: Harvard University Press, 1996.

———. *Why Deliberative Democracy?* Princeton, NJ: Princeton University Press, 2004.

Habermas, Jürgen. *The Structural Transformation of the Public Sphere: An Inquiry into a Category of Bourgeois Society*. Translated by Thomas Burger with the assistance of Frederick Lawrence. Oxford: Polity Press, 1962/1989.

Haidt, Jonathan. "Born this Way? Nature, Nurture, Narratives, and the Making of Our Political Personalities." *Reason*, May 2012, 24–33.

———. *The Righteous Mind: Why Good People Are Divided by Politics*. New York: Pantheon, 2012.

Hall, Cheryl. "Recognizing the Passion in Deliberation: Toward a More Democratic Theory of Deliberative Democracy." *Hypatia* 22, no. 4 (Fall 2007): 81–95.

Hannay, Alastair. *On the Public*. New York: Routledge, 2005.

Hargreaves, Andy, and Dean Fink. *Sustainable Leadership*. San Francisco: Jossey-Bass, 2005.

Heierbacher, Sandy. *NCDD Project Report for the Kettering Foundation, National Coalition for Dialogue and Deliberation*. Boiling Springs, PA: National Coalition for Dialogue and Deliberation, 2009.

Heifetz, Ronald. *Leadership without Easy Answers*. Cambridge, MA: Belknap of Harvard University Press, 1994.

Held, David. *Models of Democracy*, 3rd ed. Palo Alto, CA: Stanford University Press, 2006.

Hendriks, Carolyn M., John S. Dryzek, and Christian Hunold. "Turning Up the Heat: Partisanship in Deliberative Innovation." *Political Studies* 55 (2007): 262–283.

Hess, Frederick M., and Linda Darling-Hammond. "How to Rescue School Reform." *Education Week*, December 5, 2011. Accessed January 18, 2012. Available: www .nytimes.com/2011/12/06/opinion/how-to-rescue-education-reform.html?_r=2.

Higgins, Chris, and Kathleen Knight Abowitz. "What Makes a Public School Public? A

Framework for Evaluating the Civic Substance of Schooling," *Educational Theory* 61, no. 4 (2011): 365–380.

Hilmer, Jeffrey D. "The State of Participatory Democratic Theory." *New Political Science* 32, no. 1 (March 2010): 43–63.

Hirschman, Albert O. *Exit, Voice and Loyalty.* Cambridge, MA: Harvard University Press, 1970.

Holmes Group. *Tomorrow's Teachers: A Report of the Holmes Group.* Michigan: Holmes Group, 1986.

Hong, Soo. *A Cord of Three Strands: A New Approach to Parent Engagement in Schools.* Cambridge, MA: Harvard University Press, 2011.

Horvat, E. M., E. B. Weininger, and Annette Lareau. "From Social Ties to Social Capital: Class Differences in the Relations between Schools and Parent Networks." *American Educational Research Journal* 40 (2003): 319–351.

Hunter, James Davison. *Culture Wars: The Struggle to Define America.* New York: Basic, 1991.

"IAF in Action." Industrial Areas Foundation. Accessed September 11, 2009. Available: www.industrialareasfoundation.org/iafaction/iafactionschools.htm.

Irish, Charlie. *We Need to Speed Up Evolution to Stave Off Revolution.* Unpublished report, Santa Rita Collaborative, 2010.

Johnston, Bill J. "Educational Administration in the Postmodern Age." In *Postmodern School Leadership: Meeting the Crisis in Educational Administration,* edited by Spencer J. Maxcy, 115–132. Westport, CT: Praeger, 1994.

Kadlec, Alison. *Dewey's Critical Pragmatism.* Lanham, MD: Rowman and Littlefield, 2007.

Kadlec, Alison, and Will Friedman. "Deliberative Democracy and the Problem of Power." *Journal of Public Deliberation* 3, no. 1 (2007): 1–26. Accessed February 10, 2010. Available: http://services.bepress.com/jpd/vol3/iss1/art8.

Kegan, Robert. *In Over Our Heads.* Cambridge, MA: Harvard University, 1994.

Kellerman, Barbara, and Scott Webster. "The Recent Literature on Public Leadership: Reviewed and Reconsidered," *Leadership Quarterly* 12 (2001): 485–514.

Kirp, David L. "Making Schools Work." *New York Times,* May 20, 2012, Sunday Review, 1–11.

Kirst, Michael W. "The Evolving Role of School Boards: Retrospect and Prospect." In *The Future of School Board Governance: Relevancy and Revelation,* edited by Thomas L. Alsbury, 37–60. Lanham, MD: Rowman and Littlefield Education, 2008.

Klein, Daniel B. "I Was Wrong, and So Are You." *The Atlantic,* December 2011. Accessed May 12, 2012. Available: www.theatlantic.com.

Klein, Joel, Michelle Rhee, Peter Gorman, Ron Huberman, Carole R. Johnson, Andrés Alonso, Tom Boasberg, Arlene Ackerman, William R. Hite Jr., Jean-Claude Brizard, José M. Torres, Terry B. Grier, Paul Vallas, Eugene White, and LaVonne Sheffield. "How to Fix Our Schools: An Education Reform Manifesto." *New York Times,* October 10, 2010. Accessed December 2010. Available: www.washingtonpost.com/wp-dyn/content/article/2010/10/07/AR2010100705078.html.

Knight Abowitz, Kathleen. "A Pragmatist Revisioning of Resistance Theory." *American Educational Research Journal* 37, no. 4 (2000): 877–907.

———. "Reclaiming Community," *Educational Theory* 49, no. 2 (1999): 143–159.

———. "What's Pragmatic about Community Organizing?" *Philosophical Studies in Education* 41 (2010). Accessed October 10, 2010. Available: http://ovpes .org/2010Final.htm.

Knops, Andrew. "Debate: Agonism as Deliberation—Mouffe's Theory of Democracy." *Journal of Political Philosophy* 15, no. 1 (2007): 115–126.

KnowledgeWorks Foundation and Harwood Institute for Public Innovation. *Engaging Citizens through Conversation: Reconnecting Communities and Schools in the Plain Local School District.* Cincinnati, OH: KnowledgeWorks Foundation and the Harwood Institute for Public Innovation, 2004.

Kristen, Katherine. "Our Schools Can Do a Far Better Job of Teaching Patriotism." Center of the American Experiment, September 11, 2002. Accessed October 22, 2010. Available: www.americanexperiment.org.

Kuyper, Jonathan W. "Deliberative Democracy and the Neglected Dimension of Leadership." *Journal of Public Deliberation* 8, no. 1 (2012): 1–32.

Labaree, David F. "Consuming the Public School." *Educational Theory* 61, no. 4 (2011): 381–394.

———. *Education, Markets, and the Public Good: The Selected Works of David F. Labaree.* New York: Routledge, 2007.

———. "Public Goods, Private Goods: The American Struggle over Educational Goals." *American Educational Research Journal* 34, no. 1 (Spring 1997): 39–81.

Laing, Bonnie Young. "The Universal Negro Improvement Association, Southern Christian Leadership Conference, and Black Panther Party: Lessons for Understanding African American Culture-Based Organizing." *Journal of Black Studies* 39, no. 4 (March 2009): 635–656.

Lee, Caroline W. "Five Assumptions Academics Make about Public Deliberation, and Why They Deserve Rethinking." *Journal of Public Deliberation* 7, no.1 (2011): 1–48.

Leighninger, Matt. "How Should Citizens and Public Managers Use Online Tools to Improve Democracy?" *National Civic Review,* Summer 2011, 20–29.

———. *The Next Form of Democracy: How Expert Rule Is Giving Way to Shared Governance ... and Why Politics Will Never Be the Same.* Nashville: Vanderbilt University Press, 2006.

———. *Using On-Line Tools to Engage—and Be Engaged by—the Public.* Washington, DC: IBM Center for the Business of Government, 2011.

Levinson, Meira. *No Citizen Left Behind.* Cambridge, MA: Harvard University Press, 2012.

Liu, Eric. "Democracy Is for Amateurs: Why We Need More Citizen Citizens." *The Atlantic,* May 11, 2012. Available: www.theatlantic.com.

Lopez, M. Elena. *Transforming Schools through Community Organizing: A Research Review.* Cambridge, MA: Family Involvement Network of Educators, Harvard Family Research Project, 2003.

Lutz, Frank, and Laurence Iannaccone. "The Dissatisfaction Theory of American Democracy." *The Future of School Board Governance: Relevancy and Revelation,* edited by Thomas L. Alsbury, 3–24. Lanham, MD: Rowman and Littlefield, 2008.

Lynd, Robert S., and Helen Merrell Lynd. *Middletown: A Study in Modern American Culture.* New York: Harcourt Brace Jovanovich, 1929/1959.

Macedo, Stephen. *Diversity and Distrust.* Cambridge, MA: Harvard University Press, 2000.

MacIntyre, Alisdair. *After Virtue: A Study in Moral Theory.* Notre Dame, IN: Notre Dame University Press.

Malen, Betty. "The Promises and Perils of Participation on Site-Based Councils." *Theory into Practice* 38, no. 4 (Autumn 1999): 209–216.

Mangu-Ward, Katherine. "Public Is Now a Four-Letter Word." *Reason Hit and Run,* July 12, 2007. Available: http://reason.com/blog.

Mansbridge, Jane. "Practice—Thought—Practice." In *Deepening Democracy: Institutional Innovations in Empowered Participatory Governance,* edited by Archon Fung, Erik Olin Wright, and Rebecca Abers, 175–199. New York, NY: Verso, 2003.

Mansbridge, Jane, with James Bohman, Simone Chambers, David Estlund, Andreas Føllesdal, Archon Fung, Cristina Lafont, Bernard Manin, and José Luis Marti. "The Place of Self-Interest and the Role of Power in Deliberative Democracy." *Journal of Political Philosophy* 18, no. 1 (2010): 64–100.

Marres, Noortje. "Issues Spark a Public into Being." In *Making Things Public: Atmospheres of Democracy,* edited by Bruno Latour and Peter Weibel, 208–217. Cambridge, MA: MIT Press, 2005.

Marsh, Julie A. *Democratic Dilemmas: Joint Work, Education Politics, and Community.* Albany: State University of New York Press, 2007.

Mathews, David. *Is There a Public for Public Schools?* Dayton, OH: Kettering Foundation, 1997.

———. "The Lack of a Public for Public Schools," *Phi Delta Kappan* 78, no. 10 (June 1997): 740–743.

McAlister, Sara. "Community Organizing as an Education Reform Strategy." AISR: Commentary on Urban Education. Annenberg Institute for School Reform, Brown University, February 3, 2011. Accessed December 20, 2011. Available: http://annenberginstitute.org.

McCarthy, Thomas. "Practical Discourse: On the Relation of Morality to Politics." In *Habermas and the Public Sphere,* edited by Craig Calhoun, 51–72. Cambridge, MA: MIT Press, 1992.

McDermott, Kathryn A. *Controlling Public Education: Localism versus Equity.* Lawrence: University of Kansas Press, 1999.

McNeil, Linda M. "Private Asset or Public Good: Education and Democracy at the Crossroads." *American Educational Research Journal* 39, no. 2 (Summer 2002): 243–248.

Meadows, Elizabeth, and Katherine Blatchford. "Achieving Widespread Democratic Education in the United States: Dewey's Ideas Reconsidered." *Education and Culture* 25, no. 1 (2009): 36–51.

Mediratta, Kavitha. "A Rising Movement." *National Civic Review* 95, no. 1 (Spring 2006): 15–22.

Mediratta, Kavitha, and Norm Fruchter. *Mapping the Field of Organizing for School Improvement: A Report on Education Organizing in Baltimore, Chicago, Los Angeles, the Mississippi Delta, New York City, Philadelphia, San Francisco, and Washington, D.C.* New York: Institute for Education and Social Policy, New York University, 2001. [ERIC Document ED 471 052]

Mediratta, Kavitha, Seema Shah, and Sara McAlister. *Building Partnerships to Reinvent School Culture: Austin Interfaith.* Providence, RI: Annenberg Institute for School Reform at Brown University, 2009. Accessed February 21, 2010. Available: http://annenberginstitute.org.

————. *Community Organizing for Stronger Schools: Strategies and Successes.* Cambridge, MA: Harvard Education Press, 2009.

Mediratta, Kavitha, Seema Shah, Sara McAlister, Norm Fruchter, Christina Mokhtar, and Dana Lockwood. *Organized Communities, Stronger Schools: A Preview of Research Findings.* Providence, RI: Annenberg Institute for School Reform at Brown University, March 2008. Accessed February 19, 2010. Available: www.annenberginstitute.org.

Mendelberg, Tali, and John Oleske, "Race and Public Deliberation." *Political Communication* 17 (2000): 169–191.

Mengual, Gloria. "Portsmouth, N.H.: Where Public Dialogue Is a Hallmark of Community Life." *Everyday Democracy*, June 1, 2003. Accessed October 12, 2009. Available: www.everyday-democracy.org.

Meyer, John, and W. Richard Scott. *Organizational Environments: Ritual and Rationality.* Beverly Hills, CA: Sage, 1983.

Miron, Gary, and Christopher Nelson. *What's Public about Charter Schools? Lessons Learned about Choice and Accountability.* Thousand Oaks, CA: Corwin, 2002.

Mouffe, Chantal. "Deliberative Democracy or Agonistic Pluralism." *Political Science Series* 72, edited by Christine Neuhold, 1–17. Vienna: Institute for Advanced Studies, 2000. Accessed October 19, 2009. Available: www.ihs.ac.at/publications/pol/pw_72.pdf.

————. "Democracy as Agonistic Pluralism." In *Rewriting Democracy: Cultural Politics in Postmodernity,* edited by Elizabeth Deeds Ermarth, 36–47. Burlington, VT: Ashgate, 2007.

————. *The Democratic Paradox.* New York: Verso, 2000.

National Center for Schools and Communities. *From Schoolhouse to Statehouse: Community Organizing for Public School Reform.* New York: Fordham University, 2002.

National Coalition for Dialogue and Deliberation. *Resource Guide on Public Engagement,* October 2010. Accessed October 29, 2009. Available: www.ncdd.org.

Niquette, Mark. "Ohio's Voter Turnout Rebounds." *Columbus* (OH) *Dispatch,* November 5, 2009. Accessed January 20, 2010. Available: www.dispatch.com.

Oakes, Jeannie, John Rogers, and Martin Lipton. *Learning Power.* New York: Teachers College Press, 2006.

Offe, Claus, and Ulrich Preuss. "Democratic Institutions and Moral Resources." In *Political Theory Today,* edited by David Held, 143–171. Cambridge: Polity, 1991.

Palmer, Parker. *The Courage to Teach.* San Francisco: Jossey-Bass, 1998.

Parker, Walter C. "Constructing Public Schooling Today: Derision, Multiculturalism, Nationalism." *Educational Theory* 61, no. 4 (2011): 413–432.

————. *Teaching Democracy: Unity and Diversity in Public Life.* New York: Teachers College Press, 2003.

Pateman, Carole. *Participation and Democratic Theory.* Cambridge: Cambridge University Press, 1970.

Perczynski, Piotr. "Active Citizenship and Associative Democracy." In *Democratic Innovation: Deliberation, Representation and Association,* edited by Michael Saward, 161–171. New York: Routledge, 2000.

Pew Research Center. "Partisan Polarization Surges in Bush, Obama Years: Trends in American Values: 1987–2012." June 4, 2012. Accessed June 10, 2012. Available: http://pewresearch.org.

Pink, Daniel H. *A Whole New Mind.* New York: Penguin/Riverhead, 2005.

Polletta, Frances. *Freedom Is an Endless Meeting: Democracy in American Social Movements.* Chicago: University of Chicago Press, 2002.

Preskill, Stephen, and Stephen D. Brookfield. *Learning as a Way of Leading: Lessons from the Struggle for Social Justice.* San Francisco: Jossey-Bass, 2009.

"Privatization." Education Commission of the States. Accessed January 4, 2009. Available: www.ecs.org.

"Public Change of Heart: Superintendent Wise to Respond to Naming Concern." Editorial, *Pittsburgh Post-Gazette,* Monday, July 23, 2007. Accessed October 19, 2009. Available: www.post-gazette.com/pg/07204/803688-192.stm.

Public Education Network. "Supporting Local Education Funds." Accessed May 12, 2011. Available: www.publiceducation.org/lefs.asp.

Puriefoy, Wendy D. "Public Engagement and Education Excellence." *Baltimore Sun,* February 8, 2012. Accessed February 9, 2012. Available: www.baltimoresun.com.

Putnam, Robert. *Better Together: Restoring the American Community.* New York: Simon and Schuster, 1999.

Rancière, Jacques. "Introducing Disagreement." *Angelaki: Journal of Theoretical Humanities* 9, no. 3 (2004): 3–9.

Reese, William. *America's Public Schools: From the Common School to "No Child Left Behind."* Baltimore: Johns Hopkins University Press, 2005.

———. *History, Education, and the Schools.* New York: Palgrave-MacMillan, 2007.

———. "Public Schools and the Elusive Search for the Common Good." In *Reconstructing the Common Good in Education: Coping with Intractable American Dilemmas,* edited by Larry Cuban and Dorothy Shipps, 13–31. Palo Alto, CA: Stanford University Press, 2000.

Rifkin, Jeremy. *The Empathic Civilization.* New York: Penguin/Tarcher, 2009.

Rishel, Nicole M. "Digitizing Deliberation: Normative Concerns for the Use of Social Media in Deliberative Democracy." *Administrative Theory and Praxis* 33, no. 3 (September 2011): 411–432.

Rittel, Horst W. J., and Melvin M. Webber. "Dilemmas in a General Theory of Planning." *Policy Sciences* 4 (1973): 155–169.

Rose, Mike. *Why School? Reclaiming Education for All of Us.* New York: New Press, 2009.

Rothwell, Jonathan. "Housing Costs, Zoning, and Access to High-Scoring Schools." Brookings Institute, April 19, 2012. Accessed May 15, 2012. Available: www.brookings.edu.

Ruitenberg, Claudia W. "Educating Political Adversaries: Chantal Mouffe and Radical Democratic Citizenship Education." *Studies in Philosophy and Education* 28 (2009): 269–281.

———. "What if Democracy Really Matters." *Journal of Educational Controversy* 3, no. 1 (Winter 2008). Accessed October 15, 2009. Available: www.wce.wwu.edu/Resources/CEP/eJournal/v003n001/a005.shtml.

Ruscio, Kenneth P. *The Leadership Dilemma in Modern Democracy.* Northampton, MA: Edward Elgar, 2004.

Ryfe, David Michael. "The Practice of Deliberative Democracy: A Study of 16 Deliberative Organizations." *Political Communication* 19 (2002): 359–378.

Salvato, Nancy. "And to the Republic for Which It Stands." GOPUSA. Accessed on May 24, 2011. Available: www.gopusa.com.

Schott Foundation for Public Education. "Executive Summary, *A Rotting Apple: Education*

Redlining in New York City." New York: Schott Foundation for Public Education, 2012. Accessed May 29, 2012. Available: http://schottfoundation.org/publications -reports/education-redlining.

Schutz, Aaron, and Marie Sandy. *Collective Action for Social Change: An Introduction to Community Organizing.* New York: Palgrave MacMillan, 2011.

———. "Home Is a Prison in the Global City: The Tragic Failure of School-Based Community Engagement Strategies." *Review of Educational Research* 76, no. 4 (2006): 691–743.

———. "Power and Trust in the Public Realm: John Dewey, Saul Alinsky, and the Limits of Progressive Democratic Education." *Educational Theory* 61, no. 4 (2011): 491–512.

———. "Rethinking Domination and Resistance: Challenging Postmodernism." *Educational Researcher* 33, no. 1 (January/February 2004): 15–23.

———. "Social Class and Social Action: The Middle-Class Bias of Democratic Theory in Education." *Teachers College Record* 110, no. 2 (February 2008): 405–442.

Senge, Peter. *The Fifth Discipline: The Art and Practice of the Learning Organization,* rev. ed. New York: Currency Doubleday, 2006.

Shaker, Paul, and Elizabeth E. Heilman. "The New Common Sense of Education: Advocacy Research versus Academic Authority." *Teachers College Record* 106, no. 7 (July 2004): 1444–1470.

Shirley, Dennis. "Community Organizing and Educational Change: A Reconnaissance." *Journal of Educational Change* 10 (April 2009): 229–237.

———. "Community Organizing for Educational Change: Past Illusions, Future Prospects." In *The Future of Educational Change: International Perspectives,* edited by Ciaran Sugrue, 89–105. New York: Routledge, 2008.

———. *Community Organizing for Urban School Reform.* Austin: University of Texas Press, 1997.

———. "Promoting Participatory Democracy through Community Organizing." In *Partnering to Prepare Urban Teachers: A Call to Activism,* edited by Francine P. Paterman, 59–75. New York: Peter Lang, 2008.

———. "Teacher Education and Community Organizing." In *Teacher Education with an Attitude: Preparing Teachers to Educate Working-Class Students in Their Collective Self-Interest,* edited by Patrick J. Finn and Mary E. Finn, 79–94. Albany: State University of New York, 2007.

Shirley, Dennis, and Michael Evans. "Community Organizing and No Child Left Behind." In *Transforming the City: Community Organizing and the Challenge of Political Change,* edited by Marian Orr, 109–132. Lawrence: University Press of Kansas, 2007.

Smith, Aaron. *Government Online.* Pew Research Center, April 2010. Accessed May 15, 2012. Available: http://pewinternet.org/Reports/2010/Government-Online.aspx.

Smith, Michael. "New Principals: You Can't Say I Didn't Warn You." The Principal's Page. Available: www.principalspage.com/theblog/archives/2009/08.

Smydo, Joe. "Pittsburgh Schools Drop 'Public' from Name to Boost Image." *Pittsburgh Post-Gazette,* July 11, 2007. Accessed August 20, 2009. Available: www.post-gazette .com.

Somerville, Rich. "Future Generations: 'Citizens' or 'Consumers'?" In *Co-Creating a Public Philosophy for Future Generations,* edited by Tai-Chang Kim and James A. Dator, 162–172. Westport, CT: Praeger, 1999.

Spillane, James P. *Distributed Leadership.* San Francisco: Jossey-Bass, 2006.

Spring, Joel. *The American School: 1642–1993*, 3rd ed. New York: McGraw-Hill, 1994.

Stall, Susan, and Randy Stoecker. "Community Organizing or Organizing Community? Gender and the Crafts of Empowerment." *Gender and Society* 12, no. 6 (December 1998): 729–756.

Stark, Cynthia. "Hypothetical Consent and Political Legitimacy." *Paideia*. Accessed March 29, 2010. Available: www.bu.edu/wcp/Papers/Poli/PoliStar.htm.

Starrat, Robert J. *The Drama of Leadership*. New York: Routledge, 1993.

Stitzlein, Sarah M. *Teaching for Dissent: Citizenship Education and Political Activism*. Boulder, CO: Paradigm, 2012.

Stitzlein, Sarah, Walter Feinberg, Jennifer Greene, and Luis Miron. "Illinois Project for Democratic Accountability." *Educational Studies*, 42, no. 2 (2007): 139–155.

Stolberg, Sheryl Gay. "When It Comes to Scandal, Girls Won't Be Boys." *New York Times*, June 11, 2011. Available: www.nytimes.com.

Strike, Kenneth A. *Ethical Leadership in Schools: Creating Community in an Environment of Accountability*. Thousand Oaks, CA: Corwin, 2007.

———. "Liberty, Democracy, and Community: Legitimacy in Public Education." In *American Educational Governance on Trial: Change and Challenges*, 102nd Yearbook of the National Society for the Study of Education, part 1, edited by William Lowe Boyd and Debra Miretzky, 37–56. Chicago: University of Chicago Press, 2003.

———. Review of *Class and Schools: Using Social, Economic, and Educational Reform to Close the Black-White Achievement Gap*, by Richard Rothstein. *American Journal of Education* 111, no. 3 (May 2005): 414–420.

Stuhr, John J. *Pragmatism, Postmodernism, and the Future of Philosophy*. New York: Routledge, 2003.

Su, Celina. *Streetwise for Book Smarts: Grassroots Organizing and Education Reform in the Bronx*. Ithaca, NY: Cornell University Press, 2009.

Surowiecki, James. *The Wisdom of Crowds*. New York: Doubleday, 2004.

Tainter, Joseph A. *The Collapse of Complex Societies*. Cambridge: Cambridge University, 1988.

Talisse, Robert. "Liberty, Community, and Democracy: Sidney Hook's Pragmatic Deliberativism." *Journal of Speculative Philosophy* 15, no. 4 (2001): 286–304.

Tamarkin, Sally. "What ACORN and the New Right Can Teach Us about Current Trends in Community Organizing." *Social Policy*, Spring 2009, 48–50.

Tannen, Deborah. *The Argument Culture: Moving from Debate to Dialogue*. New York: Random House, 1998.

Thomas, Craig W. "Habitat Conservation Planning." In *Deepening Democracy: Institutional Innovations in Empowered Participatory Governance*, edited by Archon Fung and Eric Olin Wright, 144–172. New York: Verso, 2003.

Thomas, Nancy. "Educating for Deliberative Democracy: The Role of Public Reason and Reasoning." *Journal of College and Character* 9, no. 2 (November 2007): 1–13.

Thompson, John B. "Shifting Boundaries of Public and Private Life." *Theory, Culture, and Society* 28, no. 4 (2011): 49–70.

Thompson, Steven R. *Engaging Citizens through Conversation: Reconnecting Communities and Schools in the Plain Local School District*. Cincinnati: KnowledgeWorks Foundation and the Harwood Institute, 2004.

Tyack, David. "School Governance in the United States: Historical Puzzles and Anomalies." In *Decentralization and School Improvement: Can We Fulfill the Promise?*

edited by Jane Hannaway and Martin Carnoy, 1–32. San Francisco: Jossey-Bass, 1993.

Underwood, Julie, and Julie F. Meade. "A Smart ALEC Threatens Public Education." *Phi Delta Kappan* 93, no. 6 (2011): 50–55.

UNICEF. *Child Poverty in Rich Countries 2005.* Innocenti Research Centre Report Card No. 6. Florence, Italy: UNICEF Innocenti Research Centre, 2005. Accessed July 20, 2009. Available: www.unicef-irc.org.

US Department of Education. *Fast Facts: Dropout Rates.* Washington, DC: National Center for Education Statistics, 2011. Accessed June 12, 2012. Available: http:// nces.ed.gov/fastfacts/display.asp?id=16.

Vitale, Denise. "Between Deliberative and Participatory Democracy: A Contribution on Habermas." *Philosophy and Social Criticism* 32, no. 6 (September 2006): 739–766.

Waks, Leonard J. "Dewey's Theory of the Democratic Public and the Public Character of Charter Schools." *Educational Theory* 60, no. 6 (2010): 665–681.

Waldrop, M. Mitchell. *Complexity: The Emerging Science at the Edge of Order and Chaos.* New York: Simon and Schuster, 1992.

Walsh, Mark. "School Boards Struggle with Sunshine Laws," *Education Week* 22, no. 4 (September 25, 2002): 1–15.

Walzer, Michael. "Deliberation, and What Else?" In *Deliberative Politics: Essays on Democracy and Disagreement,* edited by Stephen Macedo, 58–69. New York: Oxford University Press, 1999.

Warner, Michael. *Publics and Counterpublics.* New York: Zone, 2002.

Warren, Mark E. *Democracy and Association.* Princeton, NJ: Princeton University Press, 2000.

———. "Democracy and the State." In *The Oxford Handbook of Political Theory,* edited by John S. Dryzek, Bonnie Honig, and Anne Phillips, 382–399. New York: Oxford University Press, 2006.

———. "What Can Democratic Participation Mean Today?" *Political Theory* 30, no. 5 (Octobewr 2002): 677–701.

———. "What Should and Should Not Be Said: Deliberating Sensitive Issues." *Journal of Social Philosophy* 37, no. 2 (Summer 2006): 163–181.

Warren, Mark R. "Communities and Schools: A New View of Urban Education Reform." *Harvard Educational Review* 75, no. 2 (Summer 2005): 133–173.

———. *Dry Bones Rattling.* Princeton, NJ: Princeton University Press, 2001.

Warren, Mark R., Soo Hong, Carolyn Heang Rubin, and Phitsamay Sychitkkhong Uv. "Beyond the Bake Sale: A Community-Based Relational Approach to Parent Engagement in Schools." *Teachers College Record* 111, no. 9 (September 2009): 2209–2254.

Weatherford, M. Stephen, and Lorraine M. McDonnell. "Deliberation with a Purpose: Reconnecting Communities and Schools." In *Deliberation, Participation, and Democracy: Can the People Govern?* edited by Shawn W. Rosenberg, 184–218. New York: Palgrave-MacMillan, 2007.

Westbrook, Robert B. *John Dewey and American Democracy.* Ithaca, NY: Cornell University Press, 1991.

"What Parents Need to Know." Common Sense Media. Accessed September 13, 2010. Available: www.commonsensemedia.org/movie-reviews/American-Beauty.html.

Wheatley, Margaret J. *Leadership and the New Science: Discovering Order in a Chaotic World,* 3rd ed. San Francisco: Berrett-Koehler, 2006.

Williams, Melissa S. "Citizenship as Identity, Citizenship as Shared Fate, and the Functions of Multicultural Education." In *Citizenship and Education in Liberal-Democratic Societies*, edited by Kevin McDonough and Walter Feinberg, 208–247. New York: Oxford University Press, 2003.

Williamson, Abigail, and Archon Fung. *Mapping Public Deliberation: A Report for the William and Flora Hewlett Foundation*. Cambridge, MA: Taubman Center for State and Local Government, John F. Kennedy School of Government, Harvard University, 2005. Accessed May 21, 2011. Available: www.hewlett.org/library/mapping-public-deliberation.

Woods, Philip A. *Democratic Leadership in Education*. Thousand Oaks, CA: Paul Chapman, 2005.

Young, Iris Marion. *Inclusion and Democracy*. New York: Oxford University Press, 2000.

Young, Michelle D., and Linda Skrla, eds. *Reconsidering Feminist Research in Educational Leadership*. Albany: State University of New York, 2003.

Index

About the Author

Kathleen Knight Abowitz is a professor in the Department of Educational Leadership at Miami University in Oxford, Ohio. She is the author of *Making Meaning of Community in an American High School* (Hampton Press, 2000). Her scholarship on questions of community, public life, critical pragmatism, and charter schooling policies has appeared in *Educational Theory, Educational Policy, Journal of Teacher Education, Educational Studies, Teachers College Record, American Educational Research Journal, Review of Educational Research, Philosophical Studies in Education,* and the *Urban Review.*

CPSIA information can be obtained at www.ICGtesting.com
Printed in the USA
LVOW04s0848260515

439688LV00012B/99/P